T0289580

Anthropology Goes Public in the VA

Karen Besterman-Dahan and Alison Hamilton

Volume Coeditors

David Himmelgreen and Satish Kedia

General Editors

NATIONAL ASSOCIATION FOR THE PRACTICE OF ANTHROPOLOGY
A SECTION OF THE AMERICAN ANTHROPOLOGICAL ASSOCIATION

Annals of Anthropological
Practice 37.2

Annals of Anthropological Practice (2153-957X) is published in May and November on behalf of the American Anthropological Association by Wiley Subscription Services, Inc., a Wiley Company, 111 River St., Hoboken, NJ 07030-5774.

Mailing: Journal is mailed Standard Rate. Mailing to rest of world by IMEX (International Mail Express). Canadian mail is sent by Canadian publications mail agreement number 40573520. POSTMASTER: Send all address changes to Annals of Anthropological Practice, Journal Customer Services, John Wiley & Sons Inc., 350 Main St., Malden, MA 02148-5020.

Publisher: Annals of Anthropological Practice is published by Wiley Periodicals, Inc., Commerce Place, 350 Main Street, Malden, MA 02148; Telephone: 781 388 8200; Fax: 781 388 8210. Wiley Periodicals, Inc. is now part of John Wiley & Sons.

Information for Subscribers: Annals of Anthropological Practice is published in two one-issue volumes per year. Institutional subscription prices for 2013 are: Print & Online: US$67 (US), US$65 (Rest of World), €42 (Europe), £34 (UK). Prices are exclusive of tax. Australian GST, Canadian GST and European VAT will be applied at the appropriate rates. For more information on current tax rates, please go to www.wileyonlinelibrary.com/tax-vat. The institutional price includes online access to the current and all online back files to January 1st 2008, where available. For other pricing options, including access information and terms and conditions, please visit www.wileyonlinelibrary.com/access.

Delivery Terms and Legal Title: Where the subscription price includes print issues and delivery is to the recipient's address, delivery terms are Delivered Duty Unpaid (DDU); the recipient is responsible for paying any import duty or taxes. Title to all issues transfers FOB our shipping point, freight prepaid. We will endeavour to fulfil claims for missing or damaged copies within six months of publication, within our reasonable discretion and subject to availability.

Back Issues: Single issues from current and recent volumes are available at the current single issue price from cs-journals@wiley.com. Earlier issues may be obtained from Periodicals Service Company, 11 Main Street, Germantown, NY 12526, USA. Tel: +1 (518) 537-4700, Fax: +1 (518) 537-5899, Email: psc@periodicals.com.

Journal Customer Services: For ordering information, claims and any inquiry concerning your journal subscription please go to www.wileycustomerhelp.com/ask or contact your nearest office.

Americas: Email: cs-journals@wiley.com; Tel: +1 781 388 8598 or +1 800 835 6770 (toll free in the USA & Canada).

Europe, Middle East and Africa: Email: cs-journals@wiley.com; Tel: +44 (0) 1865 778315.

Asia Pacific: Email: cs-journals@wiley.com; Tel: +65 6511 8000.

Japan: For Japanese speaking support, Email: cs-japan@wiley.com; Tel: +65 6511 8010 or Tel (toll-free): 005 316 50 480.

Visit our Online Customer Get-Help available in 6 languages at www.wileycustomerhelp.com

Associate Editor: Shannon Canney
Production Editor: Sarah J. McKay, Email: napa@wiley.com
Advertising: Kristin McCarthy, Email: kmccarthy@wiley.com

Print Information: Printed in the United States of America by The Sheridan Press.

Online Information: This journal is available online at *Wiley Online Library*. Visit www.wileyonlinelibrary.com to search the articles and register for table of contents e-mail alerts.

Access to this journal is available free online within institutions in the developing world through the AGORA initiative with the FAO, the HINARI initiative with the WHO and the OARE initiative with UNEP. For information, visit www.aginternetwork.org, www.healthinternetwork.org, and www.oarescience.org.

Aims and Scope: The Annals of Anthropological Practice (AAP) is dedicated to the practical problem-solving and policy applications of anthropological knowledge and methods. AAP is peer reviewed and is distributed free of charge as a benefit of NAPA (National Association for the Practice of Anthropology) membership. Through AAP, NAPA seeks to facilitate the sharing of information among practitioners, academics, and students, contribute to the professional development of anthropologists seeking practitioner positions, and support the general interests of practitioners both within and outside the academy. AAP is a publication of NAPA produced by the American Anthropological Association and Wiley-Blackwell. Through the publication of AAP, the AAA and Wiley-Blackwell furthers the professional interests of anthropologists while disseminating anthropological knowledge and its applications in addressing human problems.

Author Guidelines: For submission instructions, subscription and all other information visit: www.wileyonlinelibrary.com

ISSN 2153-957X (Print)

ISSN 2153-9588 (Online)

Contents

ANTHROPOLOGISTS IN THE VA: A GENERATIVE FORCE

ELISA J. SOBO
San Diego State University

Practicing anthropology within the Veterans Health Administration of the Department of Veterans Affairs (VA) has, until recently, received little serious consideration as a respectable career option for anthropology postgraduates. But times are changing. Anthropologists employed by the VA are responsible for some of the most important and actionable anthropologically informed health research today. Far from being a marginal pursuit, VA anthropology is in fact a generative force for medical anthropology and, indeed, the discipline as a whole. [applied anthropology, public anthropology, military, Veterans, health services, health care]

This collection lays open what has until recently been a well-kept secret: the Veterans Health Administration (VHA) of the Department of Veterans Affairs (VA) is a great place to work. As VA employees, anthropologists can make the kind of difference that most academically employed anthropologists only can dream of and that even practicing anthropologists who do contract work rarely get to enjoy. One key reason for this is that change at the VA, when fomented by an anthropologist who also is a VA employee, is change *from the inside*. The difference this makes is palpable, both in terms of practical outcomes and in the way it affects anthropology. The papers in this collection make it no longer possible to pretend otherwise.

That is not to say that publishing on VA anthropology in such a decidedly anthropological forum as the *Annals of Anthropological Practice* was an obvious move. The primary responsibility of VA employees is service to Veterans. Although publishing in high-impact, PubMed-indexed health care or health services journals can be justified as part of the service cycle, publishing in anthropological journals much less squarely fits this mandate. This is because, from the typical VA researcher's perspective, anthropological mediums are, put briefly and politely, too low profile. Besterman-Dahan, Hamilton, and the other contributors are to be commended for placing a disciplinary contribution before concern for within-VA advancement—and for working within the VA to dislodge the bias (more of which later).

The editors and contributors should also be commended for stepping away bravely from the traditional tenure track. Academic anthropologists have not always seen serving the public directly as honorable. In a conference session organized by Reisinger and Ono, I recommended (Sobo 2010) that VA anthropologists, of which I once was, leave behind the defensive corner into which this fact has, historically, placed them. I noted then that

ANNALS OF ANTHROPOLOGICAL PRACTICE 37.2, pp. 1–4. ISSN: 2153-957X. © 2014 by the American Anthropological Association. DOI:10.1111/napa.12036

engaging in debates about whether or not VA anthropology has value perpetuates the myth that it may not. But it is worth taking time here to outline briefly the history of that myth because doing so will allow us to better appreciate the revolutionary nature of anthropology in the VA.

PRACTICAL WORK: A PUBLIC GOOD

That academic chauvinism has been institutionalized by anthropology's ruling elite in the United States is no new discovery. Anthropology's defensive anti-practice bias was seen, for instance, in the late 1960s when efforts at convening a medical anthropology interest group—diligently fostered by Hazel Weidman—led to an invitation from the Society for Applied Anthropology (SfAA) to affiliate. Although the invitation was accepted as a practical solution to the challenges of maintaining cohesion, the endorsement of and by applied anthropology was "something of an embarrassment" (Good 1994:4). Applied anthropological work, and literature, was seen as "superficial, impressionistic, and nontheoretical" (Scotch 1963:32). Many saw applied anthropologists as mere "technicians" (Scotch 1963:42). Even George Foster, a key founding figure in both medical and applied anthropology, had to work through ambivalences here. "We were trained to despise applied anthropology," he once said; recalling that he did not join the SfAA himself until eight years after it was established, he elaborated, "I would have nothing of it" (Foster 2000:120, quoted in Kemper 2006:4). Accordingly, when the possibility of affiliating with the American Anthropological Association (AAA) arose for the fledgling medical anthropology interest group in the early 1970s, it jumped at the chance (see also Sobo 2011).

The fear of becoming a "technician," however, still has power. Some have linked this, and disdain for practice, to the field's discomfort with its own emergence as part of a colonial and imperial legacy (e.g., McCullough, Ono, and Hahm, this volume). The recounted experiences of VA anthropologists interviewed by Fix (this volume) confirm that academics still frequently think work carried out beyond a university will be "coopted and corrupted." VA anthropologists are doubly damned here because of their employer's military ties. The military is by definition suspect within U.S. anthropology due to a prevalent post-Vietnam abhorrence of all things associated with power, dominance, and oppression (see D'Andrade 2000:222). Of course, the business of higher education in the United States has ties to the military too, and its workers are subject to constraints such as those regulating its industrial mode of (graduate, workforce, consumer) production (see Giroux 2007). But questions regarding which group is more beholden or has less control over the fruits of its labor are unhelpful at best. The real question concerns the value, to science and the public, of what is produced.

As applied or practicing anthropologists employed beyond academia have pushed their way into seats at anthropology's head tables in the AAA, the significance of what they produce has become more apparent. Concurrently, there has been increasing acknowledgment that academically employed anthropologists—even those who self-identify as "applied"—cannot and do not speak for actual practitioners.

Practicing anthropologists' rising status has of course been aided by the changing landscape of academia itself and decreasing member interest in a totally academic association. As Fix notes (this volume), by the mid-1990s, there were more opportunities for employment beyond academia than within it. By the mid-2000s, most anthropology programs had some kind of applied aspect. They had to if departments were to stay afloat: students had begun to demand it.

More importantly, the discipline's insights have come to rely on applied endeavors. It is in application, not intellectualization, that theory really gets put to the test so that it can be refined. VA anthropology is clearly in the forefront in this regard. The articles in this collection demonstrate how our practicing colleagues are building rather than simply borrowing or sharing anthropological knowledge. They are in this sense the profession's life blood, adding vigor to what might have otherwise become a petrified field.

In addition, because they work beyond the world of academics, our VA peers are defining anthropology's use and boundaries for outsiders, serving as exemplars and providing a public face for anthropology. Anthropologists who work for the VA are helping return anthropology to the world as a public good. Their work is in fact very important, and not just for Veterans. The VA administers the largest integrated health care system in the nation. As such, the VHA often sets the standard for care and for approaches to it (such as in implementation science); it trains a huge segment of the clinical and health services workforce. In this alone, there is a great chance for VA anthropologists to make a widespread difference.

DEMONSTRATING THE POSSIBLE

The articles assembled here represent one cut of the very wide range of activities that come under the VA's research umbrella. The VA deals, by definition, with a vulnerable population (Veterans) and within that broad group there are subsets of doubly vulnerable persons (substance using Veterans, women Veterans, Veterans who serve as chaplains, homeless Veterans, Veterans with post-traumatic stress disorder [PTSD], Veterans with injured spinal cords, etc.). Because of this fact, the VA was among the first to recognize the value of patient-centered care. It was among the first health care organizations to recognize the shortcomings of single-disease frameworks. It revolutionized electronic medical record keeping and clinical support system standards. The VA understands the value of a holistic and context-sensitive systems perspective and of multidisciplinary teamwork. It understands the benefit to patients, and systems (including the clinical, administrative, and other workers that staff them) of projects *designed and owned by stakeholders within*. What could be more anthropological than that?

Indeed, it is internal ownership and the prospect of being engaged in "responsive" research with "intrinsic value" for participants (Solimeo 2010) that I miss the most when I think back to my own VA and other health services system employment. Being *part* of the target organization makes an immeasurable difference to the difference anthropologists can make.

In the past, VA anthropologists worked in isolation. But their ranks have expanded, in part due to the demonstrated results they have achieved and the impact this had on VA hiring strategies. With increased numbers, and through dedicated self-organizing, VA anthropologists are now a force to be reckoned with. The contents in this collection demonstrate how important it is, to the discipline as a whole, that our VA colleagues stand up to be counted and that we rejoin their voices into the mainstream of anthropology. The generative potential of their contribution is not to be underestimated.

REFERENCES CITED

D'Andrade, Roy
  2000 The Sad Story of Anthropology 1950–1999. Cross-Cultural Research 34(3):219–232.
Good, Byron J.
  1994 Medicine, Rationality, and Experience: An Anthropological Perspective. Cambridge, UK: Cambridge University Press.
Giroux, Henry A.
  2007 On Critical Pedagogy. New York: Continuum Books.
Kemper, Robert V.
  2006 Foster, George McClelland, Jr. (1913–2006) (Obituary). Newsletter: Society for Applied Anthropology 17(4):3–15.
Scotch, Norman A.
  1963 Medical Anthropology. Biennial Review of Anthropology 3:30–68.
Sobo, Elisa J.
  2010 'Anthropologists in the VHA: So What?' Discussion presented for 'Anthropologists in the Veterans Health Administration (VHA),' organized by H. Reisinger and S. Ono for the 109th Annual Meeting of the American Anthropological Association, New Orleans, November 18.
  2011 Medical Anthropology in Disciplinary Context: Definitional Struggles and Key Debates (or Answering the Cri du Coeur). In A Companion to Medical Anthropology. Merrill Singer and Pamela I. Erickson, eds. Pp. 9–28. Oxford, UK: Wiley-Blackwell.
Solimeo, Samantha
  2010 The Lone Anthropologist vs. Big Brother: How I Became a Medical Anthropologist for the VHA. Paper presented at the 109th Annual Meeting of the American Anthropological Association, New Orleans, November 18.

OBSERVERS OBSERVED: EXPLORING THE PRACTICE OF ANTHROPOLOGY IN THE VA

MEGAN B. McCULLOUGH
Center for Healthcare Organization and Implementation Research (CHOIR), a VA HSR&D Center of Innovation, and Brandeis University

BRIDGET HAHM
HSR&D/RR&D Center of Innovation on Disability and Rehabilitation Research, James A. Haley Veterans Hospital

SARAH ONO
Center for Comprehensive Access and Delivery Research and Evaluation (CADRE) Veterans Rural Health Resource Center-Central Region (VRHRC-CR)

From our position as publicly funded anthropologists in the Veterans Affairs, we discuss how anthropological research on Veterans health care offers an opportunity to critically engage with ideas about what constitutes public anthropology. As public sector anthropologists, we are conducting theoretically and ethnographically innovative work. In this chapter, we discuss the implications of this work in regard to anthropological theory and practice. [applied anthropology, health care, public sector, Veterans]

> So when I think about what it means to be an anthropologist in the 21st century, what it means to be an anthropologist now. I don't want to be an applied anthropologist or a practicing anthropologist or a perfect anthropologist. I simply want to be an anthropologist because I think that is the most exciting thing I can think of doing.
> Dr. Genevieve Bell, Australian Anthropological Society, September 2012

Public anthropology, practicing anthropology, applied anthropology, engaged anthropology, collaborative anthropology—these labels are charged within the discipline as are the old, tired (and tiring) debates about the value and merit of categorizing and subdividing anthropological work, especially along the lines of "applied" and "academic" anthropologies. We see these internal disciplinary debates as contestations over what counts as anthropological knowledge and practice and the valuing of some forms of anthropological knowledge and practice over others for a variety of social, political, and economic reasons. Through our experience working as anthropologists in the Department of Veterans Affairs (VA), we acknowledge this discourse and seek to move beyond it, or at least advance the conversation.

While we acknowledge the legacies of language and power that afflict these terms (public, engaged, applied, etc.), we have no wish to enter into arguments about

ANNALS OF ANTHROPOLOGICAL PRACTICE 37.2, pp. 5–19. ISSN: 2153-957X. © 2014 by the American Anthropological Association. DOI:10.1111/napa.12031

defining what counts as applied or public anthropology. Instead we engage in a theoretical, ethnographic, and reflexive exploration of what it means to be an anthropologist in VA. We present and share the vibrant, complex, confounding, frustrating, intellectually challenging, and rewarding social world of public sector anthropology in and of VA. We examine our position as anthropologists in public sector health services research (HSR) and implementation science (IS) research and then we discuss the praxis of public sector medical anthropology or how we do our work. HSR is a category of research and an endeavor whose definition is in development. A good HSR working definition is "a multidisciplinary field of scientific investigation that studies how social factors, financing systems, organizational structures and processes, health technologies, and personal behaviors affect access to health care, the quality and cost of health care and ultimately health and well-being" (Lohr and Steinwachs 2002:15). IS is also a rather new field and can be roughly understood as the study of the methods to promote integration of research findings and evidence into health-care policy and practice; the study of translating science to practice (Brownson et al., 2012:3–22). Anthropology is one of those disciplines that has contributed and will continue to contribute to IS and HSR. As anthropologists in and of VA, we question the usefulness of and the disciplinary fascination with subdividing, categorizing, and stratifying kinds of anthropology. Through its holistic character, anthropology acknowledges multiple factors that influence health and well-being; therefore, public anthropologists are well positioned in VA to vastly contribute to new directions within HSR and IS and to continue to demonstrate why anthropology matters.

HIERARCHIES OF KNOWLEDGE AND PRACTICE IN ANTHROPOLOGY

In our meditations on being and doing anthropology in and of VA, we want to briefly ground our discussion by placing ourselves and our work in relation to some of the explicit and implicit debates about the applied/academic relationship in anthropology. As VA anthropologists, our relationships with academic departments are varied. Some of us work entirely in the public sector as researchers within VA. Others do almost all of their research work in VA but have some affiliation with an academic institution. The majority of these affiliations are in departments other than anthropology like medical departments, schools of public health and nursing, and interdisciplinary programs such as gerontology.

In placing our work, we cannot neglect to acknowledge and comment on the structures of power that characterize or subtly imply that applied anthropological work is lesser anthropology. Public sector anthropology is not rejected, so much as rarely even considered. Drawing on the classic idea of marked and unmarked categories of identity, applied anthropologists are in the marked category (Battistella 1996.). The constructed hierarchy of anthropological knowledge is naturalized wherein academic anthropology has traditionally been more highly valued than applied work (Friedl 1978; McIntosh 1990). Because of our markedness, aspects of our practice, both real and imagined, are subject to evaluation in ways that differ from academic anthropology.

For example, anthropologists who work for the Department of Defense (DoD) are often perceived as betraying the discipline, research ethics, and research subjects. However, these claims, often lodged at social scientists (not just anthropologists) working for the Human Terrain System (HTS), do not fully consider the complexity of the work archaeologists do on military bases or the multifaceted work of anthropologists who teach at military academies (Rubinstein et al., 2013). This is not to say that there should not be moral and ethical debates about anthropology (both academic and applied) or that all VA anthropologists think in unitary ways that preclude our own participation in disciplinary debates about research ethics. Rather, we resist the simplistic analysis that working for the state makes us somehow the state's technicians. The work in this volume illustrates the ways that anthropologists bring critical anthropological knowledge to bear on exposing and discussing issues such as power imbalances, stigmatization, and marginalization within the delivery of VA health care. The same skills we use to uncover complex issues, also enable us to help craft solutions to those problems.

Academic anthropology in the United States has long-standing and lively debates on research ethics, power dynamics, and the complexities of representation (Baer et al., 1986; Fluehr-Lobban 2013; Marcus and Fisher 1999). However, for applied anthropologists there has often been a direct or indirect imputation which suggests that anthropologists working *within* medical care and the public sector can be co-opted and curtailed in ways that anthropologists who do work *on* or *of* medical care and the public sector cannot (Browner 1999; Purcell 2000; Scheper-Hughes and Bourgois 2004:7–8 as quoted in Rylko-Bauer et al., 2006:178–179).

We acknowledge that our work in public policy has stakeholders and may have parameters as well as it values certain results over others that we, as anthropologists, may or may not share. However, we have not been prevented from writing for our work and of our work. Elisa J. Sobo's book, Culture and Meaning in Health Services Research (Sobo 2009), stands out as an excellent case in point as does her article studying VA implementation researchers (Sobo et al., 2008). We are not the only anthropologists who operate under parameters in our work and within our institutions. Academic anthropologists increasingly face constraints themselves and are arguably part of the public sector if employed at state universities and colleges.

Recent employment trends in academic anthropology, such as increased reliance on adjunct faculty positions and a decrease in the availability of tenure-track academic positions, problematize the work of being anthropologists in U.S. academic institutions. There is less job security than hoped for at universities, wages at universities and colleges may have stagnated, and in some institutions tenured faculties are facing increasing attempts to fetter their speech and their scholarship (Ferner 2013; Schmidt 2013). We know that there are increased bureaucratic burdens and performance metrics among many other issues facing faculty along with increased pressure for research and publications. Academia is not isolated from larger trends in the labor market, such as the large compensation packages for university presidents and the increased growth of administrative positions (Ginsberg 2013).

There are serious consequences for training the next generation of anthropologists. A decrease in government subsidization of higher education, the increased costs of graduate-level education and the subsequent increases in student debt load are also issues of concern facing anthropology departments. Such inequalities are beginning to provoke deep and complicated questions for anthropology departments whose primary focus has been, and in many cases still is, on training students to pursue academic jobs; jobs that exist only for the few. Given the current situation in the academy for graduate students and adjuncts, the means by which academic anthropology reproduces itself bear scrutiny. We suggest that it is time for more engagement with applied anthropology within academic departments for the sake of graduate students and for the health of the discipline itself.

Academic anthropology in the United States is not monolithic and neither is applied work, public sector, or otherwise. The application of anthropology and its theoretical development have gone hand in hand for much of the discipline's history (Rylko-Bauer et al., 2006). Perhaps it is time for a broader acknowledgement that we do more than share a history, but that we share a present and should share a future, albeit one, we hope, with a reconfiguration of the cultural capital afforded certain kinds of anthropological work.

PUBLIC SECTOR ANTHROPOLOGISTS

What does it mean to be a VA anthropologist? As VA researchers, we are publicly funded through federal dollars, both in terms of VA research monies and through federally funded institutions such as the National Institutes of Health (NIH). Being explicitly publically funded, we are accountable not only to our colleagues in anthropology, but also to multiple publics on a national scale. We are "public" anthropologists in a manner which goes beyond Borofsky's understanding of public anthropology as something in which anthropology addresses contemporary problems to shed light on the issues of major concern and to use anthropological knowledge to facilitate social change (2000, 2011). He also still sees the academy as a major seat from which public anthropology, as he defines it, can be practiced (Borofsky 2000). Some of us have affiliations with an academic institution and many do not. However, we are funded by the public, deliver research to benefit the public, engage in policy and leadership discussions that address key health issues and health service delivery for the public, and our work, not only has the potential to change health care for the public but in a sense also belong to them.

Anthropology in VA is both the anthropology *of* medicine and public policy and anthropology *in* medicine and public policy. We are paid employees of the U.S. federal government and we are employed as anthropologists in HSR work. However, as anthropologists who work in and of VA, we do not withhold critique of the institution because the U.S. government pays our salary. In this volume, we explore the ways VA struggles to identify gaps in care and makes efforts to address them (Besterman-Dahan et al., 2014 and Lind et al., 2014). VA as an institution also recognizes that it needs to try harder to meet the needs of certain populations, especially women Veterans and

Veterans belonging to marginalized groups (Hamilton et al., 2014 and Cheney et al., 2014).

THE CONTEXT OF THE VA

"Government" work may be suspect in anthropology maybe because such work intersects or resonates with anthropology's discomfort with its own colonial and imperial past (Rylko-Bauer et al., 2006). Our work is often linked to anthropology's discomfort with its past connection to the military in WWII (Price 2008). But we are not working for the military, we are working with and for Veterans who were in the military, though it may be helpful to have a certain fluency in military culture to be effective VA researchers. We continue here to place our work in anthropology by grounding our work in its context, the Department of Veterans Affairs.

First and foremost, VA itself is a cultural construct, a context, a research participant, a player in our work. Much of the ethnographic description and discussion in this piece is about the organization itself. It is our attempt to unravel and make comprehensible the large bureaucracy that we work within. If, as a reader, you struggle to understand the structure of VA, or in discussing our work, you begin to feel that it is complicated, multifaceted, and diverse as well as pervasive and encompassing, then we have succeeded in reflecting some of what it is like to work in such a large, complex, living organization. We are always studying the organization around us as a field site even as we work within it.

National policies and programs often put forth an image of "One VA" with the goal that Veterans will be able to obtain the same or similar quality health-care services at any VA facility they go to throughout the network. Due to factors such as geography and population variation, the provision of services is variable. That is not unexpected in large health-care organization that stretches across such a large and diverse country such as the United States. As anthropologists we certainly understand that organizational culture is not monolithic or uniform. While the speed with which national mandates about care can be implemented when the political will is present can be amazing, for most policies and programs, change often moves slowly with a great deal of local interpretation and control. Prior to the 1990s when Ken Kizer revolutionized care in VA, the organization of VA facilities at the national and regional levels was very loosely organized and individual hospital directors had wide degrees of latitude in operating the hospitals (Longman 2007). Although the shift toward a national network of care has been 20 years in the making, vestiges of these days still exist in many ways due to the longevity of VA employees. Bureaucratic lines of authority and traditions that have built up locally over long periods of time (decades in some cases) result in idiosyncrasies across facilities. An additional factor contributing to differences among VAs is the politicization of VA health care which creates a more reactive environment for providing health-care services rather than a systematic, strategic one. For example, VA leadership, such as hospital administrators, are under public scrutiny and any adverse event could trigger ripples of political consequences that could potentially go all the way up to Capitol Hill.

While public accountability is absolutely necessary in a government organization, it may occasionally tacitly support more moderate approaches to implementing health care and quality improvement innovations. While one VA hospital may be able to systematically implement a new program, another one may be hastily and imperfectly implementing a change because resources are needed to address other local health priorities and goals. VA has a great deal of organizational awareness about all of these issues, which is in part why it studies itself to improve care.

Contrary to the "One VA" idea, it is a long-standing and rather pedestrian saying in VA that, "If you have seen one VA, you've seen one VA." This is an insider joke about the great diversity that exists in this one complex bureaucracy. VA is the largest integrated health system in the United States with 21 Veterans Integrated Service Networks (VISNs). These VISNs oversee long-term care facilities, mental health units, hospitals, primary care outpatient clinics, and small community-based outpatient clinics. Moreover, VA has an entire division, the Veterans Health Administration (VHA), with its own Office of Research and Development (ORD) composed of four departments or service lines at the time of this writing: Health Services Research & Development (HSR&D), Rehabilitation Research & Development (RR&D), Clinical Science Research & Development (CSR&D), and Biomedical Laboratory Research & Development (BLR&D). For the purposes of this article, we will mostly be focusing on HSR&D. HSR&D is the department that studies Veterans' health care, and it is through various grants and funding mechanisms associated with these departments that the majority of anthropologists are employed.

As researchers who study difference and the implementations to improve care, we are based in interdisciplinary research centers that are spread across the country. VA's research centers have different research foci and different areas of expertise. For example, the Center of Innovation on Disability and Rehabilitation Research (CINDRR) located at the James A. Haley Veterans Hospital in Tampa, Florida (i.e., Tampa VA) specializes in disability and rehabilitation research, as the name implies. Each of the authors is based at very different research centers attached to very different VA health systems. We would like to take a moment here to convey some of the contextual flavor of each of these VA sites as well as some of their special areas of research and the populations their facilities serve.

Sarah Ono's VA home is the Center for Comprehensive Access and Delivery Research and Evaluation, more commonly referred to as CADRE in Iowa City. Iowa City's HSR&D research center is in its third iteration, second name, and a new building since leaving the main hospital in 2010. The building itself is pretty nondescript, containing the HSRs, as well as various labs and an RR&D center for the Prevention and Treatment of Vision Loss. Sarah works with a team of ten anthropologists, five of whom have Ph.D.s in anthropology. The work space could just as easily be an insurance company—gray is the predominant décor color and there is a sea of cubicles inside a ring of offices. There is water cooler talk, but along with discussion of popular media there is more clinical chit chat—something new to most anthropologists coming to VA from academic settings. Elements of our work translate from site to site, but other pieces are very site-specific. When it comes down to it, the Iowa City VA Health Care System, which includes research, serves a largely rural population in a region that covers the upper-Midwestern states. In Iowa there are more pigs than people, and while Washington, D.C. may close for weather, it is rare to get a snow day at the Iowa City VA. In fact, once during a particularly bad snowstorm, a patient came to the hospital on his tractor. While this is not a common occurrence, it is common in Iowa. The population served and the geography of the region plays an important role in the kind of research that is done here. This can be said of any of VA research centers.

Under the hot, humid Florida sun, Bridget Hahm works at the CINDRR located at the James A. Haley Veterans Hospital in Tampa, Florida (i.e., Tampa VA). Tampa's research center is jointly funded with the North Florida/South Georgia Veterans Health Care System located in Gainesville, Florida. The goal of the CINDRR is to conduct research to improve rehabilitation and disability services for Veterans of all ages through a focus on community reintegration, informatics and measurement, and technology. Bridget currently works with seven anthropologists (some with Ph.D.s and others with an MA) who carry out the research to help CINDRR fulfill its care goals. These facilities are located within VA Sunshine Health Care Network (VISN 8) which covers a geographic range from South Georgia to Puerto Rico; it is the largest VISN in the VHA and serves more than half a million Veterans annually. The population served is highly diverse, ranging from predominantly white, rural areas to densely populated urban areas with large, diverse populations. The Tampa VA is home to one of four regional polytrauma centers that treat Veterans and active duty soldiers returning from combat and focuses on the treatment of traumatic brain injuries. The Tampa VA also provides other specialty care programs such as spinal cord injury and disorder treatment and rehabilitation, mental health services for Post Traumatic Stress Disorder (PTSD), substance abuse and other mental health disorders, and women Veterans.

Megan McCullough works at the Center for Healthcare Organization and Implementation Research (CHOIR) currently with five anthropologists (again some with Ph.D.s and others with an MA). CHOIR is based in Massachusetts and composed of two research centers, one in Bedford and the other in Boston, that used to be separate but that have now joined together to form one large, multidisciplinary research center whose mission is to improve Veterans health outcomes by studying health-care issues and implementing evidence-based practices to improve care not only in the urban, rural, and suburban areas of New England but also at other VAs across the nation. Two areas of specialty in CHOIR are organizational science and IS. Currently, there are three research foci at CHOIR: medication optimization, recovery in vulnerable populations (especially homeless Veterans), and public health communication. There are also ongoing study areas that focus on community living centers (nursing homes), patient safety, and patient-centered care.

Bedford has a focus on mental health, long-term care, and rehabilitation. Boston is a referral hospital for all of New England, and offers all kinds of specialty and subspecialty care, in addition to an emergency department (ED), full-service OR (operating room) suite, ICUs (intensive care units), and a large inpatient ward, etc. Some VA facilities are more driven by a "top down" leadership structure and others less so, some are innovative and flexible and others less so, while some places and lines of care are exemplars and others are not. The microcultures and local biologies (Lock and Nguyen 2010:90) that exist and live in every hospital, long-term care facility, psychiatric unit, and research center are myriad. Patients and staff interact in their daily lives embedded in their local moral worlds (Kleinman 1995) as the work of health, healing and care are embodied and practiced. Every facility is as alike as it is different and this is true vertically and horizontally. We remind ourselves and our fellow anthropologists to question all assumptions they may have had about government institutions. One VA is truly only one VA; or more accurately VA is many VAs.

MANAGING MULTIPLE IDENTITIES IN VA

As anthropologists, we are often grouped with other social scientists at VA and broadly labeled "qualitative researchers." However, doing social science in VA calls for a "bridging" of identities (Hamilton 2013) between being a qualitative researcher, being a medical anthropologist, and being an expert in specialized areas, such as co-occurring disorders, patient-centered care, disease state management, and the implementation of health-care innovations among many others. Anthropologists bring different ways of understanding, observing, and analyzing social phenomena that complement and sometimes challenge our clinical health services colleagues (Hamilton 2013). For example, health services and IS are very concerned with context and daily lived experience as an influence on the uptake of health-care improvement implementations. Anthropology shares a deep concern with context although we understand the concept of context quite differently. As anthropologists not only are we bridging our identities in VA, we are also trying to call attention to the way the structure of VA itself contributes to, confines, or shapes our studies.

The emergent modes for sharing information in VA push us to develop new skills to deliver our findings in virtual meetings and cyber-seminars, along with peer-reviewed manuscripts and papers delivered at professional HSR, IS, and medical meetings. VA anthropologists are nimble; it is an appropriate adjective for anthropologists in the public sector. The environment is one that is often reactive to a changing political climate and requires both agility and adaptability. The expected pace of qualitative work is often more rapid than we are accustomed to, but the nature of anthropological practice supports a level of flexibility that is well suited to a steady stream of emergent questions and associated tasks.

Often working at the frontlines of care does not leave much time for anthropological theoretical articles about what we are doing. While anthropological theory may not be sought out as such in VA, we use it conceptually, to think with, and often alone or in small discussions with other anthropologists. The research approach of VA is still very centered on biomedicine, clinical outcomes, evidence-based care, HSR, and health-care implementations. This is appropriate for a health-care setting and unlikely to change. However, it can become hard to maintain connections with the anthropological mainstream. Theory has a very different meaning in HSR and implementation research.

However complicated the relationship between applied and academic anthropologies, most of us find it enriching to stay engaged with the larger anthropology community in the United States through meetings such as the annual American Anthropological Association, Society for Medical Anthropology and Society for Applied Anthropology meetings. We sometimes wish that our work, which is broadly read in HSR and implementation journals, would be read and appreciated by other anthropological audiences.

BEING AND DOING ANTHROPOLOGY IN VA

In this section, we will discuss how we do our work in VA. First, we will discuss how we are funded and then move onto to discuss the embodied praxis of VA work. We conclude this section by discussing what is expected of us by our coworkers and supervisors, and the challenges these requirements present to our keeping in touch with anthropology as a discipline.

Anthropologists, along with many other kinds of VA researchers, are funded through soft money. Very few VA researchers have permanent jobs in the federal government; the typical model is a temporary or term appointment contingent upon grant funding. VA anthropologists are typically expected to obtain grants such as those specifically available through VA or through other government agencies, NIH or National Science Foundation (NSF). Because of these institutional barriers to funding, and because we are part of the "applied" world, the academic world knows very little about the kinds of grants we earn; and therefore our grants possess less cultural capital within the field of anthropology. Some VA research centers have worked with investigators on contract with universities whose VA time did not "count" as productivity in their academic departments. VA investigators who work part-time at both institutions may find themselves in a liminal status at both places which may affect their access to the benefits of full-time employment (e.g., levels of employer coverage of health-care insurance, prorated paid time off). It can also be challenging working on many projects in order to maintain our salaries. We frequently face the challenge of dividing our time between contributing to other peoples' projects (as a co-investigator or methodologist) and forging ahead in development of our own research program as principal investigators. Sometimes the research centers where we work have expectations and directions they want us to pursue, such as becoming a self-funding principal investigator. Other centers are less directive and place less emphasis on having anthropologists become principal investigators.

The degree to which we work in teams in VA research introduces a very different dynamic to anthropological work, which is often solo—or imagined to be conducted a "lone" anthropologist fashion. Projects in VA involve teams, even if one's role is as an "independent investigator," there is a team not far away. This trait of HSR (Sobo 2009; Sobo et al., 2008) can have a number of effects on a newly employed VA anthropologist. We are not accustomed to sharing our data and, if we are, there is often still a line drawn so that personal field notes remain, well, personal. Throughout graduate training, many of us experience the less-is-more approach to guidance and mentoring when it comes to study design, methodological development, planning analysis, and last but not least, writing. Things are left vague so that each of us can go out and see what we find and figure out how to do anthropology. Figuring things out is a critical element in the rite of passage for an anthropologist and, whether or not we recognize it, the process cultivates a unique skill set.

For many of us, we find a balance between the autonomy of working as a lone anthropologist and the collaborative nature of team-based work. On the one hand, it can be hard to hand over field notes for incorporation into a data set, or know that transcribers are listening to your interviews full of "um"s, "er"s, and unfinished sentences. On the other hand, there is reassurance that comes with knowing an interview guide has been reviewed by other team members who deploy the rigor of their own disciplines. In a multidisciplinary team, the necessary feedback to improve even the smallest of research tasks is available and is productive. It is a different experience to sit with a group of colleagues where everyone is familiar with the data at hand. The connection is not just because one works in Oaxaca or the Pacific Islands, as it is in more academic circles, but because you are all looking at the same set of data at the same time. It is data that you have collected and analyzed *together*. There can be engaged debate about what someone talked about in an interview or discussion when it comes to deciding most relevant themes and their application when coding. This is not a theoretical exercise, but rather, a collective effort to get it right. The work we do in VA is shared. We adhere to limits established by Institutional Review Boards (IRBs), in place to protect privacy, and acknowledge that we do not "own" our data; if we go, the data stays. These data are the product of publicly funded grants and the property of the organization that employs us. The role of anthropologist as public servant is another piece to consider when we think about who we are and the function of the work we do.

As anthropologists, we are frustrated by a wide range of things that vary according to personality, training, and approach. Our major constraint, something equally as unlikely to change as the conventions of HSR, is VA bureaucracy itself, which is full of rules and paperwork. Things move slowly. Sometimes good ideas and important research insights are never implemented. Sometimes changes we wish would happen, do not happen. These kinds of frustrations and concerns are shared by many HSR&D researchers.

We have times where our holistic understanding of health is constrained in the way health care is divided and subdivided. We also face colleagues who appreciate us and what we bring to the table, but sometimes fear that anthropology is too subjective, too prone to bias, and not evidence-based enough. We face the fact that sometimes other researchers do not understand how labor intensive qualitative work is, and that they underestimate or do not understand how skillful one has to be to carry it out effectively. We have all had someone ask us to be on a project for 5 percent of our time but in fact they have not asked for 5 percent effort; they have asked for a large amount of work and we have to translate, to bridge, to explain what we do and why that cannot happen for the time allotted. We are often approached as only methodologists, where interviewing or ethnographic observation is seen just as a technique, rather than a complex, analytical, and conceptual approach to gathering data. We face these challenges frequently. Some days things work out better than others. Often we find that we are better, sharper anthropologists (methodologically and conceptually) because we have been challenged on how we know, what we know, and how we learned it.

As VA researchers, we are expected to publish research articles in journals that "count" and are indexed in PubMed in order to establish a track record that will make us better candidates for government research awards. Given that many anthropological journals are not indexed in PubMed, this means that VA anthropologists are not rewarded in the same way for submissions to those journals. In VA, we generate work that aims to improve aspects of Veterans' health. It might relate to health-care delivery and issues of access, or to a specific disease or condition. We evaluate implementation on small and large scales, trying to better understand why some good ideas succeed and others fail to be adopted. We may be working on a topic of national interest, such as PTSD or military sexual trauma, or on an organizational change that may only be recognized by the nurses it is affecting at one location, such as the contributors to this special issue explore. In our work, we find problems with the care VA delivers which is why VA has researchers—to improve care and to lead the way in changing American health care. Some problems are small, some are large, and some are controversial, but many of us struggle to make sure that the data demonstrating a gap, a problem gets out there, gets seen, and we try to help get the issue addressed and improvement made. It is not perfect, as no system is—but we find our voices and we find ways of making our voices heard and we do collaborative research with Veterans to have their voices heard.

To varying degrees, we are left to our own devices when it comes to figuring out the applications for our work as anthropologists. As the authors in this special issue can attest, there is variety among institutions and programs, especially when it comes to addressing applied anthropology (Fix, this volume). Each of us is a combination of our influences—what brought us to anthropology in the first place; who we chose (or who chose us) to be mentors; the area of specialization that we connected with; and the people who spoke about something we were compelled to listen to. For each of us we decide what it is to be an anthropologist. We figure out through practice and through discourse with our VA anthropology peers how to use being an anthropologist to produce high quality research. Finally we then try to balance the often competing demands of our job as qualitative researchers with our own interests as anthropologists to write up and share our results.

EXPLODING ANTHROPOLOGICAL CATEGORIES

We ethnographically explored how we perform our job as public sector anthropologists. We have also described the context of VA, our complex and multiple identities as anthropologists and how we do, be and embody anthropology in VA. Now, we have come full circle to discuss how we see our work advancing discussions in anthropology about public anthropology.

Public sector medical anthropology is placed in a double bind. On one hand, applied anthropology, including public sector work, is often viewed as producing less intellectually rigorous work. On the other hand, the perceived lack of rigor (and sometimes real) lack of theory is made up for by the importance of doing public good and bringing anthropological insights to help solve problems in real time and to participate in public debates. In VA, we feel this double bind acutely. We are doing research that, at its best, really helps people. It can radically change the health-care Veterans receive. Though we often use theory to approach our work, there is often insufficient time (or it is not practical) to publish in anthropological journals. Public sector medical anthropology can and does enrich the discipline but it is a struggle for us to keep up with trends in anthropology and find the time to publish in anthropology journals, which as we noted earlier, are not as highly valued as IS journals or health service journals in VA.

For some time now, certainly the past 15–20 years, there has been increased interest in marking the "sea change" in anthropology (Checker et al., 2010) which seeks to have anthropology "serve the public good" (Borofosky 2011), or make "anthropology public" (Scheper-Hughes 2009:1), or "reclaim" applied anthropology's past to forge a future discipline composed of applied social theory and pragmatic engagement (Rylko-Bauer et al., 2006), or perhaps to suggest that there is already a convergence of applied, practicing, and public anthropology that points the ways forward for innovative anthropological work and significant contributions to public policy (Lamphere 2004). We highlight that none of these approaches are particularly dichotomous or mutually exclusive, although all the authors cited may not be in agreement with this supposition. VA anthropology is public, practicing, and applied.

Work in the federal system is perceived to be distinct from the academy. However, these separations are debatable depending on the lens you use. The richness of the work comes from what we do in VA and this richness is a result of the other two labels that can be used to describe our work—*collaborative* and *engaged*. These are terms readily associated with fieldwork-based ethnographic practice and without them we would not get far in our efforts at participant-observation. In the public sector generally, and VA specifically, there are different limitations on our use of true participant-observation, but this does not result in our work being less collaborative and engaged. The setting in which we work may look different from most fieldwork, but the assets we bring as anthropologists and the richness of our findings are very much the same.

VA anthropologists partner, in the best anthropological sense of the word, with other researchers, with Veterans, and with health-care providers to improve care. In this volume, Cotner et al., discuss their work with the PrOMOTE study whose goal is to evaluate the success of a supported-employment model for Veterans with spinal cord injury. Lind et al., examined Veterans' perceptions of dignity while being moved using safe patient handling equipment such as slings and ceiling lifts. Finley and Besterman-Dahan both seek to better understand Veterans dealing with PTSD. Hamilton et al., and Cheney et al.'s work focuses on sensitive issues such as homelessness and substance use. Haun's research seeks to understand how Veterans are using new electronic means of communicating with their care providers such as a secure messaging system.

CONCLUSION

VA anthropological work is focused on improving patient-centered care from the patient point of view and improving staff performance by understanding what staff do in regard to care and implementing changes to improve that care for Veterans. Health services are action oriented and VA engages in research that touches on crucial medical issues of the day, such as how to serve vulnerable populations, how to use technology and social media to improve health, how to address disparities, how to contain costs and meet health-care needs, how to implement evidence-based practices to improve care, how to provide patient-centered care, et cetera. VA helps set the direction and the standard of care for health care generally for the United States. Anthropological insights into context, culture, power dynamics, gender, race, class, social organization, social networks, kinship, practices of care, explanatory models of illness, local moral worlds, et cetera inform every project we undertake with the explicit goal of actively changing the health-care experience and health outcomes for patients in VA each and every day. What we have learned, and continue to learn, is how critical anthropology is to HSR and how well positioned we are as anthropologists to do this work. Public sector anthropology is an exciting, exasperating, exceptional thing to do as an anthropologist; for that is what we are, who we are, and we cannot think of anything more worthwhile to be.

NOTE

Acknowledgements. This material is based upon work supported by the Department of Veterans Affairs, Veterans Health Administration, Office of Research and Development. The views expressed in this article are those of the authors and do not necessarily reflect the position or policy of the Department of Veterans Affairs or the U.S. government.

The authors would like to acknowledge our special issue editors, Karen Besterman-Dahan and Alison Hamilton. Thanks! We also wish to thank David Himmelgreen and Satish Kedia for their support of this special issue. We appreciate the feedback from three anonymous reviewers who helped improve our work. Ann Cheney and Gemmae Fix also gave us early valuable feedback. We would like to thank each other for the fun time we have had collaborating. We thank our families and loved ones for their support. We would also like to sound a note of appreciation for all the other HSR&D researchers with whom we collaborate and who are dedicated, smart, and inspiring peers. VA providers and staff are often deeply dedicated and determined to provide excellent care and we appreciate their willingness to participate in research. Lastly, we would like to thank the Veterans who share their health-care experiences with us. We are honored and privileged to serve you in some modest way as you have served us in so many.

REFERENCES CITED

Baer, Hans, Merrill Singer, and John H. Johnsen
   1986   Toward a Critical Medical Anthropology. Social Science and Medicine 23(2):95–98.
Battistella, Edwin L.
   1996. The Logic of Markedness. New York: Oxford University Press.
Besterman-Dahan, Karen, Jason Lind, and Theresa Crocker
   2014   "You never heard Jesus say to make sure you take time out for yourself": Military chaplains and the
          stigma of mental illness. Annals of Anthropological Practice.
Borofsky, Robert
   2000   Public Anthropology: Where to? What Next? Anthropology Newsletter 41(5):9–10.
   2011   Why a Public Anthropology? Center Public Anthropology. Hawaii Pacific University.

Browner, Carole H.

    1999 On the Medicalization of Medical Anthropology. Medical Anthropology Quarterly 13(2):135-140.

Brownson, Ross C., Graham A. Colditz, and Enola K. Proctor, eds.

    2012 Dissemination and Implementation Research in Health: Translating Science to Practice. Oxford, UK: Oxford University Press.

Checker, Melissa, David Vine, and Alaka Wali

    2010 A Sea Change in Anthropology? Public Anthropology Reviews 112(3):5–6.

Cheney, Ann M., Audrey Dunn, Brenda M. Booth, Libby Frith, and Geoffrey M. Curran.

    2014 The intersections of gender and power in women Veteran's experiences of substance use and VA care. Annals of Anthropological Practice 27(2):353–375.

Cotner, Bridget A. Jennie Keleher, Danielle R. O'Connor, John K. Trainor, and Lisa Ottmanelli

    2014 The role of social networks for Veterans with spinal cord injury in obtaining employment. Annals of Anthropological Practice 27(2):244–260.

Ferner, Matt

    2013 Patricia Adler, CU-Boulder Professor Allegedly Forced Out Over Prostitution Lecture. Huffington Post on-line. http://www.huffingtonpost.com/2013/12/16/patricia-adler-deviance_n_4454652.html, accessed December 23, 2013.

Fix, Gemmae

    2014 Anthropologist and government employee:career paths to becoming an applied anthropologist. Annals of Anthropological Practice 27(2):224–243.

Finley, Erin

    2014 Moving the national dialogue around PTSD forward: the role of the VA and other cultural institutions in empowering Veterans for the next generation. Annals of Anthropological Practice 27(2):279–295.

Fluehr-Lobban, Carolyn

    2013 Ethics and Anthropology: Ideas and Practice. Lanham, Maryland: AltaMira Press.

Friedl, Ernestine

    1978 Society and Sex Roles. Human Nature 1(4):68–75.

Ginsberg, Benjamin

    2013 The Fall of the Faculty. 2nd edition. New York: Oxford University Press.

Hamilton, Alison

    2013 Bridging Anthropology and Health Services Research. Anthropology News. http://www.anthropology-news.org/index.php/2013/03/01/bridging-anthropology-and-health-services-research/, accessed December 23, 2013.

Hamilton, Alison B., Jessica Zuchowski and Donna L. Washington

    2014 Gendered social roots of homelessness among women Veterans. Annals of Anthropological Practice 27(2):296–311.

Haun, Jolie, Jason D. Lind, Stephanie Shimada, and Steven Simon

    2014 Secure messaging as a tool to facilitate Veteran-provider communication. Annals of Anthropological Practice 27(2):261–278.

Kleinman, Arthur

    1995 Writing at the Margin: Discourse between Anthropology and Medicine. Berkeley, CA: University of California Press.

Lamphere, Louise

    2004 The Convergence of Applied, Practicing and Public Anthropology in the 21st Century. Human Organization 63(4):431–443.

Lassiter, Luke Eric

    2008 Moving Past Public Anthropology and Doing Collaborative Research. NAPA Bulletin 29:70–86.

Lind, Jason D., Gail Powell-Cope, Margeaux A. Chavez, Marsha Fraser, and Jeffery Harrow.

    2014 Negotiating domains of patient dignity in VA spinal cord injury units: Perspectives from multidisciplinary care teams and Veterans. Annals of Anthropological Practice 27(2):334–352.

Lock, Margaret, and Vinh-Kim Nguyen

    2010 An Anthropology of Biomedicine. Malden, MA: Wiley-Blackwell.

Lohr, Kathleen, and Donald M. Steinwachs
  2002 Health Services Research: An Evolving Definition of the Field. Health Services Research February
    37(1) 15–17.
Longman, Phillip
  2007 Best Care Anywhere: Why VA Health Care is Better than Yours. Sausalito, CA: PoliPointPress, LLC.
Marcus, George E., and Michael M. Fischer
  1999 Anthropology as Cultural Critique: an Experimental Moment in the Human Sciences. Chicago, IL:
    University of Chicago Press.
McIntosh, Peggy
  1990 White Privilege: Unpacking the Invisible Knapsack. Independent School 90(2):31–36.
Price, David H.
  2008 Anthropology Intelligence: The Deployment and Neglect of American Anthropology in the Second
    World War. Durham, NC: Duke University Press.
Purcell, Trevor W.
  2000 Public Anthropology: An Idea Searching for a Reality. Transforming Anthropology 9(2):30–33.
Rubinstein, Robert A., Kerry Fosher, and Clementine Fujimura, eds.
  2013 Practicing Military Anthropology: Beyond Expectations and Traditional Boundaries. Kumerian Press.
Rylko-Bauer, Barbara, Merrill Singer, and John Van Willigen
  2006 Reclaiming Applied Anthropology: Its Past, Present Future. American Anthropologist 108(1):178–190.
Scheper-Hughes, Nancy
  2009 Making Anthropology Public. Anthropology Today 25(4):1–3.
Scheper-Hughes, Nancy, and Philippe Bourgois
  2004 Introduction: Making Sense of Violence. In Violence in War and Peace: An Anthology. Nancy
    Scheper-Hughes and Philippe Bourgois, eds. Pp. 2–31. Malden, MA: Blackwell Publishing.
Schmidt, Peter
  2013 Unfettered Academic Speech: Not in Kansas Anymore. Chronicle of Higher Education. December
    20. http://chronicle.com/article/Unfettered-Academic-Speech-/143697/, accessed December 23, 2013.
Sobo, Elisa J.
  2009 Culture and Meaning in Health Services Research. Walnut Creek, CA: Left Coast Press, Inc.
Sobo, Elisa J., Candice Bowman, and Allen L. Gifford
  2008 Behind the Scenes in Health Care Improvement: The Complex Structures and Emergent Strategies
    of Implementation Science. Social Science and Medicine 67(10):1530–1540.
VHA Office of Research and Development
  2013 About the Office of Research and Development. http://www.research.va.gov/about/, accessed
    December 6, 2013.

ANTHROPOLOGIST AND GOVERNMENT EMPLOYEE: A DESCRIPTION OF CAREER PATHS TO BECOMING AN APPLIED ANTHROPOLOGIST WITH THE U.S. DEPARTMENT OF VETERAN AFFAIRS

GEMMAE M. FIX

Center for Healthcare Organization and Implementation Research (CHOIR), a VA HSR&D Center of Innovation, and Boston University School of Public Health

The U.S. government is the largest employer of anthropologists, with an increasing presence in the Department of Veteran Affairs (VA). However, there has been limited discussion of the path from graduate school to an applied career. This article describes the motivations and trajectories of anthropologists employed by VA. Interviewees described their VA work as embodying the principles of anthropology and the ability to see the results of their work as deeply gratifying. [applied anthropology, federal government, health services research, medicine, interdisciplinary]

INTRODUCTION

I am an anthropologist. I work for the U.S. federal government, in the Department of Veteran Affairs (VA) as a "Research Health Scientist." I am continually and increasingly having conversations with other anthropologists about careers outside of academia, specifically in relation to how I came to work in the VA. Since becoming a VA employee, I have met other VA anthropologists and I ask them this same question. The purpose of this article is to provide the reader with the answers to this question from a group of anthropologists working for the U.S. Department of Veteran Affairs and to learn how each came to be both anthropologist and VA employee.

I was first introduced to the VA as an anthropology graduate student. Through a fortuitous connection, I was able to use the VA hospital in the city in which I lived as a doctoral research "field site," where I investigated Veterans' experiences recovering from open-heart surgery (Fix 2008). I enjoyed conducting research in the VA. The clinicians were supportive and curious about my research, the staff consistently went out of their way to help, and the Veterans were simply amazing to work with. I also knew I wanted to be a practicing anthropologist; I was not interested in a traditional academic career. This positive, applied experience encouraged me to pursue working in the VA. However, I was unfamiliar with how VA research functioned. Even though my research was conducted at the VA, I worked independent of other VA researchers and knew little about the organization. As I neared completion of my doctorate, I looked for a VA position that

ANNALS OF ANTHROPOLOGICAL PRACTICE 37.2, pp. 20–39. ISSN: 2153-957X. © 2014 by the American Anthropological Association. DOI:10.1111/napa.12035

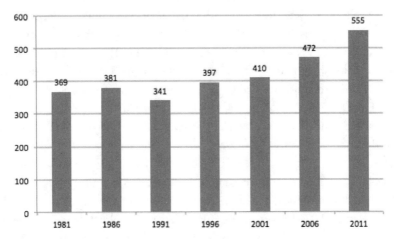

FIGURE 1. Annual number of doctoral recipients in anthropology.
Source: National Science Foundation, Survey of Earned Doctorates
http://www.nsf.gov/statistics/srvydoctorates/.

would provide further training in "health services research"—a discipline I learned about during my doctoral work, as I was able to fund my dissertation through an Agency for Healthcare Research and Quality (AHRQ) health services research grant. My doctoral experience taught me that both the VA community and the field of health services research were receptive to my anthropological perspective.

At the VA Health Services Research and Development (HSR&D) Center of Excellence in Bedford, MA, I became a VA health services postdoctoral fellow. The VA has several HSR&D centers located throughout the United States (see http://www.hsrd.research.va.gov/centers/). HSR&D is a division of the U.S. Department of Veteran Affairs that investigates patient care, health care delivery, outcomes, and quality through intramural research funding mechanisms (see http://www.hsrd.research.va.gov). The organization is composed of medical doctors, health economists, and social scientists, working to improve VA health care through grant funded research. I now work as a researcher in this collaborative, national organization where I use my anthropological perspective to inform health services research.

As an independent doctoral student, I was unaware there were other anthropologists working in the VA. But now, I have met dozens of other anthropologists who found themselves on a career path similar to my own, as both anthropologist and VA employee.

Over the past several decades there has been an increase in anthropology program graduates (see Figure 1). However, the number of academic career opportunities has not increased to meet their employment needs. The percentage of anthropologists obtaining academic positions has dropped precipitously. In the early 1970s, the vast majority (88 percent) of anthropologists with doctoral degrees went on to academic positions in anthropology or comparable departments (Givens et al., 1997). By the mid-1990s, there were more nonacademic career opportunities (i.e., federal government or private industry) available to anthropologists with Ph.D.s than academic positions (Givens et al., 1997). Between 1981 and 2011, the number of anthropology Ph.D.s conferred annually increased from 369 to 555. For the 555 doctorates conferred in 2011, 191 were seeking employment, 103 were continuing postgraduate work through positions such as postdoctoral fellowships, and 185 reported "definite employment" upon graduation" (see Table 1). Of these respondents, a little more than half reported teaching as a primary activity. Thus, many anthropologists are finding nonacademic career paths.

A U.S. Bureau of Labor Statistics report, which includes anthropologists with all levels of education, notes that "scientific research and development" (29 percent) and the "federal government" (25 percent) are the largest industries employing anthropologists and archeologists, followed by "management, scientific and technical consulting services" (11 percent) and then "educational services; state local and private" (7 percent) (Bureau of Labor Statistics, U.S. Department of Labor 2013). Within the federal government, an institutional presence of anthropologists has been identified at five federal agencies, including the U.S. Census Bureau, the National Park Service, National Marine Fisheries Service, Centers for Disease Control and Prevention, and USAID (Fiske 2008). There is also a substantial presence of anthropologists in the Department of Veteran Affairs, where these anthropologists are writing about their research findings in both traditional medical journals and anthropologically oriented publications (e.g., Besterman-Dahan et al., 2012; Cheney 2012; Finley 2011; Finley et al., 2013; Fix and Bokhour 2012; Hamilton et al., 2013; McCullough and Hardin 2013; True 1998; True et al., 2013). However, there is a little reflective information about these anthropologists' career experiences, aside from Sobo's (2009) book describing the intersections of anthropology and health services research, where she includes who own experiences as an anthropologist and health services researcher. Anthropologists working in the VA's motivations to seek federal employment, graduate school experiences, and their relationship with the discipline of anthropology are largely unknown. This information may be instrumental to other anthropologists seeking nonacademic positions. Therefore, this article describes experiences of anthropologists employed by the Department of Veteran Affairs. This may serve as a record of both how they became VA anthropologists and the landscape of their current work lives.

METHODS

A list of anthropologists working in the U.S. Department of Veteran Affairs was generated from the table of contents of a proposed special issue of the *Annals of Anthropological Practice*, devoted to profiling anthropological research being conducted in the VA. The table of contents listed 26 unique names, including my own. The sampling strategy was to interview all first authors. I contacted each first author and invited him or her to be interviewed. Interviews took place over the telephone or in person, between August and October 2013. With the interviewee's consent, the interviews were audio-recorded.

The semistructured interview guide focused on both anthropological background and VA work. It began with an open-ended question, asking the interviewee to describe her or himself. They were then asked how they became an anthropologist, with probes about undergraduate and graduate school experiences. Interviewees were asked to describe how

TABLE 1. Postgraduation Plans of 2011 Doctorate Recipients in Anthropology

	Number
All doctorate recipients[a]	555
Postgraduation status[b]	
Definite postgraduation study	103
Definite employment	185
Seeking employment or study	191
Other[c]	18
	Percent
Definite postgraduation study[d]	
Postdoc fellowship	71.8
Postdoc research associateship	27.2
Other/unknown[e]	1.0
Definite employment[f]	
Academic[e]	73.0
Government	8.6
Industry/business[g]	4.9
Not-for-profit organization	10.3
Other/unknown[h]	3.2
Primary activity[i]	
Research and development	24.6
Teaching	54.3
Management or administration	10.9
Professional services	6.9
Other	3.4
Secondary activity[i]	
Research and development	48.0
Teaching	18.3
Management or administration	6.9
Professional services	4.0
Other	2.3
No secondary activity	20.6
Activity unknown	5.4

[a]Respondents who did not report sex.

[b]Only respondents who responded to postgraduation status.

[c]Respondents who indicated that they did not plan to work or study, respondents who indicated some other type of postgraduation plans, and respondents who indicated definite plans for other full-time degree program.

[d]Respondents who indicated plans for other full-time degree program were excluded. Percentages are based on number of doctorate recipients reporting definite postgraduation plans for study.

[e]"Other" includes respondents who indicated definite postgraduation study plans for traineeship, internship/clinical residency, or other study.

[f]Percentages based on number of doctorate recipients reporting definite postgraduation plans for employment.

[g]Doctorate recipients who indicated self-employment.

[h]"Other" is mainly composed of elementary and secondary schools.

[i]Percentages based on number of doctorate recipients reporting definite postgraduation plans for employment and primary work activity.

Note: Due to rounding, percentages may not sum to 100.

Source: Adapted from Survey of Earned Doctorates, 2011. http://www.nsf.gov/statistics/srvydoctorates/

they learned about their VA position and work responsibilities. They were also asked to reflect on both their relationship with anthropology as a discipline and how their VA work relates to anthropology. The interviews concluded with a broad question about additional areas not already discussed. The interview guide was used flexibly; questions were asked in an order that best fit the conversation flow.

Interviews took about one hour. Audio-recordings were imported into the qualitative data management software, NVivo 10 (QSR 2014). I wrote field notes in a separate Microsoft Word document for each interview. Detailed, descriptive field notes were written as the audio-recording was played back, to create a detailed account of the interview (Bernard 2002). The field notes contained a combination of paraphrasing and verbatim passages. Analytic notes were written later, in a separate, single Microsoft Word document, synthesizing analysis from all interview data. I analyzed the field notes iteratively, as the field notes were written, using tenets of grounded theory and an a priori strategy based on my own experiences as a VA anthropologist (Patton 2002).

Interviewees were not compensated for their time. This study was reviewed by the Bedford VA Institutional Review Board, and determined to not be human subjects research. All interviewees were invited to review this manuscript prior to submission.

FINDINGS

The following findings are from interviews with ten anthropologists working in VA: Besterman-Dahan, Cheney, Cotner, Finley, Hamilton, Haun, Lind, McCullough, Ono, and True. I also include my own views and reflections as appropriate. I knew most of the interviewees prior to the interview. McCullough works in the same VA research center as I do. I met Besterman-Dahan, Finley, Hamilton, and Ono when we were on a panel at the 2010 American Anthropological Association annual meeting at a session composed of individual research presentations about VA research studies. I knew True through exchanges on a mailing list used by VA anthropologists. I had not previously spoken with Cotner, Lind, or Haun.

Graduate School

Most interviewees received doctorates in anthropology (see Table 2). Cotner has a master's degree in anthropology and self-identifies as an anthropologist, however she chose to pursue a doctorate in education to enhance methodological aspects of her training (e.g., evaluation and quantitative methods). Haun, who has a doctorate in health behavior, was included in these interviews to inform how nonanthropologists working in VA perceive anthropologists. True has a doctorate in folklore. She used to refer to herself as an anthropologist, but is now "owning" her identity as a folklorist.

Nearly all interviewees had undergraduate degrees in anthropology. Finley, Hamilton, and Lind also received Master of Public Health (MPH) degrees. Besterman-Dahan worked as a clinical dietitian and received a master's in adult education before proceeding to a doctorate in anthropology. Besterman-Dahan, Cheney, Cotner, Finley, Lind, Ono, and I went directly from graduate school to being employed by the VA. McCullough

TABLE 2. Interviewee Education and Employment

Interviewee	Degree	Anthropological Subfield	Degree Year	University	Other Advanced Degree	Began Working in VA
Besterman-Dahan, Karen, Ph.D., RD	Ph.D. Applied Anthropology	Biocultural anthropology	2008	University of South Florida	MA Adult Education	2008
Cheney, Ann M., Ph.D.	Ph.D. Anthropology	Medical Anthropology	2010	University of Connecticut		2010
Cotner, Bridget A., Ph.D.	Ph.D. Curriculum and Instruction, College of Education	Applied Anthropology	2014	University of South Florida	MA Applied Anthropology	2011
Finley, Erin P, Ph.D., MPH	Ph.D. Medical Anthropology	Medical Anthropology	2009	Emory University	MPH	2009
Fix, Gemmae, Ph.D.	Ph.D. Anthropology	Human Biology	2008	University at Buffalo		2008
Hamilton, Alison, Ph.D., MPH	Ph.D. Anthropology	Medical and Psychological	2002	University of California, Los Angeles	MPH	2002 contract; 2006 VA employee
Haun, Jolie, Ph.D., EdS	Ph.D. Health Behavior	N/A	2007	University of Florida	MS, EdS Counseling in Human Systems	2009
Lind, Jason D., Ph.D., MPH	Ph.D. Applied Anthropology		2009	University of South Florida	MPH	2009
McCullough, Megan, Ph.D.	Ph.D. Anthropology	Medical Anthropology	2006	New York University		2012
Ono, Sarah, Ph.D.	Ph.D. Anthropology	Cultural Anthropology	2010	University of Iowa		2009
True, Gala, Ph.D.	Ph.D. Folklore (BA Anthropology)		2000	University of Pennsylvania		2008

was a visiting professor between graduating and working for the VA. Hamilton and True had non-VA research positions before becoming VA employees.

Most started working for the VA within the past few years. Hamilton has the longest tenure. She began working part-time for the VA as a "contractor" in 2002; she did not transition to being a VA employee until 2006. True began working part-time for the VA in 2007, when a colleague asked her to join a VA study. Hamilton, McCullough, and True learned about their VA positions from professional connections; Besterman-Dahan, Cotner, Lind, and Ono saw positions posted on e-mail distribution lists; Cheney saw a position posted on the American Anthropological Association website. Finley and I continued on with the VA through formalized postdoctoral programs, after conducting our independent doctoral research at a VA hospital.

Interviewees discussed graduate school both in terms of the formal curriculum and their doctoral research. (In the remainder of the paper, I will refer to the people I interviewed as interviewees, as they were not traditional, deidentified research subjects. Additionally, quotes will not be linked to individuals to maintain confidentiality and in appreciation of our candid conversations.) Interviewees described a range in the amount of theoretical and methodological coursework with some heavily methodological and others very theoretical. Only one described a program strong in both methodological and theoretical training, "I had very good exposure to different kinds of methods, but I also had very good theory." All of the interviewees brought up their methodological training because of the relevance to their current position, where their methodological skills were seen as a key aspect of VA work. The amount of methods courses varied from an intensive to negligible amounts. Of note, three authors graduated from the University of South Florida's applied anthropology program—each remarking during the course of the interview that it was the first such program in the United States. Those who felt they had received minimal methodological training now felt deficient because the VA positions were namely for "qualitative" skills. One interviewee reflected that, "I did not get diddly-squat for methods training and that has been an issue over time." She later stated, given her current work needs, "I would have pushed harder to find more methods training." However, she noted receiving more training would have been difficult because she was not judged as a doctoral student on her methodological expertise; methods were viewed as a small facet of earning a doctorate in anthropology.

Several interviewees described programs that emphasized informal training as opposed to formal coursework. One interviewee noted her graduate program did not teach method courses, instead students received "individual attention" from faculty. She characterized this as an older style of anthropology where students "jump off the deep end; if you can swim, great." Interviewees noted the benefit of unstructured programs, "I was allowed a lot of freedom to do things." Another added her program provided "a lot of hands on experience with ethnographic data." And yet another concurred, explaining: "So much of grad school, maybe in particular for anthropology, is the having-done-it." She noted the unstructured nature of anthropology programs encourage creativity and self-motivation. These interviewees each emphasized that learning methods through hands-on experience was a critical part of anthropological training.

A few interviewees brought up their theoretical training or their own inclination to using theoretical approaches to inform their current VA research. One interviewee stated, "I am crazy about theory," in contrast to another who described herself as not being a "theory person." She went on to say "[I] feel like I have to force a conceptual framework" when designing research.

Early Career Plans

As graduate students, some interviewees assumed they would have traditional teaching positions in anthropology departments upon graduation while others felt they always knew they would have an applied career. (The terms "applied," "practicing," and "public" anthropology have historically complicated meaning [see McCullough, Hahm, and Ono, this issue]. For the purpose of this article, I will use the term applied.) Some interviewees said that their graduate programs seemed to have an implicit assumption that students would follow academic career paths: "There was an implication that somehow applied was a lesser form of anthropology. Even though there was this larger argument that anthropology offers so many insights the world can use." In particular, this program made it difficult to receive training for an applied career. This interviewee was frustrated by what she felt was the tension in anthropological programs that eschewed applied work, but at the same time anthropology is a discipline in which contributing to the larger world is central. Several interviewees felt anthropology programs poorly prepared students for nonacademic positions: "I think that anthropology comes up short when it comes to training people to get jobs. There are biases in the academy when it comes to applied work. It would benefit as a discipline from giving real thought to how to prepare students for other kinds of jobs besides classic academic teaching, writing positions."

Others discussed having a "vague notion that I wanted to go into academia and teach. I did not think I would be doing what I am now, by any stretch. I envisioned a very traditional path that probably wasn't right for me, but it was the only one I was aware of... That was the only model I had. I had no idea that people did what we do." Another interviewee added conceptualizing a nonacademic career was difficult, "I assumed I was going to go the regular academic route because I lacked a vision of other possibilities." To prepare for an applied career, one interviewee identified professors with applied positions as role models. Several interviewees described graduate school as focused on academic careers, "I imagined that I would teach. I think I had a fantasy of some sort of small four year institution. It was not a fantasy I was alone in having." This interviewee added that path was frustratingly narrow because, "There seems to be a very strict rule—dissertation, book, baby—in anthropology, if you are a woman." She underscored "baby" as last in this series of events, and saw her decision to have children as affecting her ability to secure a tenured teaching position. Successful women she knows that got tenure track positions in anthropology departments had not varied from this path, unless children were taken out of this progression of events.

Others reflected that they knew early in graduate school that a traditional, academic path was not for them: "I knew that I probably wasn't a good fit for a strictly cultural anthropology environment. I can play a cultural anthropologist and I am one to some extent, but I knew that I wasn't going to be happy if teaching were my only options. I knew that the broader I set up my skill set, the more chance I would have finding something else."

Doctoral Research

Interviewees' doctoral research spanned a range of topics and locations. Field sites were both U.S. and non-U.S. based; some topics were medical, others were not. Only Finley's and my dissertation focused on Veterans. Despite the range of topics, doctoral experiences affected interviewees' decisions to seek VA employment.

All of the interviewees described their doctoral experiences and then linked how those experiences informed the work they now do. Several described changing dissertation topics as they embarked on or completed doctoral data collection. One changed her topic immediately before going into the field because plans "fell apart." Another had a remote field site, but "then life intervened" and a U.S.-based field site was chosen. And yet another changed topics after returning from the field, when her committee told her that writing up the data she had collected would be difficult; they suggested instead using existing data from another study. None of these interviewees expressed concern about their experiences of shifting dissertation topics, rather they saw their flexibility as informing how they manage current research challenges. After describing multiple bureaucratic issues commencing dissertation data collection, one interviewee said, "It ended up working out beautifully."

Several spoke of departmental support pursuing nonacademic careers. But this was not universal: "I got so much crap from some of the people within my department who really think if you go outside academia and work at an institution, that you will be co-opted and your work will be co-opted and corrupted. There is a lot of suspicion about those of us who wanted to do applied work, a view that we were not pure."

Becoming a VA Anthropologist

The decision to seek VA employment was described as resulting from the job market, life events, a desire for a work-life balance, and as a means to apply anthropological knowledge. The lack of academic positions was attributed to the "changing economy, a changing academic structure. All of those Baby Boomers they told us were going to retire, when we were looking at grad schools in the 90s didn't. Those job lines went away." Another interviewee described a "window" for finding an academic position and described the difficulty of finding tenure-track positions beyond this "shelf-life." The lack of preparation for the nonacademic job market made this particularly frustrating, "You're on your own." The limited job market pushed interviewees toward applied positions: "I finished my dissertation during a period when the career opportunities in academics were at an all-time low. In anticipation of that I started thinking of other places where I thought anthropology would be really applicable."

Almost all of the interviewees used the term "practical" to describe the decision to become a VA employee: "It meant not uprooting my family, which was probably the biggest draw." A number of interviewees recounted personal life events that led them to

VA. Some had serious medical issues either personally or within their immediate family. Others simply wanted to start or had started a family, and viewed applied work as being more conducive to marriage and family life. Wanting a traditional job became more salient as the interviewees transitioned from graduate student to job seeker. Maintaining an overseas field site seemed untenable given family responsibilities. Having a set schedule, within the confines of a traditional work-week provided a work-life balance. An interviewee noted that working for the VA "definitely feels like a real job." Additionally, there were financial aspects to consider, "I needed to make money, and I needed to work." One interviewee noted traditional academic jobs did not pay as well as positions with the federal government or international agencies.

A VA position met interviewees' employment needs and provided the opportunity to be explicitly employed as an anthropologist: "On a very pragmatic level, the best thing is having a job, having that stability, and having it be a job as an anthropologist." This left interviewees feeling appreciative: "I feel like I am an anthropologist. I love anthropology. I see how many of my friends can't get jobs. I think about how fortunate I've been. How incredibly welcoming people are. When I say I am a medical anthropologist, people say, 'Oh, that's fabulous.'" Interviewees linked their anthropological training, their career aspirations and their current work tasks: "There is a very direct connection between what I was trained to do, what I set out to do, what I would like to do, and the position I'm in. It's not a big stretch."

Almost all of the interviewees brought up being unaware positions for anthropologists existed in VA, "I didn't know anything about the VA. I didn't know that they hired anthropologists." Another remarked: "As an anthropologist, you're graduating with your doctorate, or even your master's degree. It would be nice to know that you could look at the VA."

The Principles of Anthropology

Important to the interviewees, working in the VA was viewed as embodying principles of anthropology. The work was seen as professionally and emotionally rewarding, "I love my job. I get to do work that I think actually has the potential to make a difference." When describing their research populations, interviewees invoked social justice and critical feminist anthropological traditions. Many linked their graduate school research with their current work. Only Finley and I worked directly with Veterans during our doctoral research, but many others identified doctoral topics related to mental health, trauma, or women's health on which they continue to focus.

Interviewees were drawn to work in VA in part because of a perceived moral obligation they attributed to their anthropological perspective. They described feeling compelled to work with marginalized populations such as Veterans experiencing homelessness, or those who suffered from traumatic brain injuries, posttraumatic stress, serious mental illness, or struggled with addiction: "What was intriguing to me, why I applied [for the position], was because I love the Veteran aspect. And I love helping people who are marginalized." Additionally, several interviewees had family connections to the military.

A VA research career was especially appealing because it could positively affect Veterans: "We work for the VA. The bottom line is it is all about making the Veterans' lives better, in whatever that means for the Veteran. That's critical." Interviewees noted that in VA their work had the potential to have tangible outcomes and could change health care delivery: "[VA] work has real translatability; that's exciting." Research results could have a "direct impact on policy—that's every applied anthropologist's dream. It's to not just talk about what the issue is, but have a direct line to the policy makers." Having research affect Veterans was deeply gratifying: "I can see where my contribution might do something to actually improve things in real time, not like in 20 years, and that is the most gratifying thing for me about what I do now." Having tangible, actionable research results was viewed as an extension of this moral obligation to research participants: "My big thing is I wanted to make a difference in people's lives immediately."

Being a VA Employee

While interviewees strongly identify as anthropologists, they are also federal employees. Being a VA researcher entails traditional office-based work, where time is spent attending to administrative tasks and developing, conducting, and disseminating research findings. More traditional, anthropological fieldwork frequently takes the interviewees out of the office to collect data. Some interviewees work on a limited number of research studies, while others juggle a range of projects.

Almost all of the interviewees work full time as VA employees, with a few devoting a percentage of time to an academic position with comparable research responsibilities. These non-VA positions are similar in that interviewees work on grants to cover a percentage of their salary. Interviewees have affiliations with medical schools or schools of public health; some have courtesy appointments in anthropology departments, however none are professors in anthropology departments. Some of these appointments were largely symbolic and uncompensated, with few of the traditional obligations to the academic department, such as teaching. Many found the dual relationships with the VA and an academic affiliate complicated and without defined rules.

While VA's Health Services Research and Development (HSR&D) group is not a traditional academic department, the environment mirrors many aspects of academic departments: writing grants, publishing in academic journals, and attending professional conferences are key aspects of VA careers and markers of professional success. However, there are also key differences. Employees rarely have teaching responsibilities and salary support is grant dependent. In general, the VA HSR&D infrastructure compensates Ph.D. research investigators in a system based on a percentage of time devoted to a particular work task. Salary support may be covered through either "soft" research grant money or "hard," "core" funds allocated in a research center's annual budget. "Soft" money is composed of funding from research grants. Salary support from grants is calculated in percentages. An individual grant might cover anywhere from 5 to 100 percent of a person's salary. As a rough calculation, 20 percent coverage means that there would be an expectation to work on that grant, about one day a week—or 20 percent of a week. The weekly amount of work may vary, but over the course of the grant, this would be an average "percent effort." VA grants often last between one and five years. The salary coverage needed, and number and duration of grants, can make calculating effort confusing even for seasoned VA researchers. Complicating this, grants have different start and end dates. From the time of first grant submission to actual funding can be as long as 18 months.

Some interviewees were "principal investigators [PIs]," meaning they took primary responsibility, as part of a team, leading a research grant. The role of PI entails conceptualizing, writing, and then carrying out a grant—bearing ultimate responsibility for all aspects of a study. Others worked as "investigators" or "analysts" on other people's grants or were part of their research center's "core." These categories are not mutually exclusive. Interviewees' work roles were often a combination of PI, investigator, or analyst, with some having responsibilities in their site's "qualitative core." Despite differing titles, work tasks encompassed "doing the nitty-gritty of research." Interviewees described writing grants, working on other people's studies, collecting data through interviews or focus groups, and writing manuscripts for publication in academic journals.

Being a principal investigator often carries the responsibility of ensuring salary coverage—either on your own grant, or others, or a mixture of both. As might be imagined, achieving consistent, 100 percent salary coverage is complicated, challenging, and demanding: "One thing that is incredibly stressful is working in a world of soft money. I sometimes think if I were in an academic setting, would I really have to worry about getting grant money?" The percentage of funding could be below or above 100 percent. Therefore it was possible to not receive a full paycheck, although no interviewee said this happened.

In calculating percent effort, some interviewees described difficulties determining how much effort they were contributing to a project, and reflected on past occasions they had poorly calculated the amount of work. One interviewee recounted sarcastically, "'Okay, I'll do 15 focus groups for 10% effort.' If you do that one too many times, you may not make it." She explained this might mean uncompensated work, because 15 focus groups could equal several days a week of work, far more than the half-day one would be compensated through 10 percent funding. This calculation had been particularly challenging for her because there were no other anthropologists, or even qualitative researchers, where she worked to help explain how to calculate effort.

The presence and amount of anthropology ebbed and flowed. When asked how anthropology fit into VA work, one interviewee responded, "It's always there. It's my foundation. It's where all the other things come to. It's where I am grounded." She then carried on the analogy to describe "geysers" as events that come up, which provide a direct link to anthropology, such as interacting with other VA anthropologists, presenting at the American Anthropological Association's annual meeting, or writing a chapter for the *Annals of Anthropological Practice*.

VA Work-Life

As in all professions, VA work-life has challenges. Interviewees noted difficulties they saw as inherent in a 9–5 job with a set "tour of duty." Interviewees described working in cubicles and having to follow rules such as formally requesting time off. This was juxtaposed against an academic environment, where, for example, bringing small children to work was permissible. Despite there being a set schedule, interviewees also mentioned autonomy in scheduling their time. Many interviewees still identified with a more flexible academic schedule, driven by grant and paper deadlines: "Yes, 9–5 'tour of duty,' it's like that some of the time, but it's still research. If an article is due, the work still needs to be done. It is a set tour of duty, but it doesn't mean you aren't thinking about the work at other times."

Interviewees described bureaucratic challenges to accomplishing research tasks: "It's like the VA has two heads and neither head is paying attention to what the other one is doing." This interviewee went on to explain, "The research head gives us the money; 'This is fantastic and innovative.' Then you've got the other head: [administrative departments]. You've got this other head; they work at complete cross purposes with you. You better have thick skin and take some breaks." While interviewees were frustrated by VA regulations, they viewed it as part of the job, "Bureaucracy is a pain in the ass. That's just part of the territory."

Interviewees struggled with competing work demands and furthering career aspirations. One interviewee described how she worked as a methodologist on other people's grants while trying to "carve out time to think about my own work, instead of always running on the treadmill." She described her work-life as "always go, go, go," which made it difficult to find time to pursue her own research.

Interviewees had to explain anthropology to nonanthropology colleagues. While anthropologists were seen as valuable contributors to VA HSR&D research, there was still confusion about the details of anthropology as a disciplinary perspective. Anthropologists were primarily viewed as qualitative methodologists. A typical response to my question about who an interviewee was, garnered responses like: "My business card says, 'anthropologist, qualitative researcher.' That's my professional identity." One interviewee further explained she saw herself as an "applied medical anthropologist, but people are more comfortable with 'qualitative researcher.'" However, one interviewee noted at her research center: "People are saying we need an anthropologist on our team. It's not just, 'We need a qualitative methodologist.'"

Being viewed as a qualitative methodologist was compounded by confusion about qualitative research. Interviewees were frustrated by the lack of understanding: "Everyone tries to compare me with the quantitative people in my office. That's apples and oranges. They don't collect the data. They analyze the data, but that is way different than coding."

The need for VA professionals to publish in "health services" journals was new and challenging. One interviewee described her experiences learning a new writing style, where the content and organization was vastly different than the anthropology journals she was accustomed to. She worried about doing a disservice to both the participants and the rich data she had collected and felt constrained by the paper limitations: "It is a shift for me, as I sort of struggle to learn to cut. Part of what I was trained to do as an anthropologist is look broadly and deeply, and here the depth is fine, but it has to be much narrower."

Further, interviewees described difficulties competing for VA research grant money. This was particularly challenging because these anthropologists felt disadvantaged competing for health services research grants. This in turn shaped how interviewees incorporated anthropology into their grants: "This constraint of having to get our own salary, and having to do so through a mechanism that isn't necessarily anthropologically friendly, that creates stress and influences the way I do anthropology." This interviewee then described how writing in a traditional anthropological style was a poor fit for a health services research grant. Therefore, she wrote grants that focused on the qualitative aspects of her work: "My experiences of writing grants and applying to NIH-like mechanism, it's more about 'qualitative.' I will write this as an expert in qualitative methods, but when I do the research I am going to be an anthropologist." Another interviewee complained that nonanthropological grant reviewers "just want interventions, without really wanting to back up and see what the issues are" in contrast to anthropologists who are trained to "find out what the problems are instead of assuming." She saw the anthropological perspective as critical to informing successful health interventions.

Ultimately, interviewees felt welcomed and appreciated in VA: "I see this favorable response, very often they're like, 'Oh, you're an anthropologist! That's great.' There is a lot of respect for anthropology in health services research, and I think it's because of what we bring to the table, that's unique to our training." In particular, there has been a transition in VA funding allocation, toward "implementation science research." Implementation science is a field of research devoted to putting evidence-based findings into clinical practice (Damschroder et al., 2009; Davies et al., 2010; Helfrich et al., 2010; Powell et al., 2012). Implementation research projects are often conducted in clinical settings; the messiness of conducting research in an uncontrolled environment is embraced. Anthropologists are seen as particularly adept at conducting implementation research, "VA work—especially implementation work—is a great fit for anthropologists. It is a great fit for what anthropologists are trained to do—account for complexity, messiness. That is what we thrive in." The implementation portfolio of VA research funds many of the interviewees.

Being an Anthropologist in VA

Interviewees strongly identified as anthropologists and saw their work as anthropology. An anthropological perspective was seen as enhancing VA research: "For me it means that I bring a particular perspective to the types of work we do." Interviewees saw their anthropological insight as adding to a traditionally narrow, VA research framework. Anthropologists brought in a holistic, critical perspective, "It's about the critical lens I can bring, how I contextualize and situated their experiences. 'Okay, I'm an anthropologist, what can I bring to this project?' It's that lens we bring from our discipline. It's our contextualized understanding." Interviewees saw anthropologists as particularly adept at being, "really careful and thoughtful about how what we put out in the world is going to affect the communities and individuals we work with. That is one thing I like about the VA anthropology community."

There were also reflections on being an anthropologist in a large organization: "All VAs are different. They all have a flag, pictures of [President] Obama and [Secretary of Veteran Affairs] Shinseki. There is a lot of work by other anthropologists who are looking at institutions and bureaucracies around the world, but not as much in the U.S. It's fascinating to be a part of looking at VA institutional culture." Another interviewee likened working in the VA to working on one big ethnography, where all of the research taken together creates a singular, rich ethnography. Another reflected on how anthropologists study other organizations, looking for complexity. She felt this same lens was not turned to federal agencies, which were viewed as homogeneous: "How as anthropologists can we write off something as big as the U.S. federal government as one monochromatic thing?"

VA Research

In turn, anthropologists saw VA as a place with a lot of potential: "It's like this really great place for anthropologists to work. It's probably a little bit untapped." With another interviewee adding: "I feel like there are a lot of interesting people doing interesting, innovative, outside the box things. Even though it's really hard, and you feel like you're swimming upstream. People are doing really neat stuff. One thing I love about the VA, if you come up with a good idea, and you explain it clearly enough, then you can get funded to do something unusual—in the VA. There is support for coming up with new, innovative approaches."

Working in VA pushed interviewees to be good stewards of anthropology and exemplify anthropological practices. An interviewee described the need to explain her work to nonanthropological colleagues: "In an anthropology department, for academic anthropologists, who spend most of their time with other academic anthropologists there are certain things about the ways anthropology sees the world that don't get questioned and they do get questioned here, all the time." Working in VA necessitated reflecting on what an anthropological perspective brought to a research problem. This was seen as promoting rigorous anthropology. The act of being in the VA made being an anthropologist an explicit part of who someone was: "Sometimes I learn more about what it means to be an anthropologist by people telling me what I bring to the table as an anthropologist." One interviewee reflected on the group of anthropologists working in the VA, and noted the diversity of anthropological graduate schools represented: "Anthropologists in VA are being drawn from both large and small programs."

Relationship with Anthropology

None of the interviewees was employed by anthropology departments. This left them figuring out ways to maintain a relationship with the discipline and reflecting on what it means to be an anthropologist. Despite not being embedded in traditional anthropological departments, interviewees saw themselves as anthropologists. From their VA vantage point, interviewees felt they could now better reflect on anthropology. Interviewees described complicated feelings about their connections with the discipline: "It's a bit fraught, my relationship with anthropology. I alternate between being incredibly grateful for it and loving it, and seeing it as a huge part of who I am, and wanting to smack it upside the head." While they were comfortable describing themselves as anthropologists to their VA colleagues, they had a difficult time explaining what they did to their anthropological peers: "When I go to the AAAs I feel like an outsider. I don't really feel like an academic anthropologist and that is kind of largely how I see my interactions with other anthropologists within that context, but when I am with VA anthropologists I feel like an applied anthropologist and I feel a really strong connection." One interviewee described feeling compelled to project an academic identity: "When I am around anthropologists I want to put forth that identity that I am an academic still, even though I am in this applied world."

Interviewees were frustrated and conflicted. They felt like they had to prove they were anthropologists but also felt they were at the forefront of anthropology: "Outside academia is such an exciting place to be an anthropologist right now. Inside academia, it's really not." This interviewee went on to explain that in traditional academic departments and in traditional academic journals, anthropologists were applying old theories to new populations: "I see us repeating the same questions and calling on the same theory over and over and over, and you put it in a new environment, 'Who cares? What does that add?'" Whereas VA anthropological work is, "good for anthropology as a field because it forces us to deal with the fact that we have gotten stuck, particularly within medical anthropology. We haven't pushed ourselves past this on a lot of topics because we haven't forced ourselves to engage in the real world."

Interviewees wondered about the role of anthropology departments. One interviewee noted the need for academic departments to sustain and promote the diversity of anthropological practice. Interviewees were frustrated by what they felt was a disconnected, unengaged discipline: "For anthropology to remain viable as a field, I see this [VA work] as the direction that it needs to go in. There's too much going on in the world. There are too many problems and issues and challenges that we need to address as human beings, for anthropologists with so much to offer, to sit back and say, 'Oh, that's interesting.'"

Maintaining Anthropological Engagement

Interviewees sought to stay engaged with the discipline of anthropology through reading and submitting publications, presentations, and social networks. Within the VA there is a growing community of anthropologists. Several VA research centers have multiple anthropologists, which facilitates communication. There is a VA-wide anthropology research group, with an e-mail list for questions, information sharing, and periodic conference calls. This list has generated research conference panels at the American Anthropological Association and Society for Applied Anthropology meetings that are organized around VA research, as well as this special issue of *Annals of Anthropological Practice*. Many interviewees were pleasantly surprised to find a network of VA anthropologists, including other anthropologists at their work site: "One of the reasons I am so happy as an anthropologist within VA is because of the other anthropologists. I really feel like I'm part of a community who helps me do my job better. It helps me feel at home in VA; I take that for granted sometime. If I were trying to do this all by myself, I would not be nearly as happy as I am."

Being a VA anthropologist is rewarding and challenging. Each interviewee underscored the importance of his or her work, the anthropology it embodied, and the significance of improving the lives of vulnerable populations through good anthropology. Interviewees repeatedly emphasized their VA work was the work they wanted to do; choosing to work in VA was not a concession. Rather, it allows the interviewees to be employed *as anthropologists*. Notably, because these anthropologists are part of the VA system, research findings can directly affect Veteran health care.

Interviewees were initially unaware of VA work. Many did not realize VA hired anthropologists; jobs were discovered fortuitously. Graduate programs should better prepare students for the changing job market by informing students about opportunities outside of colleges and universities, and then prepare students to fill these positions. However, anthropology professors may have difficulty preparing students for nonacademic careers, since by definition they are academics. One solution would be to better engage applied anthropologists in anthropology departments and expose students to the range of professional opportunities. This relationship may have the added benefit of softening the suspicion surrounding applied anthropologists.

Interviewees struggled to maintain and integrate two identities: anthropologist and VA employee. While the interviewees had not followed traditional anthropological career paths leading to anthropology departments, they still strongly identify as anthropologists and see their work as anthropology. However, they feel conflicted by how the discipline views them. Many perceived a tension between their VA work and a more traditional anthropological career. From the anthropological end, some felt conflicted in that they constantly had to prove they were real anthropologists. Yet, VA work exemplifies many aspects of anthropology. Interviewees are working with marginalized populations and research results have a direct impact on health care. VA HSR&D research is informed by theories of human behavior, an area anthropologists are uniquely situated to understand. In an anthropology department, anthropological perspectives are assumed. But because VA colleagues are often nonanthropologists, we have to think critically about how anthropological theories and perspectives contribute to research problems. These experiences are pushing us VA anthropologists to move the field of anthropology forward.

It is also hard to be an anthropologist in VA. Grant-funded work is competitive and stressful, as several interviewees noted. The economy and concomitant reduction in federal grant funding may exacerbate an already difficult environment, as detailed by Sobo (2008). Our struggles maintaining funding in a "soft money" environment is not unique to VA anthropologists. Strategies such as crafting grants to reflect "qualitative" aspects of our work may yield more funding opportunities, and then a more anthropological lens can be applied once a grant is awarded.

Still, interviewees described struggling with the moniker, "qualitative." Interviewees were often seen by VA colleagues as qualitative researchers, which minimizes the richness of an anthropological perspective. This results in a paradox for the interviewees. They were hired because of their methodological skills, but at the same time many described taking limited methods courses. Instead, graduate programs encouraged independence, an important skill they identified as allowing them to adapt to the VA research environment. However, academic training in many graduate programs leaves a significant portion of graduates with training that is at an angle to what they are currently doing. Graduate programs might better prepare students for the job market by offering methods courses and explicitly linking anthropological skills to nonacademic jobs.

Nonetheless, overly focusing on one's "qualitative" skills can be confining. It is important that qualitative methods are part of a broader, anthropological view. This perspective was seen as critical, but more problematic to integrate into VA research. Several interviewees spoke about difficulties incorporating anthropology into more traditional VA HSR&D grants and instead felt compelled to describe their work as qualitative health services research. To combat this, these interviewees are actively working to make VA research more anthropological.

Having a network of VA anthropologists provides professional support among this growing cadre. Instead of losing their anthropological identity when leaving academia, the connection to anthropology is in some ways strengthened. These anthropologists have effectively establishing a new kind of academic home, embedded in the VA.

This manuscript has limitations. I only spoke with ten anthropologists who currently work in VA and are writing about that work. There are undoubtedly anthropologists who have left VA; their perspectives have not been included. Notably, almost all of the interviewees are female. They brought up the importance of family, children, and the need to earn an income. One interviewee specifically noted the difficulties of starting a family while also embarking on a career and the challenges for women who stray from the "dissertation, book, baby," path. Working as a VA anthropologist provided these women the opportunity to have a work-life balance, while employed as an anthropologist.

In this volume, McCullough and colleagues ask us to think about the words used to qualify anthropology, "applied," "practicing," "public." I ask, what does it mean to be an anthropologist? The interviewees represent an accomplished group. Many have achieved indicators of a successful academic career. They have published in a range of prestigious journals, received awards, and are recipients of grants from the National Institutes of Health, National Science Foundation, as well as now taking on the role of principal investigator in VA funded grants—a system with many parallels to other federal funding mechanisms. Real, rich anthropology is happening in VA.

Within the VA, the growth of anthropology may shift VA research culture. We are being recognized explicitly for our important, anthropological contributions to VA research. This recognition goes up to leadership. In a recent newsletter for VA HSR&D researchers, the national director of VA HSR&D research wrote, "Both HSR&D and [the implementation research group] benefit from the presence of anthropologists on various research teams" (Atkins 2013). Within anthropology, as traditional career models shift, there is tremendous potential for growth and new opportunities.

NOTE

Acknowledgments. This material is based upon work supported by the Department of Veteran Affairs, Veterans Health Administration, Office of Research and Development. The views expressed in this article are those of the author and do not necessarily reflect the position or policy of the Department of Veteran Affairs or the U.S. government. I thank Renee Cadzow and Bridget Cotner for reviewing drafts of this manuscript. I am especially thankful for the interviewees who assumed a very different role, as interviewee instead of interviewer, and shared their experiences. And finally, I am thankful to be an anthropologist in a rich, collaborative, and supportive research environment.

REFERENCES CITED

Atkins, David
   2013 Director's Letter. http://www.hsrd.research.va.gov/publications/forum/oct13/oct13-director.cfm, accessed January 11, 2014.
Bernard, H. Russell
   2002 Field Notes: How to Take Them, Code Them, Manage Them. *In* Research Methods in Anthropology: Qualitative and Quantitative Approaches (3rd edition). Pp. 365–389. Walnut Creek, CA: AltaMira Press.
Besterman-Dahan, Karen, Susanne W. Gibbons, Scott D. Barnett, and Edward J. Hickling
   2012 The Role of Military Chaplains in Mental Health Care of the Deployed Service Member. Military Medicine 177(9):1028–1033.
Bureau of Labor Statistics, U.S. Department of Labor
   2013 Occupational Outlook Handbook, 2014–15 Edition, Anthropologists and Archeologists. U.S. Department of Labor, Washington, DC.
Cheney, Ann M.
   2012 Emotional Distress and Disordered Eating Practices Among Southern Italian Women. Qualitative Health Research 22(9):1247–1259.
Damschroder, Laura J., David C. Aron, Rosalind E. Keith, Susan R. Kirsh, Jeffery A. Alexander, and Julie C. Lowery
   2009 Fostering Implementation of Health Services Research Findings into Practice: A Consolidated Framework for Advancing Implementation Science. Implementation Science 4:50.
Davies, Philippa, Anne E. Walker, and Jeremy M. Grimshaw
   2010 A Systematic Review of the Use of Theory in the Design of Guideline Dissemination and Implementation Strategies and Interpretation of the Results of Rigorous Evaluations. Implementation Science 5:14.
Finley, Erin P.
   2011 Fields of Combat: Understanding PTSD among Veterans of Iraq and Afghanistan (The Culture and Politics of Health Care Work). Ithaca, NY: Cornell University.
Finley, Erin P., Jacqueline A. Pugh, Holly Jordan Lanham, Luci K. Leykum, John Cornell, Poornachand Veerapaneni, and Michael L. Parchman
   2013 Relationship Quality and Patient-Assessed Quality of Care in VA Primary Care Clinics: Development and Validation of the Work Relationships Scale. Annals of Family Medicine 11(6):543–549.
Fiske, Shirley J.
   2008 Working for the Federal Government: Anthropology Careers. NAPA Bulletin 29(1):110–130.
Fix, Gemmae Maya
   2008 When the Patient Goes Home: Understanding Recovery from Heart Surgery. Ph.D. Dissertation, Department of Anthropology, State University of New York at Buffalo.
Fix, Gemmae M., and Barbara G. Bokhour
   2012 Understanding the Context of Patient Experiences in order to Explore Adherence to Secondary Prevention Guidelines after Heart Surgery. Chronic Illness 8(4):265–277.

Givens, David B., Patsy Evans, and Timothy Jablonski

1997 1997 AAA Survey of Anthropology Ph.D.s. http://www.aaanet.org/resources/departments/97Survey.cfm, accessed March 13, 2014.

Hamilton, Alison B., Amy N. Cohen, Dawn L. Glover, Fiona Whelan, Eran Chemerinski, Kirk P. McNagny, Deborah Mullins, Christopher Reist, Max Schubert, and Alexander S. Young

2013 Implementation of Evidence-Based Employment Services in Specialty Mental Health. Health Services Research 48(6 Pt 2):2224–2244.

Helfrich, Christian D., Laura J. Damschroder, Hildi J. Hagedorn, Ginger S. Daggett, Anju Sahay, Mona Ritchie, Teresa Damush, Marylou Guihan, Philip M. Ullrich, and Cheryl B. Stetler.

2010 A Critical Synthesis of Literature on the Promoting Action on Research Implementation in Health Services (PARIHS) Framework. Implementation Science 5:82.

McCullough, Megan B., and Jessica A. Hardin, eds.   2013 Reconstructing Obesity: The Meaning of Measures and the Measure of Meanings. Vol. 2. New York: Berghahn.

National Science Foundation, Survey of Earned Doctorates

2013 http://www.nsf.gov/statistics/srvydoctorates/, accessed October 29, 2013.

2011 Survey of Earned Doctorates.

Patton, Michael Quinn

2002 Qualitative Research and Evaluation Methods. Thousand Oaks, CA: Sage Publications, Inc.

Powell, Byron J., Curtis McMillen, Enola K. Proctor, Christopher R. Carpenter, Richard T. Griffey, Alicia C. Bunger, Joseph E. Glass, and Jennifer L. York

2012 A Compilation of Strategies for Implementing Clinical Innovations in Health and Mental Health. Medical Care Research and Review 69(2):123–157.

QSR International Pty Ltd.

2014 NVivo, Version 10. Victoria, Australia: QSR International Pty Ltd.

Sobo, Elisa J.

2009 Culture and Meaning in Health Services Research: A Practical Field Guide. Walnut Creek, CA: Left Coast Press.

Sobo, Elisa J., Candice Bowman, and Allen L. Gifford

2008 Behind the Scenes in Health Care Improvement: The Complex Structures and Emergent Strategies of Implementation Science. Social Science & Medicine 67(10):1530–1540.

True, Gala

1998 Introducing the Patient's Voice: An Applied Folklore Approach to Autonomy in Adolescent Health Care. Journal of Folklore Research 35(3):223–239.

True, Gala, Anneliese E. Butler, Bozena G. Lamparska, Michele L. Lempa, Judy A. Shea, David A. Asch, and Rachel M. Werner

2013 Open Access in the Patient-Centered Medical Home: Lessons from the Veterans Health Administration. Journal of General Internal Medicine 28(4):539–545.

THE ROLE OF SOCIAL NETWORKS FOR VETERANS WITH SPINAL CORD INJURY IN OBTAINING EMPLOYMENT

BRIDGET A. COTNER
HSR&D Center of Innovation on Disability and Rehabilitation Research (CINDRR), James A. Haley Veterans' Hospital, Tampa, FL

JENNIE KELEHER
HSR&D Center of Innovation on Disability and Rehabilitation Research (CINDRR), James A. Haley Veterans' Hospital, Tampa, FL

DANIELLE R. O'CONNOR
HSR&D Center of Innovation on Disability and Rehabilitation Research (CINDRR), James A. Haley Veterans' Hospital, Tampa, FL

JOHN K. TRAINOR
HSR&D Center of Innovation on Disability and Rehabilitation Research (CINDRR), James A. Haley Veterans' Hospital, Tampa, FL

LISA OTTOMANELLI
HSR&D Center of Innovation on Disability and Rehabilitation Research (CINDRR), James A. Haley Veterans' Hospital, Tampa, FL

The purpose of this article is to demonstrate the use of ethnographic methods to explore the types of social support provided to Veterans with spinal cord injuries (SCIs) who are participating in an employment program. Interview data with Veterans and their social support members along with employment narratives written after a job was secured are used to document the types of support provided to Veterans with SCI to facilitate obtaining and maintaining employment. The impact of social support on mental and physical health is well documented in the literature; however, there is a need for research on the influence of social support on employment. As applied in VA spinal cord care, the "individual placement and support (IPS)" model of supported employment for vocational rehabilitation integrates vocational services into clinical treatment, and includes social support members in the pursuit of employment goals. Guided by theories of social capital, the types of social support provided to Veterans were classified into three types: instrumental, informational, and emotional. Analysis of data showed that for all Veterans with SCI, some form of social support was needed to aid in finding and maintaining employment, demonstrating the need for evidence-based supported employment (EBSE) services in the VA spinal cord

ANNALS OF ANTHROPOLOGICAL PRACTICE 37.2, pp. 40–56. ISSN: 2153-957X. © 2014 by the American Anthropological Association. DOI:10.1111/napa.12034

system of care. [evidence-based supported employment, social capital, social support, and work]

INTRODUCTION

It is well documented in the literature that social support promotes physical and mental well-being (Helgeson and Cohen 1996; Isaksson et al., 2005; Jacobson 1987; Uchino 2006), life satisfaction (Lidal et al., 2008; van Leeuwen et al., 2012), and overall quality of life (Karana-Zebari et al., 2011). While social support from a network of people can be essential to overcome a variety of limitations, "there is very limited research about the importance of the social network for occupation" (Isaksson et al., 2005:1014). Further, for persons with physical disabilities, who have additional limitations, especially to employment, social support may be even more critical. Yet, little is known about the role of social support for employment outcomes in general, let alone for those with disabilities. Spinal cord injury (SCI) is a disability that creates significant life disruption that can clearly affect occupational and social functioning as well as health status. Thus, social support plays an important role in helping these persons adjust to the new conditions that SCI imposes on their lives (van Leeuwen et al., 2012). SCI affects more than 225,000 people in the United States; of these, the Veterans Health Administration (VHA) provides care to over 25 thousand (Veterans Health Administration 2012). Ethnographic research with Veterans with SCI provided an opportunity to address the overarching question: In what ways do social network members support employment for Veterans with SCI?

Incorporating ethnographic methods in health sciences research facilitated understanding of programmatic outcomes on the people most affected, the Veterans and their families. We used ethnographic data, interviews, and employment narratives from a mixed method, longitudinal study, the Spinal Cord Injury-Vocational Integration Program: Predictive Outcome Model over Time to Employment (PrOMOTE), to address the guiding research question. PrOMOTE is studying the translation of the "individual placement and support (IPS)" model for employment from the severe mental illness population to Veterans with SCI. This study examined employment and other rehabilitation outcomes over a two–year period for 280 Veterans with SCI at seven Veteran Administration Medical Centers' (VAMC) SCI centers across the country. An overview of the IPS model of supported employment (SE) is provided below.

IPS and Employment Outcomes

Vocational rehabilitation for Veterans is available, based on eligibility, from several sources. In the VHA, vocational rehabilitation is available through compensated work therapy programs. Historically, Veterans in this program participated in sheltered workshops or transitional work experiences in environments where the VA has secured contracts. Eligible Veterans with service-connected disabilities may also be served by the Veterans Benefits Administration (VBA) Vocational Rehabilitation and Employment and Chapter 31 programs, which offer education assistance and job leads, and/or contracts vocational services out to state vocational rehabilitation agencies.

IPS is a standardized form of vocational rehabilitation originally developed to help persons with severe mental illness obtain competitive employment in the community. The Department of Veterans Affairs adopted the IPS model in 2003 (Hamilton et al., 2013) and began implementation in 2004 (Resnick and Rosenheck 2009) as part of the recovery model for Veterans with severe mental illness because of its patient-centered focus (Pagoda et al., 2011). IPS has proven to be more effective than conventional vocational rehabilitation methods by applying the eight main evidence-based principles described below (Drake et al., 2012).

Jobs are competitive

Vocational rehabilitation specialists (VRSs) assist Veterans to find paid employment rather than volunteer, take unpaid work, or work in sheltered environments for persons with disabilities. Competitive jobs are those for which anyone can apply, regardless of disability, with compensation that equals at least minimum wage.

Eligibility based solely on client choice

This principle is sometimes referred to as "zero exclusion," meaning that anyone who wants a competitive job is eligible regardless of physical or psychological diagnosis, substance-use history, or legal history. In the PrOMOTE research study, Veterans had to meet certain eligibility criteria to participate: have an SCI, live within 100 miles of the VA (to ensure the VRS can provide community-based services), and have a desire to work competitively.

Integration of rehabilitation and health care

The VRS is attached to the clinical treatment team working with each Veteran to foster integrated care. Vocational services are elevated to the same level as other clinical services, with the VRS participating in regular team meetings and consulting with individual providers to exchange information on how to improve or address health issues as they arise during the employment process.

Client preferences determine job selection

A Veteran's personal preferences for work guide the employment process. The VRS conducts an individualized job search based on input from the Veteran and people in the Veteran's life. The VRS also speaks with the clinical treatment team to identify any factors that may influence the type of job, such as the number of hours a Veteran can sit without compromising his or her health.

Personalized benefits counseling

As part of the IPS model, the VRS arranges benefits counseling for Veterans so that they are informed about how different work schedules and pay could affect benefits they receive. This assistance may be provided at any time during a Veteran's participation in IPS.

Rapid job search

The search for a job begins as soon as a Veteran expresses the desire to work rather than prioritizing training and pre-assessments to determine strengths, as is more common in traditional vocational rehabilitation. Typically, the VRS begins contacting employers within the first 30 days of a Veteran's enrollment in IPS.

Community-based services

The VRS builds a network of employers based on Veterans' interests. Job development focuses on building relationships with potential employers in the Veteran's community.

Ongoing individualized job support

Once a Veteran becomes employed, ongoing support, referred to as follow-along support, is provided by the VRS to continue to meet the needs of the Veteran while employed.

Until a large randomized clinical trial, called the Spinal Cord Injury Vocational Integration Program (SCI-VIP), studied the IPS SE approach to employment with Veterans with SCI, it had not been implemented and evaluated with persons with physical disabilities. This study demonstrated that IPS SE was two and half times more effective than referrals to traditional vocational rehabilitation in returning these Veterans to competitive employment (Ottomanelli et al., 2012). A number of reasons may explain why the IPS model benefited the SCI Veteran population more than traditional methods of vocational rehabilitation. For one, the IPS model integrates vocational services within the medical setting by including the assigned VRS as a provider on the Veteran's primary health care team, so barriers can be addressed as they arise during job search as well as after a job is obtained (Ottomanelli et al., 2012). Second, Veterans with SCI had greater access to vocational services through the VRS assigned to them at the SCI center. The intensity of the one-on-one vocational assistance provided by the VRS through the IPS SE program represented an increase in vocational services over traditional vocational services (Ottomanelli et al., 2012). However, further research is needed to document facilitators and barriers to employment for Veterans with SCI through the IPS approach. The ethnographic research conducted as part of the PrOMOTE study is charged with documenting the experiences of Veterans with SCI and clinicians to identify facilitators and barriers to enhance future program implementation.

Theoretical framework

We situated our ethnographic study around how social capital, specifically social support provided by Veterans' social networks, influences the ability of Veterans with SCI to obtain employment. Social capital refers to "attempts to explain how some people gain more success in a particular setting based on the nature and qualities of their connections to others" (Johnson et al., 2011:11). The concept of social capital emerged out of work on culture by Bourdieu (1986), who defined social capital as "the aggregate of the actual or potential resources which are linked to possession of a durable network of more or less institutionalized relationships of mutual acquaintance and recognition" (Bourdieu 1986:248). Building on Bourdieu's work, research in education found a causal linkage between social capital and access to resources and identified that who we know and who they know makes certain achievements possible (Coleman 1988). For instance, the wealthy remain wealthy through their contacts with other wealthy people. Thus, social relations provide capital resources. Putnam (2000) popularized the concept of social capital through his book, "Bowling Alone," which identified a decline in the level of social capital in the United States. Putnam (2000) identified two types of social capital: social support (bonding) and social leverages (bridging). "Bonding social capital refers to links between like-minded people … Bridging social capital, by contrast, refers to the building of connections between heterogeneous groups" (Baron et al., 2000:10). Social support (bonding social capital) assists people in managing their daily lives by providing material and emotional assistance, such as transportation and encouragement, whereas social leveraging (bridging) helps people widen their social contacts and open access to more information and resources (Johnson et al., 2011). In anthropological research, social network analysis stresses the relationships among social entities to identify patterns and implications of these relationships (Baron et al., 2000). A critical feature of a social networks, as a form of social capital, is their interrelatedness, or what Scott (1991:3) calls "contacts, ties, and connections."

In this study, social capital is defined as social support that includes social leveraging by social network members. Emerging out of the work by Bourdieu (1986) and Coleman (1988), resources provided by social support members were classified into three main types: instrumental, informational, and emotional (House 1981; House et al., 1985; Thoits 1985):

- Instrumental: Provision of material goods, such as money, assistance with daily chores, and transportation.
- Informational: Provision of guidance or advice.
- Emotional: Verbal and nonverbal communication of caring and concern, such as "being there" and providing reassurance to help restore self-esteem or reduce feelings of inadequacy (Helgeson and Cohen 1996:135; Muller et al., 2012).

These three classifications of resources provided by social support members were used as an a priori organizing framework to distinguish the types of support provided to Veterans with SCI in this study as identified inductively from the qualitative data.

METHOD

An ethnographic study design was used to understand Veterans' experiences in obtaining and maintaining employment as part of the IPS program implemented at seven VAMC SCI centers. Three applied anthropologists served as the qualitative research team who conducted ethnographic research as part of the PrOMOTE study. The qualitative team alternated who went to each of the seven participating SCI sites, with two members conducting a site visit together. There were two site visits a year, approximately every six months. Each site visit was three to five days long, depending on the schedule. To date, four visits to each site have occurred with two more visits scheduled for a total of six site visits over the course of three years while the IPS SE program is being implemented.

Data collection at each site visit consisted of interviews, participant observations, and observations of physical spaces and resources. Semistructured interviews were conducted with four types of people: clinical staff members who were involved in or knowledgeable about the IPS SE program, Veterans participating in the IPS SE program, Veterans who chose not to participate in IPS SE, and social support members that the Veterans identified as being involved in their lives. Interviews typically lasted one hour and were audio-recorded using encrypted and password-protected digital recorders. Participant observations were conducted at meetings the VRS attends, such as interdisciplinary team meetings (IDTs) and meetings with Veterans on their caseload. Additionally, observations of physical space and of the resources available were conducted at each SCI Center; in Veterans' homes, Veterans' places of employment; and at community locations Veterans described in their interviews, such as of local public transportation depots. Field notes were written for all observations. A more detailed description of the seven sites, sample, and data collection procedures are provided below.

Sites and Sample

The seven participating sites are briefly described in Table 1. The seven SCI centers are geographically dispersed across the United States: site 1 is located in the Northeast; site 2 in the Midwest; sites 3 and 4 are located in the Southwest; site 5 is in the West; site 6 is located in the mid-Atlantic; and site 7 is in the Southeast.

At six of the sites, the beginning of the implementation of the IPS SE program ranged from August to November 2011, while at site 1, implementation began after the first year (July 2012). Three of the sites, sites 2, 3, and 4 participated in the randomized controlled trial, the SCI-VIP study that implemented the IPS SE model from 2005 to 2010. The other four sites (sites 1, 5, 6, and 7) were added in the PrOMOTE study to implement the IPS SE model in SCI centers that did not have an existing SE program.

Within the 18-month enrollment period of the IPS SE program in PrOMOTE, 280 Veterans with SCI, 66 from the original SCI-VIP cohort, met the eligibility criteria and were enrolled in the IPS SE program. One site, site 1, only had nine months of open enrollment due to their later start-up (July 2012) compared to the other sites and the end of enrollment date (April 1, 2013). The eligibility criteria for participation in the SE program were that Veterans have an SCI injury, be under the age of 65, be unemployed at the time of enrollment, live within 100 miles of the SCI center, and desire competitive employment. The age cap of 65 years old was to ensure Veterans were not over retirement age. The 100 mile radius criterion was set to ensure a large enough sample of Veterans while allowing the VRS to serve the Veteran in his or her community. Veterans outside of the 100 mile radius were excluded. The IPS SE program as part of the PrOMOTE study is for unemployed Veterans who desired to become employed with the assistance of a VRS. Previous SCI-VIP participants (66 of the 280 in PrOMOTE) were enrolled irrespective of age or employment status for longitudinal analyses across studies. Of the 280 Veterans with SCI who participated in the IPS SE program across all seven sites, 43 started working within the first 12 months of the implementation of IPS SE at their site. These 43 employed Veterans with SCI and 4 of their social support members comprised the sample for this analysis.

Analysis of the demographics of the Veterans with SCI revealed that the average age of the 43 Veterans with SCI who were employed was 50 years old, and the majority (95 percent) were male. While the number of female Veterans has been projected to double from 2010 to 2040, from approximately 9 percent to 18 percent (Department of Veterans

TABLE 1. Description of Study Sites, Number of Visits, Employed Veterans with SCI in the First 12 Months of Implementation, and Interviews with Employed Veterans and Social Support Members

Study Site	Site Description	No. of site visits	No. of employed Veterans in first 12 months	No. of employed Veterans interviewed	No. of social support interviews
1	Location: Northeast United States. Number served in 2012: 323 SCI and disorder (SCI/D) patients. SE services start date: July 2012.	2	7	7	0
2	Location: Midwest United States. Number served in 2011: Approximately six hundred SCI/D patients. *SE services start date: November 2011.	4	4	3	1
3	Location: Southwest United States. Number Served in 2011: Approximately one thousand two hundred twenty SCI/D patients with 30 inpatient beds. *SE services start date: September 2011.	4	6	5	2
4	Location: Southwest United States. Number Served in 2011: Approximately six hundred sixty-seven SCI/D patients with 40 inpatient beds. *SE services start date: October 2011.	4	17	14	1
5	Location: West coast of the United States. Number Served in 2011: 800 SCI/D patients. SE services start date: August 2011.	4	2	1	0
6	Location: East coast of the United States. Number Served in 2011: 665 SCI/D patients with 100 inpatient beds, including 20 long-term beds. SE services start date: August 2011.	4	4	3	0
7	Location: Southeast United States. Number Served in 2011: 2013 SCI/D patients with 100 inpatient beds, including 30 long-term beds. SE services start date: August 2011.	4	3	3	0
Total		26	43	36	4

Note *indicates that the site participated in SCI-VIP.

Affairs 2011), the number of female Veterans with SCI remains small, representing less than three percent in 2007–08 (Curtin et al., 2012). The Veterans were well represented by the three main ethnic groups: Black/African American, 48 percent; Hispanic, 13 percent; and White, 38 percent. Over half (55 percent) of the Veterans were divorced, 25 percent were married, and 15 percent were never married. The Veterans' level of SCIs varied: five percent had high tetraplegia (C1–4 vertebrae injured, resulting in no functional ability below the neck); 19 percent were low tetraplegia (C5–8 vertebrae injured, resulting in increased use of arm muscles with each vertebra); 33 percent paraplegia (no or limited use of legs); and 40 percent ambulatory (ability to stand and walk to varying degrees). Of the 43 Veterans who were employed, 53 percent had been employed within the last five years but were unemployed at the time of entering the IPS program. The majority of the Veterans had earned a high school diploma (58 percent), another 13 percent having completed a GED. While some of the Veterans with SCI completed some college (18 percent earned an associate's degree, 7.5 percent a bachelor's degree. and 3 percent a master's degree), the average number of years of education for this group of Veterans with SCI was 14 years.

For a social support member to be eligible to participate in a qualitative interview, Veterans were asked to identify people involved in their life who he or she would allow the research team to contact. Only four social support members were identified and, subsequently, interviewed. The low number of identified support people to be interviewed may result from Veterans protecting the time of the people in their life. The four social support members consisted of one significant other, two friends, and one Veteran's mother. The significant other and Veteran had spent the majority of their lives together, having met in school and dated when young and then reunited after a number of years separated. They currently live together with the Veteran's brother. Both friends who were interviewed had long histories with their Veteran friend and currently spend time together. The Veteran's mother provides full-time care for her son at home since his SCI.

Data Collection

As applied anthropologists studying the experiences of Veterans with SCI in the employment program, it is critical to learn from the participants what barriers and facilitators they have experienced in obtaining and maintaining employment in order to improve the program. The data collection procedure is described below.

To allow documentation of participant experiences through time, qualitative site visits were conducted approximately every six months. The first site visit occurred within the first three months of implementation of the IPS SE model at each of the seven sites. Following the first site visit, subsequent visits occurred approximately every six months (ranging between four and eight months in between site visits). Each site visit was scheduled for one week (ranging from three to five days on-site). As of July 2013, four rounds of qualitative site visits have been conducted at six of the participating sites who began implementation of the IPS model at the beginning of the study (2011), and two rounds of data collection have been conducted at site 1 due to their start in 2012.

The following types of qualitative data were collected during site visits: interviews conducted with Veterans (both those participating in IPS SE and those who did not participate), their social support members and clinicians, participant observational data (field notes), and observations of physical spaces and resources (also documented through field notes). In this article, Veterans in the IPS SE program and social support interview data collected during site visits and employment narratives, written once a Veteran with SCI obtained employment, are used in the analysis to address the research question. Both data sources are described below.

Open-ended, semistructured interviews were conducted with Veterans with SCI participating in the IPS SE program and social support members of the Veterans to document the experiences of the Veterans in the program from the Veteran and social support member perspectives. With Veteran permission, social support interviews were conducted with family, friends, and care providers. A total of 36 Veterans with SCI who were participating in the IPS SE program and employed within the first 12 months of participation were interviewed along with four social support members of those employed Veterans (Table 1). All interviews were digitally audio-recorded with permission from the participants, and lasted approximately one hour. When possible, two experienced qualitative researchers were present, with one researcher leading the interview and the second researcher providing follow-up questions as needed. Veterans and their social support members were informed and consented into the qualitative research and received a $20 voucher for participating in the interview, per Institutional Review Board approval at each participating site's institution and the VA's research and development review board.

Once a Veteran with SCI obtained employment, a narrative ($n = 43$) was written by the PrOMOTE National Clinical Coordinator who provides one-on-one and group training to the study VRSs as well as oversight on clinical activities to ensure the principles of the IPS SE model are being implemented with as much fidelity to the model as possible. Each employment narrative, referred to as a "success story," followed the same format: background, which includes a description of the Veteran's daily life prior to participation in the IPS SE program, why the Veteran enrolled in the program, and the Veteran's vocational goal(s). The second section focused on the Veteran's employment: a description of the job, accommodations and supports provided, and a quote from the Veteran about what the job means to him or her. The third section highlighted the IPS SE evidence-based principles that are illustrated in the success story narrative. Once written, the National Coordinator shared the narrative with the specific VRS who worked with the Veteran in the case. The VRS reviewed and edited the narrative as needed.

Analysis

Inductive and deductive methods guided the analysis of the Veterans' employment narratives and interviews to allow for the development of themes from the data and to classify the themes according to the three types of social support: instrumental, informational, and emotional (House 1981; House et al., 1985; Thoits 1985). A code book, consisting of known constructs, such as the eight principles of evidence-based SE, and constructs that emerged inductively from the data, was generated with new codes added as needed. A qualitative analysis software program, ATLAS.ti v. 6.2.28, (Scientific Software 2012) was used to code data using a constant comparative approach (Glaser and Strauss 1967; Lincoln and Guba 1985). Two of the qualitative researchers coded the Veteran ($n = 36$) and social support ($n = 4$) interviews separately. Once at least 80 percent interrater reliability was established, every third interview was coded by both researchers and interrater reliability calculated to ensure consistency over time (Huberman and Miles 2002). Analysis for the success-story employment narratives were coded by one of the qualitative researchers while the National Clinical Coordinator reviewed the codes. Any discrepancy in coding in the narratives was discussed and amended to ensure 100 percent agreement.

To enhance credibility of the research findings, the three qualitative researchers analyzed coded interview data separately, and then compared the themes that emerged to ensure consistency. Additionally, triangulation occurred through comparison of data from the three data sources, Veteran and social support member interviews and success story narratives.

RESULTS

Veterans with SCI in the IPS SE program received a variety of social network support that assisted them in getting jobs and maintaining employment. The key finding that emerged from this research was that all 43 Veterans with SCI received support from their VRS, people in their lives, or both, that resulted in becoming employed. This finding highlights the necessity of social support to facilitate job obtainment for this population. The types of support needed to obtain a job and maintaining it were key themes that we will describe below.

Obtaining a Job

The role of the Veterans' social network was critical to obtaining a job. Below, the types of support that emerged from the data are presented.

Instrumental Support

The majority of the Veterans with SCI (31 of 40, 77.5 percent) who were employed within the first 12 months of the IPS SE program received instrumental support from people in their personal lives and their VRS. Family and friends provided instrumental support through at home health care; assistance with activities of daily living (ADLs), such as helping reach for items and cleaning; housing; and transportation for the Veteran. Persons with SCI are commonly cared for at home by family members (Schulz et al., 2009). This type of support is essential to overcome barriers to community reintegration (Sekaran et al., 2010).

The VRS, who worked directly with the Veterans to provide one-on-one assistance in searching for a job, often contacted potential employers on behalf of the Veteran and introduced the Veteran to the employer to expedite the hiring process. Over half of the Veterans (58.8 percent) discussed the types of support they received from their VRS in their interviews. One Veteran stated, "You know, at that time I was just finishing up my degree. So I was needing somebody that was going to be able to assist me in order to fulfill my plan." Individualized support provided by the VRS to conduct the job search and identify potential employers was enhanced by the Veteran's social support networks that provided care and addressed critical needs such as transportation and housing. Access to social support from members within the Veterans' personal network of family and friends is an example of bonding social capital; however, the VRS provided social leveraging (bridging social capital) by contacting employers and other people within the VRS' personal network, such as other clinicians. When combined, the Veteran benefited from the "contact, ties, and connections" (Scott 1991:3) inherent in both types of social capital.

Informational

All of the Veterans with SCI who obtained employment through the SE program got their jobs through information provided by members of their social networks and VRS. As part of the IPS SE model, the VRS accessed the Veteran's social network to learn more about the Veteran and to learn of job opportunities through contacts the Veteran already had. When asked if his social network had been involved in the SE program, one Veteran responded, "Well actually, a couple of them. The VRS has taken their information ... she wanted to kind of talk with them and see if they had kind of a, relationships they have with other people so they can kind of extend the network." While getting to know the Veterans, the VRS identified people in the Veteran's life to contact or ask the Veteran to contact. Additionally, the VRSs utilized their own networks as well as those of the clinicians at the VA, and followed up with employer contacts identified through job development activities conducted in the community. Together, these sources of information facilitated all 43 of the Veterans with SCI to reach their goal of becoming employed.

Emotional Support

Family and friends of the Veterans with SCI in the IPS SE program were mainly support- ive of the Veterans getting a job with just a few exceptions. Supportive social network members were happy for the Veteran, encouraging, and wanted the Veteran to be suc- cessful. One Veteran stated,

> My family or friends... they like the fact that I'm working. You know, that's good for them to see that. They treat me like everybody else. I'm in a wheelchair, but they don't treat me like I'm in the wheelchair. I've always been that way, so they're happy that I'm out and independent...

Another Veteran with a social network less supportive of her going back to work said the following, "I tell them I'm looking for a job and they say, 'What?! You're looking for a job?!' I say, 'Yeah, they have this thing at the VA.' 'You wanna work?!...'" After becoming employed through the program her family was surprised. "Yeah they were laughing because they said, 'you working? Really? Where you working at? Is it a real job?'" Some family members and friends were unsure what jobs are available; others expressed being worried the Veteran would lose his or her VA, social security or disability benefits if the Veteran returned to work. One Veteran explained, "[My sister] is concerned that I'm gonna let go of Social Security, [when I] start working back." While benefits counseling is provided to Veterans with SCI participating in the IPS SE program, family and friends may not receive or trust the same information and may have concerns about the impact of employment on other income benefits.

Through the job-searching process and working with their VRS, Veterans with SCI became empowered and wanted to lead the employment process. One example of this was when a Veteran identified a possible place of employment where his nephew worked, but insisted that the VRS not go through his nephew; instead, the Veteran, according to the VRS, "wanted to secure a competitive position there on his own merits." Other Veterans were empowered through volunteer opportunities at their church or in their community, such as the VA, to "want to do more." Either through participation in the IPS SE program or through positive volunteer experiences, some Veterans gained self-confidence to take charge of their employment process.

Maintaining a Job

Once Veterans with SCI were successfully employed, their VRS and other social network members worked with them to facilitate retention of the job.

Instrumental Support

The main support for all of the employed Veterans was his or her VRS. As part of the IPS SE model, the VRS provides follow-along support for each employed Veteran. The type and amount of follow-along support was dictated by Veteran needs and preference, but usually consisted of regular phone calls or meeting periodically to discuss how the job was going and if there were any concerns, and to determine whether any accommodations were needed at the work site to maximize functioning. One social support member for a Veteran explained, "[The] first day her [VRS] and [Occupational Therapist (OT)] came over. And they did an evaluation and a determination. And they worked with the scheduling and the HR people. They'd sit down. We need to figure out what it is that we needed." A job site assessment is common for VRS and the OT on the Veteran's clinical team to provide upon initial employment to ensure a healthy work environment for the Veteran. If workplace accommodations are identified, the VRS follows up with appropriate members of the clinical team to submit consults for needed resources, such as specialized tools, software, or even new wheelchairs.

In addition to the ongoing, follow-along support provided by the VRS, approximately 25 percent of the Veterans benefited from having a natural support person on the job. The natural job support person was either a supervisor or coworker who provided assistance to the Veteran as needed. For instance, one Veteran's supervisor had "taken him under his wing" according to the VRS, and the Veteran and supervisor worked side by side during the Veteran's shift. The identification of a natural job support person was either facilitated by the VRS or occurred naturally on the job site through the Veteran.

A concern that was expressed by some Veterans was the possibility of losing their jobs due to potential health issues. While health issues can be a barrier in maintaining employment in this population, many Veterans relied on their social networks for assistance with their health and addressing issues as they arose at work. One Veteran explained,

> I don't really think he [the employer] knew much about my health, really. I don't know if you knew, you know, that I still have bowel and bladder problems that I might have an accident. Like one time I was late for work. I said, Hey, I was on the train coming over here, had, you know, an accident.

Bowel and bladder concerns were just one of the health issues that arose for the employed Veterans. Other health issues, such as pressure ulcers, affected the amount of time a Veteran could sit. Through the support of the VRS, the clinical team, and natural supports on the job, health concerns are better able to be addressed.

Emotional Support

One of the most common expected and actual outcomes of employment stated by participants was an increase in social interaction. Most of the Veterans discussed the positive benefit of being able to meet new people and expand their social networks through employment. When asked what goals he would like to reach as a result of participating in the IPS SE program, one Veteran stated, "Well, I like to go out and meet people and make some more friends and co-workers and just have a good time while doing it."

The ability to get out of the house and make friends in the workplace was such a motivating factor in employment seeking for Veterans that it exceeded the expected outcome of earning money for most Veterans. What is especially compelling about this desire for increased social interaction is that both Veterans who had significant amounts of social support from close family and friends as well as those Veterans who were socially isolated looked forward to the social interaction that employment would and did bring.

As an extension of Veterans' desire for increased social interaction, just over half of the Veterans stated that employment would make them active members of society and provide purpose in their lives. This finding incorporated the ideas of income and self-esteem associated with social interaction through employment. Veterans reported a desire to use employment to contribute to society, most commonly in the form of reducing their reliance on government assistance and paying into the system, but also in that their jobs allowed them to become more independent and "give something back." One Veteran explained, "A person in a wheelchair can be productive, they not just tryin' to hedge off the system as some people think and that the chair doesn't take away from who we are as people." Some of the Veterans hoped that their participation in the PrOMOTE study and the fact that they had been employed could be helpful to other Veterans with SCI by serving as an example that they too could be employed in spite of their SCI. "Started off with, I don't even think I was making, now about $60 more than I was on disability. But

I took it [the job] because it was helping other Veterans," stated a Veteran who valued being able to "help out fellow brothers in arms" as another Veteran put it, more than the monetary amount earned from the job.

CONCLUSION

PrOMOTE is the largest study to date conducted with Veterans with SCI participating in IPS SE. As part of the mixed method design of PrOMOTE, the ethnographic study was designed to document participant experiences during implementation, and to identify facilitators and barriers to participation in the IPS SE program. Through the use of anthropological methods, such as interviews and employment narratives in this study, applied anthropologists are well positioned to identify facilitators and barriers and to act on this information to improve programs or policies (Castañeda 2010; Shuttleworth and Kasnitz 2004). A challenge to conducting multisite ethnographic research is the limitation to the amount of time at the site due to the distance and cost associated with travel. While week-long visits occurred twice a year, additional time at each site may have facilitated a deeper rapport with the Veterans and subsequently, better access to the people in their lives. The limited number of social support interviews that were conducted may be a result of that. This article examined the role of social support members and the types of support provided to Veterans with SCI as they pursued employment. Applied anthropologists concern themselves with using their anthropological knowledge and skills to solve practical problems (van Willigen 2002), in this study, what types of support facilitate Veterans with SCI to obtain employment.

Veterans with SCI who were successfully employed within the first 12 months of implementation of the IPS SE program leveraged social support through the assistance of their VRS. As part of the IPS SE model, the principle of *community-based services* encourages the VRS to use their own network of employers and build on that network through job development in the Veterans' community. VRS served as bridges to connect Veterans with SCI to people outside of their personal social network who may open up opportunity for employment. In addition to social leveraging, the VRS facilitated the Veterans reaching out to people in their personal social networks to provide instrumental support, such as transportation to and from job interviews or place of employment, or informational support by identifying the people in their lives who may know of potential employment places or contact people. The majority of people in the Veterans' personal social network offered positive emotional support and encouragement with a few exceptions where Veterans' family members expressed concern about employment and the impact earned income may have on social security or disability income. A common barrier for persons with disabilities returning to work is fear about losing his/her disability benefits (Rosenheck et al., 2006). With the IPS SE model, the principle *personalized benefits counseling* emphasizes the provision of accurate, thorough benefits counseling for those receiving employment services.

Once a job was obtained, social support continued for these Veterans through *ongoing individualized job support*, a key principle of the IPS SE model. Follow-along supports provided by the VRS included regular contact with the Veteran to identify issues to be addressed and workplace accommodations. Additionally, Veterans benefited by having a social support person on the job site to provide assistance as needed. Work provided an opportunity for the Veterans with SCI to integrate back into society. Most of the employed Veterans in this study identified meeting new people and having more social interaction as an outcome of their employment. In the SCI-VIP study, Ottomanelli et al. (2013) found that "employment" had a positive effect on an individual's ability to participate in social relationships.

Veterans with SCI in the IPS SE program who were employed all received social support originating with their VRS and personal network of family and friends that expanded through social leveraging to an employer network and coworkers. The level of social support encouraged through the IPS SE model facilitated Veterans with SCI finding and maintaining employment and demonstrates the need for IPS services in the VA spinal cord system of care.

NOTE

Acknowledgements. This material is based on work supported by the Department of Veterans Affairs, VHA, Office of Research and Development, Rehabilitation Research and Development Service and a grant from VHA Rehabilitation Research and Development Grant (RR&D O7814-R). The contents of this article do not represent the views of the Department of Veterans Affairs or the U.S. Government. We thank Gemmae Fix, Lynn Dirk, Eni Njoh, and the peer reviewers for their helpful comments.

REFERENCES CITED

Baron, Stephen, John Field, and Tom Schuller, eds.
  2000 Social Capital: Critical Perspectives. New York: Oxford University Press.
Bourdieu, Pierre
  1986 The Forms of Capital. *In* Handbook of Theory and Research for the Sociology of Education. John G. Richardson, ed. Pp. 241–258. New York: Greenwood Press.
Castañeda, Heide
  2010 Im/migration and Health: Conceptual, Methodological, and Theoretical Propositions for Applied Anthropology. NAPA Bulletin 34(1):6–27.
Coleman, James S.
  1988 Social Capital in the Creation of Human Capital. The American Journal of Sociology 94:S95–S120.
Curtin, Catherine M., Paola A. Suarez, Lisa A. Di Ponio, and Susan M. Frayne
  2012 Who are the Women and Men in Veterans Health Administration's Current Spinal Cord Injury Population? Journal of Rehabilitation Research & Development 49(3):351–360.
Department of Veterans Affairs
  2011 Veteran Population Projection Model. Washington, D.C.:Office of the Actuary. https://www.va.gov/vetdata/Veteran_Population.asp, accessed March 13, 2014.
Drake, Robert E., Gary R. Bond, and Deborah R. Becker
  2012 Individual Placement and Support: An Evidence-based Approach to Supported Employment. New York: Oxford University Press.
Glaser, Barney G., and Anselm L. Strauss
  1967 The Discovery of Grounded Theory: Strategies for Qualitative Research. Chicago: Aldine Publishing Co.
Hamilton, Alison B., Amy N. Cohen, Dawn L. Glover, Fiona Whelan, Eva Chemerinski, Kirk P. McNagny, Deborah Mullins, Christopher Reist, Max Schubert, and Alexander S. Young

2013 Implementation of Evidence-based Employment Services in Specialty Mental Health. Health Services Research 48(6pt2):2224–2244.

Helgeson, Vicki S., and Sheldon Cohen
1996 Social Support and Adjustment to Cancer: Reconciling Descriptive, Correlational, and Intervention Research. Health Psychology 15(2):135–148.

House, James S.
1981 Work Stress and Social Support. Reading, MA: Addison-Wesley Publishing Co.

House, James S., Robert L. Kahn, Jane D. McLeod, and David Williams
1985 Measures and Concepts of Social Support. *In* Social Support and Health. Sheldon Cohen and Leonard S. Syme, eds. Pp. 83–108. Orlando, FL: Academic Press.

Huberman, Michael, A, and Matthew B. Miles
2002 The Qualitative Researcher's Companion. London: Sage Publications.

Isaksson, Gunilla, Lisa Skär, and Jan Lexell
2005 Women's Perception of Changes in the Social Network after a Spinal Cord Injury. Disability and Rehabilitation 27(17):1013–1021.

Jacobson, David
1987 The Cultural Context of Social Support and Social Networks. Medical Anthropology Quarterly 1(1):42–67.

Johnson, Jennifer A., Julie A. Honnold, and Perry Threlfall
2011 Impact of Social Capital on Employment and Marriage among Low Income Single Mothers. Journal of Sociology & Social Welfare 38(4):9–31.

Karana-Zebari, Dunia, M. B. de Leon, and Claire Z. Kalpakjian
2011 Predictors of Marital Longevity after New Spinal Cord Injury. Spinal Cord 49(1):120–124.

Lidal, Ingeborg B., Marijke Veenstra, Nils Hjeltnes, and Fin Biering-Sørensen
2008 Health-related Quality of Life in Persons with Long-standing Spinal Cord Injury. Spinal Cord 46(11):710–715.

Lincoln, Yvonna S., and Egon G. Guba
1985 Naturalistic Inquiry. Beverly Hills: Sage Publications, Inc.

Muller, Rolf, Claudio Peter, Alarcos Cieza, and Szilvia Geyh
2012 The Role of Social Support and Social Skills in People with Spinal Cord Injury: A Systematic Review of the Literature. Spinal Cord 50(2):94–106.

Ottomanelli, Lisa, Scott D. Barnett, and Lance L. Goetz
2013 A Prospective Examination of the Impact of a Supported Employment Program and Employment on Health-related Quality of Life, Handicap, and Disability among Veterans with SCI. Quality of Life Research 22(8):2133–2141.

Ottomanelli, Lisa, Lance L. Goetz, Alina Suris, Charles McGeough, Patricia L. Sinnott, Rich Toscano, Scott D. Barnett, Daisha J. Cipher, Lisa M. Lind, Thomas M. Dixon, Sally Ann Holmes, Anthony J. Kerrigan, and Florian P. Thomas
2012 Effectiveness of Supported Employment for Veterans with Spinal Cord Injuries: Results from a Randomized Multisite Study. Archives of Physical Medicine and Rehabilitation 93(5):740–747.

Pagoda, Terri K., Irene E. Cramer, Robert A. Rosenheck, and Sandra G. Resnick
2011 Qualitative Analysis of Barriers to Implementation of Supported Employment in the Department of Veterans Affairs. Psychiatric Services 62(11):1289–1295.

Putman, Robert D.
2000 Bowling Alone: Civic Disengagement in America. New York: Simon & Schuster.

Resnick, Sandra G., and Robert A. Rosenheck
2009 Scaling Up the Dissemination of Evidence-based Mental Health Practice to Large Systems and Long-Term Time Frames. Psychiatric Services 60(5):682–685.

Rosenheck, Robert, Douglas Leslie, Richard Keefe, Joseph McEvoy, Marvin Swartz, Diana Perkins, Scott Stroup, John K. Hsiao, and Jeffrey Lieberman
2006 Barriers to Employment for People with Schizophrenia. American Journal of Psychiatry 163(3): 411–417.

Schulz, Richard, Sara J. Czaja, Amy Lustig, Bozena Zdaniuk, Lynn M. Martire, and Dolores Perdomo

2009 Improving the Quality of Life of Caregivers of Persons with Spinal Cord Injury: A Randomized Controlled Trial. Rehabilitation Psychology 54(1):1–15.

Scientific Software
2012 ATLAS.ti, version 6.2.28 [Computer software]. Berlin.

Scott, John
1991 Social Network Analysis: A Handbook. Newbury Park, CA: Sage Publications.

Sekaran, P., F. Vijayakumari, R. Hariharan, K. Zachariah, Susan E. Joseph, and R. K. Senthill Kumar
2010 Community Reintegration of Spinal Cord-injured Patients in Rural South India. Spinal Cord 48(8):628–632.

Shuttleworth, Russell P., and Devva Kasnitz
2004 Stigma, Community, Ethnography: Joan Ablon's Contribution to the Anthropology of Impairment-Disability. Medical Anthropology Quarterly 18(2):139–161.

Thoits, Peggy A.
1985 Social Support and Psychological Well-being: Theoretical possibilities. In Social Support: Theory, Research, and Applications. Irwin G. Sarason and Barbara R. Sarason, eds. Pp. 51–72. Dordrecht, The Netherlands: Martinus Nijhoff.

Uchino, Bert N.
2006 Social Support and Health: A Review of Physiological Processes Potentially Underlying Links to Disease Outcomes. Journal of Behavioral Medicine 29(4):377–387.

van Leeuwen, Christel M. C., Marcel W. M. Post, Floris W. A. van Asbeck, Helma M. H. Bongers-Janssen, Lucas H. V. van der Woude, Sonja de Groot, and Eline Lindeman
2012 Life Satisfaction in People with Spinal Cord Injury During the First Five Years after Discharge from Inpatient Rehabilitation. Disability and Rehabilitation 34(1):76–83.

van Willigen, John
2002 Applied Anthropology: An Introduction. Westport, CT: Greenwood Publishing Group, Inc.

Veterans Health Administration
2012 State of VA Research 2012: Improving Veterans' Lives. Veterans Health Administration report. http://www.research.va.gov/resources/pubs/docs/state-of-va-research2012.pdf, accessed October 29, 2013.

EVALUATING SECURE MESSAGING FROM THE VETERAN PERSPECTIVE: INFORMING THE ADOPTION AND SUSTAINED USE OF A PATIENT-DRIVEN COMMUNICATION PLATFORM

JOLIE N. HAUN
HSR&D Center of Innovation on Disability and Rehabilitation Research (CINDRR), James A. Haley Veterans' Hospital, Tampa, FL

JASON D. LIND
HSR&D Center of Innovation on Disability and Rehabilitation Research (CINDRR), James A. Haley Veterans' Hospital, Tampa, FL

STEPHANIE L. SHIMADA
Edith Nourse Rogers Memorial VA Hospital; Boston University School of Public Health; and University of Massachusetts Medical School

STEVEN R. SIMON
Center for Healthcare Organization and Implementation Research and VA Boston Healthcare System

*Secure messaging (SM) is a secured asynchronous electronic e-mail system within the Veterans Health Administration web-based patient portal, My Health **e**Vet. This electronic tool is part of a national transformation initiative to create new models of care to support patient-provider communication and promote self-care management. SM is designed to empower patients to communicate with their providers, but to date little research has evaluated Veterans' perspectives on using SM as a communication tool. This article provides an overview of a qualitative mixed-methods study with 33 Veterans who opted-in to use SM. We used a combination of in-depth interviews, user-testing, three-month review of secondary SM data, and three-month follow-up phone interviews to understand Veterans' experiences using SM. Synthesizing these data, we identified high- and low-volume users and characterized their reasons for using or not using SM. These profiles illustrate the Veteran perspective, enabling clinicians, administrators, and other stakeholders to understand how to adapt marketing and educational strategies and make system changes to promote and facilitate Veteran adoption and sustained use of SM as a communication tool. [Veterans, secure messaging, patient-provider communication, mixed methods, qualitative, patient-centered care]*

INTRODUCTION

Advancements in electronic communication technologies, such as the Internet and direct messaging, have surged in the past 20 years. Americans have become increasingly reliant on the use of these technologies to facilitate daily communication. As a result,

ANNALS OF ANTHROPOLOGICAL PRACTICE 37.2, pp. 57–74. ISSN: 2153-957X. © 2014 by the American Anthropological Association. DOI:10.1111/napa.12029

communication technologies are being integrated into health care systems providing a platform for patient-provider communication; in an attempt to increase access and promote self-care management. Patient-provider communication is a central component to improving quality of care and patient outcomes (Institute of Medicine, Committee on Quality of Health Care in America 2001). Secure messaging (SM), an e-mail-like electronic resource, is designed to promote continuity of patient-provider communication (Andreassen et al., 2006; Houston et al., 2004; Roter et al., 2008). Previous research suggests that patients value SM to communicate electronically with their providers (Andreassen et al., 2006; Houston et al., 2004; Roter et al., 2008). SM use is intended to improve patient self-care management, patient-provider communication, and effective health service utilization. Houston and colleagues (2004) found 95 percent of respondents felt e-mail was a more efficient means of communication with their physicians than the telephone; and 77 percent noted being able to communicate adequately without a face-to-face appointment. Limited evidence to date suggests that SM use may also impact utilization of health care services. For example, SM use in Department of Veterans Affairs (VA) has been associated with a reduction in urgent care use (Shimada et al., 2013) and another study showed a 7–10 percent drop in outpatient visits and a 14 percent drop in telephone contacts as a result of SM (Zhou et al., 2007, 2010).

Patient use of SM has also been associated with improved outcomes for chronic conditions (Harris et al., 2009; Zhou et al., 2010). Zhou and colleagues (2010) reported in a recent study that within a two-month period, there were improvements in care as measured by the Healthcare Effectiveness Data and Information Set (HEDIS). Patients with diabetes using SM improved on all measures recommended for testing and control of glucose, cholesterol, and blood pressure levels by an average of 2.4–6.5 percent over patients not using SM. In this same study, rates of service receipt improved in the SM group compared to the control group (Zhou et al., 2010). Successful implementation of SM provides a viable means of electronic communication to promote self-care management, and continuity of care.

Based on the premise that SM can promote self-care management and continuity of care, providers in the United States are being incentivized via Stage 2 Meaningful Use requirements from the Office of the National Coordinator for Health Information Technology to use SM to communicate with at least 5 percent of their patients (HealthIT.gov n.d.). My HealtheVet (MHV), the VA online personal health record and patient portal, provides users with tools such as SM, to manage their health care. As the VA system implements Patient Aligned Care Teams in the model of patient-centered medical homes, SM is projected to be a key mechanism of communication between users and their health care team members. SM evaluation research is central to changing the patient-provider communication paradigm and transforming care delivery.

The aim of this paper is to present profiles of high- and low-volume users and describe experiential differences between users in order to understand how people use SM. These findings will inform strategies and interventions to increase adoption and sustained use of SM. This approach was designed to capture the user experience so VA physicians and administration can better understand the user perspective and facilitate a more cohesive SM experience for Veteran users.

Secure Messaging

SM is similar to other e-mail systems, but it is a secure system designed for use by Veterans and their VA health care team. Veterans must sign up for MHV, verify their identity in person at a VA facility (a process called "in-person authentication"), and then opt-in online to gain access to SM. SMs can be initiated by the Veteran user or members of the health care team. As long as the individual is signed in to his or her MHV SM account, the user can send SMs at any time. Users can select among a set of possible recipients, draft messages, provide a subject header, and categorize their message into one of four categories (i.e., test, medication, general, appointment) to inform recipient of the topic of the SM. When a Veteran sends an SM, a designated member of the VA clinical team receives the message and can either respond directly to the Veteran or triage (forward) the message to another member of the clinical team. If an SM from a Veteran does not receive a timely response once triaged to a team member, the message is automatically tagged as a high-priority message—termed "escalation" within the VA—prompting action by the team member. Though response times can vary, the established expectation for response time to Veterans SMs is three federal business days.

Understanding Sm Use From An Anthropological Perspective

Implementing SM within the VA requires systematic inquiry to identify barriers and facilitators to user adoption and utilization. As such, the Technology Acceptance Model (Mathieson 1991) and Theory of Planned Behavior (Glanz et al., 2008) have been found to be useful in predicting adoption of technology. These theoretical frameworks facilitate the evaluation of SM from the user's perspective. As such, these frameworks were used in the development of the interview items and data collection process. However, to understand the user's perspective within the context of the social and health care cultural environment, the integration of medical anthropology is needed. SM is an electronic communication phenomenon within the VA health care system, to adapt to the changing modernized health care delivery paradigm (Albrecht et al., 2003). Medical anthropology provides a multidimensional and ecological perspective that applies meaning to the understanding of SM as a communication tool within the health care culture, as an influence in health, health care communication, and self-care management (Anderson 1996; Baer and Susser 2003).

In alignment with the medical anthropological perspective, this work featured qualitative methods aimed to explore the health culture phenomena of Veteran-provider communication via SM. The mixed methods used in this study were designed to collect data using multiple data sources to arrive at a holistic understanding of Veterans' experiences. This approach reflects and develops a knowledge base on the meaning of SM as a communication and self-care management tool for Veterans (Philipsen 1992). The purpose from this perspective was to describe and interpret the shared patterns of values, behaviors, and beliefs of SM users and nonusers, and determine distinguishing factors of the two groups. Understanding SM from the Veterans' perspective is Veteran-centered and can inform interpersonal, marketing, and system-based efforts to make SM a useful and user-friendly tool for communication between Veterans and their health care team members.

METHODS

This prospective descriptive qualitative study used mixed-methods to describe Veterans' experiences using SM. In-depth interviews, user-testing, a three-month review of secondary Veteran SM data, and three-month follow-up phone interviews were used to characterize Veteran SM utilization. Computer and health literacy and patient demographics were collected using a paper-based survey. This paper reports on the initial interview and secondary data collection components of this research.

Study Sample and Data Collection Instruments

The study was conducted at two large VA Medical Centers, one in the Northeast, the other in the Southeast of the United States. Participants were identified and recruited based on MHV Administrative data. Veterans met inclusion criteria if they were SM users without any cognitive impairment that would prevent use of a personal computer or the ability to provide informed consent. Based on qualitative sampling methods, an over-recruitment strategy was used at each site to allow for attrition, resulting in 33 total participants. One participant was lost to follow-up for unknown reasons, resulting in complete data for 32 participants. Each participant received up to $50 for their participation.

Data, with exception of the secondary SM data, were collected at two time points: during a baseline in-person meeting, and during a three-month follow-up phone interview. Secondary SM data were collected from the time of consent to three months post consent.

Participant Surveys

During the initial research visit, Veterans were given a 13-item self-reporting demographic survey to assess age, gender, race/ethnicity, education level, income level, marital status, computer use, Internet use, MHV use, and SM use. Health literacy was assessed using two validated instruments: (1) the BRIEF health literacy screening; and (2) the Rapid Estimate of Adult Literacy in Medicine (REALM) survey. The BRIEF is a four-item self-report screening tool to assess health literacy skills (Haun et al., 2009). The REALM assesses health literacy by having respondents read aloud three columns of 22 health-related terms (Davis et al., 1991). Electronic Health literacy was also assessed using two instruments: (1) the eHealth Literacy Scale (eHEALS); and (2) the Computer-E-mail-Web (CEW) Fluency Scale. The eHEALS is a ten-item measure of eHealth literacy developed to measure consumers' knowledge, comfort, and perceived skills at finding, evaluating, and applying electronic health information to health problems (Norman and Skinner 2006). The CEW fluency Scale is a 21-item measure of common computer skills (Bunz 2004).

Interviews

Face-to-face, semistructured interviews were conducted with all participants focusing on their experiences using SM. The interview guide was created following the Theory of Planned Behavior framework to elicit beliefs and attitudes; subjective norms; perceived behavioral control; and behavioral intention toward SM use. Other interview questions were developed based on the Technology Acceptance Model and addressed usefulness and ease of use of SM. Interviews followed the guide but were open-ended in nature, allowing the interviewer ample ability to ask probing questions and to follow up on interesting topics and user experiences related to SM.

Secure Messaging Content

SMs were collected, both outgoing and incoming, for each participant over a three-month period following consent. Data included sender and recipient identification, date and time of delivery, subject header, category of message type (e.g., test, appointment, medication, general), and SM message content. Similar to a medical chart review, Veteran's SM content was analyzed to examine the quantity and quality of content, exchange patterns, and timing of inbound and outbound SM between participants and their health care teams. This approach allowed for analysis of authentic user content and patterns to further inform research findings.

Data Management and Analysis

All data gathered in this study were stored on a secure VA network. Participant surveys were scanned and stored as PDFs. Audio-recordings of all interviews were transcribed, and later uploaded for analysis using ATLAS.ti version 7.1 (ATLAS.ti Scientific Software Development GmbH). Descriptive statistics from Veteran surveys were managed using the statistical software suite SPSS version 21 (SPSS IBM, NY, USA). Data from SM usability testing were captured using Morae version 3.3 usability software (TechSmith Corporation, MI, USA).

We used qualitative analysis methods to analyze all interview data to identify domains and taxonomies related to participants' experiences using SM (Strauss and Corbin 1998). We used the semistructured interview guide to organize and code interview text to develop thematic categories. Categories were grouped into taxonomic relationships and then compared and contrasted across coded categories. Coding schemas were developed by two research team members to create domains and taxonomies and evaluated for inter-rater reliability and credibility. Data were then categorized and interpreted, and barriers and facilitators were identified. Quantitative data were summarized with descriptive statistics to describe sample characteristics.

FINDINGS

Survey and Assessment Findings

The majority of participants were older white males ($n = 26$, 78.8 percent), all had at least a high school education, and 63.6 percent ($n = 21$) had an annual income of \$35,001 or more. Demographic characteristics are reported in Table 1.

TABLE 1. Study Sample Demographics

$N = 33$	
Age range	27–77
Average age	59.5 (SD = 12.0)[*]
	n (%)
Male	26 (78.8)
Education	
High school	4 (12.5)
Some college/vocational	6 (18.8)
Associates degree	6 (18.8)
College degree	8 (25.0)
Graduate degree	9 (27.3)
Ethnicity	
Caucasian/white	22 (66.7)
African American/black	5 (15.6)
Hispanic/Latino	2 (6.3)
American Indian/Alaskan Native	1 (3.1)
Unknown/missing	3 (9.4)
Annual income	
$5,000–$10,000	1 (3.1)
$10,001–$15,000	3 (9.4)
$15,001–$25,000	4 (12.5)
$25,001–$35,000	2 (6.3)
$35,001–$45,000	5 (15.6)
More than $45,001	16 (48.5)
Missing	2 (6.3)

[*]SD = standard deviation.

The majority of participants had adequate health literacy and eHealth competency skills. With a possible range of 4–20 on the BRIEF, the sample range was 10–20, with a mean of 17.7 (SD = 2.5). Similarly, for the REALM, with a possible range of 0–66, the sample range was 55–66, with a mean of 63.3 (SD = 2.8). Results indicate this sample has higher levels of health literacy than the general Veteran population (Chew et al., 2008; Haun et al., 2009). Electronic health literacy scores on the eHEALS, with a possible range of 10–50, had a mean of 42.7 (SD = 5.7), with a sample range of 29–50. The CEW produced similar findings, with a possible range of 18–90, the sample range was 54–90, with a mean of 82.8 (SD = 10.4). Though comparative studies are not available for this population using these tools, scores indicate this sample had adequate computer literacy skills. At baseline, all participants (n = 33, 100 percent) reported using a computer and the Internet more than once a week. Participants reported using SM for at least the past six months (n = 10, 30.3 percent) or longer (n = 12, 36.4 percent). The majority of participants reported using SM "at least once a month" (n = 12, 36.4 percent) or "a few times a year" (n = 16, 48.5 percent). The majority of Veterans, 81.8 percent (n = 27), reported being satisfied with SM.

Interview Findings

Qualitative analysis of interviews revealed that Veterans valued SM for communicating with their health care teams. Veterans contend that SM is an excellent alternative to calling the hospital, allowing them to communicate with their primary care team at their convenience (e.g., late at night). Veterans reported the top reasons they used SM included (1) general consults; (2) medication refills; (3) appointments; and (4) test results. These participant reports were supported by the secondary content data. Veterans also expressed satisfaction with the timely manner of SM communication; generally getting a response back from their primary care team within 48 hours, if not sooner (though secondary data indicated otherwise). Veterans reported no problems understanding SM responses from their primary care team members; and few Veterans noted being uncomfortable sharing private health information through SM.

Understanding the perceptions, experiences, perceived barriers and facilitators, and recommended suggestions for improving SM is very important for making changes to increase adoption and promoting sustained use. Understanding the profiles of high- and low-volume users can provide insights on users' perspectives to inform the nature of intended use or nonuse. Thus, these findings are reported as such, with a brief review of the data domains as they surfaced in the qualitative analysis, but also as the personal perspectives that surfaced based on high- and low-volume SM use status.

Descriptive Domains

Interview themes fell into four major domains: (1) perceived benefits of using SM; (2) facilitators for using SM; (3) barriers to using SM; and (4) suggestions to improve SM.

Benefits reported by participants focused on *resource* and *communication efficiency* between Veterans and their primary care teams. SM provides users with an alternative form of communication that allows them to avoid telephone calls with long hold times, answering multiple and sometimes sensitive or redundant questions from call center staff, and unnecessary travel to a VA facility. They also reported understanding that SM saves system and personal resources. Though perceived benefits are primary motivators for SM use, two major categories surfaced around perceived facilitators for using SM— *convenience* and *SM user-friendly features*. *Convenience* included aspects such as the ability to communicate during nonclinic hours (nights and weekends) and not having to make visits to the clinic. *SM user-friendly features* covered aspects such as standard e-mail formatting and feature options, message notification option, and folders for organizing received and sent messages. Veterans expressed the ways in which these features enhanced their ability to effectively use and manage their SMs.

Barriers are a primary deterrent for technology adoption and sustained use. Participants reported barriers related to *initiation and knowledge barriers*, *privacy* and *security issues*, *prohibited personal expression*, and *clinician resistance*. These themes included several topics including not knowing how to sign up and initiate the authentication process required to use SM, not being able to locate the link within MHV to access the SM feature, not knowing how to reach specialists through MHV, and not fully understanding in what context they should use the SM tool.

Suggestions for improvements to SM included ease of use/features, navigation, screen visualization, access and awareness, education, and marketing. To improve ease of use, participants stated the need for a clearer navigation path to get from the MHV site to the SM feature. Veterans also suggested setting up a default user preference setting that requires the Veteran to provide a personal e-mail address to facilitate SM message notification. Though message notification currently exists, Veterans reported being unaware of the tool, yet found it extremely useful once made aware of its existence. In addition to simplifying the message notification feature, standard e-mail features were commonly requested by Veterans including a print option, spell check, formatting tools, and a message receipt system (an automated e-mail stating message was received). Other ease of use suggestions included improvements for those with visual needs, incorporating larger print/font (e.g., visual icons), changing web resolution to eliminate the need for scrolling, and ensuring key elements such as tabs and icons are clearly visible without magnification. Another suggested improvement was for their primary care team members to identify themselves when responding to SMs. Suggested identifiers included health team members' names, photos, clinical role, and credentials. This would help eliminate confusion regarding who among their care team were responding to their SMs.

To increase usefulness, SM respondents most commonly reported a strong desire for access to specialty clinics via SM, especially to those where they are current patients. Veterans expressed frustration not having SM access to some specialists and having to fall back on traditional methods of communication. Others cited redundancy in having to SM their primary care physician in order to communicate with their specialist.

Other innovative suggestions included voice/image options (e.g., webcam, live chat), an SM Mobile app, separate SM log-out from MHV log-out, and the ability to import/attach information from Blue Button (VA's patient accessible electronic health record) and other MHV features (e.g., test results) into their SMs when communicating with their VA health care team.

High- and Low-Volume SM User: Shared Perspectives

Identifying high- and low-volume user perspectives can help distinguish these two user groups to understand SM use within the health care context. This understanding will inform interpersonal, system-based, and marketing changes to increase SM adoption and promote sustained use within the health care culture. High-volume users were operationalized by those users who used SM five times or more in the three-month secondary data collection period, while low-volume/nonusers were those with less than five SMs in the three-month time frame, with particular attention to those with no use. Though there were differences between high- and low-volume SM users, these two groups shared issues with getting authenticated to access SM use and navigation of the MHV site to use the tool. For example, a shared theme among these two user groups was *Problems Getting Started and Navigating to the SM Tool.* Based on shared perceptions of both high- and low-volume user groups, this theme is described in the following paragraphs with relevant participant quotes.

Problems getting started and navigating to the SM tool

Though there is awareness by VA leadership that the MHV site has usability issues and a redesign is needed, site navigation issues may be negatively impacting Veterans' use of the SM tool. This is the case for high- and low-volume SM users, and was commonly expressed in participant statements regardless of high- or low-volume SM use:

> It's not so easy to get that page where your first start doing it cause it seems kind of like every time I do it I have to, I end up googling MHV and then I have to look and try and find it and then I have click here and then I have to...I don't know...it seems like it takes a few minutes to get into the system and it seems like it ought to be easier....The organization of the page should be better. That's true of the entire MHV system. When they designed it they need to have somebody who's with it, actual design and how people look at a page designing it. I don't use it that often but still...it seems like it ought to be more intuitive. (high-volume user)

> The [My HealtheVet] desktop, they have so much up there, there was so much competing with prescriptions and, messaging. I think there are even secondary windows. There's nothing on the desktop, that tells you to click for....like the one time I really needed appointments and medications I couldn't get to them cause the, the VA desktop was cluttered, it's dense...I would say again that it was very klutzy getting to it. It's a great idea but it's not smooth enough, there's too much in the front page, the front window, you know, there's everything under the sun, it's like going to a restaurant and you've got the menu and you've got the appetizers, you got the wine list, all on the one menu and I don't think there's enough thought put into that. (low-volume user)

Despite navigation issues, high-volume users overcame these barriers and continued to use SM for several reasons, while low-volume users did not. Themes of the diverse perspectives represented by these two groups are reviewed in the following sections.

High-Volume User Perspective

Dominant themes that represented high-volume SM users were SM as a Convenient Form of Communication; Knowing the Purpose for SM Use and Having a Need; Preference for Alternatives to Traditional forms of Communication. These themes and related participant quotes are provided in the following paragraphs.

SM as a convenient form of communication

When high-volume users were asked to describe the reasons for using SM, responses clearly indicated the convenience of using SM as a motivator for continued use.

> First you get quick communication with your team; 2nd reason, you can communicate from anywhere with any computer, laptop, or iPad, or any source and 3rd reason, you can request, see your feedback from your appointment from doctor right away as soon as they answer back, you can print those results, you can keep it in your inbox and you can have your medical answer right away that can help your request. Rather than make an appointment and wait a longer process, so that's my three main reasons for the SM.

Knowing the purpose for SM use and having a need

A primary perspective reported by high-volume SM users indicated understanding the purpose for SM use and having a need (e.g., health-related issue) to use SM. High-volume users reported using SM to complete several types of tasks including managing appointments, getting referrals, managing their tests, making general inquires, and refilling prescriptions.

> ... [SM] can be used to communicate everything from refills, request new prescriptions, to order new prescriptions to the team or doctor, to request your labs. To be put into the system, to request to have the doctor or team to call back the Veteran for any concern or private question that probably the Veteran need to talk or discuss either one-to-one over the phone or it can be used to provide information, health information like a glucose readings ... or to request a consult for specialty doctors.

These Veterans reported that SM saved them time and resources by providing them full access to their primary care team from anywhere. These Veterans valued the ability to send an SM late at night, instead of waiting to call during business hours.

> I like to do most of my studying at night, and if I happen to think that I got to re-order this prescription, I just get on [SM] and do it. Its 24/7 you know, and the next thing I know I got it [prescription] within a week ... It doesn't tie up personnel at the VA, it just makes life easier ... [You] access that through MHV, Veterans can login into any computer and through the VA website can communicate securely using the SM. So within the website it's secure to get into SM and, and communicate from whatever that Veteran is located, could be on vacation, could be in another place.

Similarly, Veterans expressed that SM affords them the ability and confidence to draft a question to their provider in their own time and without the pressure of having to relay the same question over the phone or in person. Thus, having an ability to draft conversations using SM helped Veterans effectively communicate with their health care team.

> In SM, you can narrate [your message] very, very precisely and have it understood by the clinical team that reads your message and it's a lot better than someone just answering the telephone and then try to decide how your call should be routed.

Preference for alternatives to traditional forms of communication

High-volume SM users appreciated SM as an alternative form of communication, avoiding the frustration of spending hours on the phone or driving long distances to communicate with their health care team face to face. Participants reported conveniently communicating with their primary care team and getting responses and results.

> Well often it's important to try to connect with your primary care doctor and that's difficult in today's world ... so SM has been a real big help for me to ask questions and get answers right away doing it through the nurse who is head of the medical team and, uh, often the doctor will call me right back within some period of time so it's been important to me.

Low-Volume User Perspective

Despite the benefits and convenience of using SM, low-volume users reported several issues that discouraged their use of SM. Themes representing the perspective of low-volume users were *Healthy and No Need for Communication with Providers*; *Limited Knowledge about the Tool and User Features*; *Defining "Secure" and Misaligned Expectations*; and *Experiencing clinician resistance*. Details and participant quotes related to these themes are reviewed in the following paragraphs.

Healthy and no need for communication with providers

A primary and perhaps obvious reason for low-volume use of SM was the perception of being healthy and without a need for communication with one's health care team. Users may understand the value of using SM, but if they are healthy and without issue, there was no perceived need for SM use. For example, when asked if SM is a useful way to communicate with health care team members, one participant replied,

> ... it's not that important to me right now, but it's possible that down the road I might need that [SM] more ... I hope I don't end up with too many more medical problems, but this makes it easier to renew prescriptions and I don't know what kind of medical issues I'm gonna have ...

Limited knowledge about the tool and user features

Several low-volume users had limited knowledge of the SM features, and for what purpose the tool should be used.

> I would say, I would say it's a good idea. I'm not 100% sure what you're supposed to use it for. The site doesn't tell you so I'm never sure if I'm supposed to ask medical questions or just, hey can I make an appointment or can I get a refill. I don't know how in-depth you're supposed to get with your provider.

Though the features are available in the current system, if users did not know they exist they perceived it as a problematic issue with the system. An example of this is when participants criticized the lack of an option to get notifications that they had SMs in their inbox, despite the current availability of this SM feature. One participant reported:

> It's [SM] klutzy, I'd tell them when you're exchanging, messages between you and your provider, you don't get any notification on your email. For instance like my email is Hotmail so I don't get any notification telling me that hey you've got a message on yours, VA has sent you a SM so I don't get any of that feedback because I'm only on the SM when I need to be and I'm on Hotmail every day. I did write him using SM about a cholesterol pill and I read about the FAA had put out a new warning on this particular, cholesterol pill so I wrote him on SM, I wrote him, and I kept waiting for an answer and, you know, I'd be looking at my hotmail account and so one day I searched there and I was looking for a medication list and there was SM and there was his response ... No, no, they didn't notify me ...

Defining "secure" and misaligned expectations

A deterrent to SM use was confusion regarding who, among the primary care team, receives their SM messages. For example, some participants reported learning from team member responses that their e-mails were not going directly to their primary care physician, and felt uncomfortable with the fact that multiple members of their primary care team had access to their SMs. As a result, these Veterans reported being discouraged and cited that it would affect the type of health information they decide to include in future SMs. Others reported being informed by VA team members that personal nonhealth-related information was also discouraged.

> ...it's not as secure as I thought it was gonna be...The one benefit that I thought that I had was that you're talking to your doctor and that turned out to be false and so I don't hold SM in the highest state that I initially held it in because there's too many players that I don't know who they are and because I don't know who these players are now I don't feel it's secure. I don't feel I can speak that freely to my doctor cause I don't know the people that are listening...it requires me to screen everything that I say. I almost have to manipulate what I feed to the team where with my doctor I can state very open and freely....but SM has great potential but it just has to be explained if they have to do away with this and stop letting you think you're talking to your doctor somehow, it has to be a little clearer...its misleading to say you're sending a message directly to your primary care provider.

Experiencing clinician resistance

Veterans who were low-volume users were more likely to note Veterans Health Administration (VHA) staff resistance to SM use as a barrier to SM use. Several Veterans cited having contacted a specialty clinic/pharmacy/primary care provider through SM and that clinic called the Veteran, rather than replying via SM. Other Veterans cited that when they asked their specialist if they could contact them through SM, they were told to just call the clinic instead. These Veterans perceived that staff was avoiding SM in favor of traditional methods of communication.

> There's another specialty clinic I went to not long ago and the [specialist] told me at this point in your treatment I want you to call me and tell me this. He said I probably won't answer the phone, so leave a message. I said, 'can I just use SM?" And he said no, no, I don't use that, I don't want to have an inbox with a thousand messages.

Secure Messaging Data Content Findings

Data were collected for 33 participants, of which $n = 18$ (54.5 percent) initiated a total of 66 SM threads during the three-month review period. Of those threads, 62 were categorized and 3 were to test the system. SM users are able to categorize their SMs into one of four categories (i.e., general, appointment, medication, test). Fifteen (45.5 percent) participants did not use SM during the three-month time frame. Fifty (75.8 percent) of the Veteran initiated SMs received responses. SM content topics are illustrated by Veteran selected category in Table 2. Due to the generic nature of the categories available to users, "general" is overused to address all topics, including those represented by the other three categories (i.e., appointment, medication, test).

TABLE 2. SM Content Topic by Veteran Selected Category

Category	n	SM Content Topic
General	36	Condition management/report, specialty/procedure request, correspondence request, medication refill request, test results, appointment requests, treatment/appointment follow-up (Two SMs sent to check if previous SMs were received; one SM to report of being removed from team on SM recipient list)
Appointment	15	Confirmations, cancellations, specialty requests
Medication	10	Refill requests, medication inquires
Test	1	Test request

Though data methods were largely convergent, some data sources indicated discrepancy between Veterans reports and objective data collection. For instance, although approximately 80 percent of participants reported using SM at least once in the past three months, SM content collection indicated only 55 percent of Veteran participants had sent or received SMs. This discrepancy may be resultant of recall bias. Another possible reason for this discrepancy is participants' confusion between the MHV portal and SM tool, such that they may have used MHV but not SM. Similarly, the majority of Veterans reported receiving SM responses within 24–48 hours, however a review of the SM content suggested that response times ranged anywhere between 8 minutes to 136 hours (>5 days). Patients are told to expect a reply within three federal business days after the original SM is sent. Several SMs sent by Veterans did not get an SM response, however some indicated response through other mechanisms (e.g., Veteran sent SM thanking team members for a call). These data support participant reports about perceived resistance to clinician use of SM.

An unexpected finding from SM content data collection was that Veterans sent messages to inquire about sensitive topics such as sexually transmitted diseases (STDs) and erectile dysfunction (ED), but these topics were not revealed in interviews. The use of mixed methods provided insight to the uses of SM related to topics of sensitive nature that were not gleaned from Veterans' self-reports.

DISCUSSION

As health care evolves from a reactive, episodic disease-based paradigm to a preventative, continuous health model, large health care systems such as the VA require the integration of electronic health resources to promote continuity and increase communication and workflow efficiency. These electronic health resources facilitate a patient-centered culture of care for Veterans and their families. SM provides a patient-driven communication platform that can empower patients to effectively engage in continuous health relationships with their health care teams through meaningful use of this electronic resource. This approach to coordination of care has great potential to change the expectations and culture of health care communication. Consumer adoption and sustained utilization is necessary to leverage these tools and their benefits to capacity. Understanding user needs and the cultural context is central to intervening and remediating any barriers to adoption and sustained use of SM. To understand and contextualize Veterans' experiences using SM, we used mixed methods in a prospective study design. Our results illustrate the primary domains related to benefits, facilitators, barriers, and suggestions for improvements as well as themes represented by high- and low-volume users.

Overall, data indicate that Veterans who participated in this study are satisfied with SM and find it relatively easy to use. Perceived benefits of SM most commonly related to convenience and ease of communication with their primary care team. The ability to avoid telephone triage, using SM when they choose, and the ability to edit SMs before sending them to their primary care teams were strong motivators for continued SM use. Similar findings were reported in another study that found patients preferred SM over phone calls to communicate their health care needs (Liederman and Morefield 2003). Though participants reported understanding the benefits of using SM and a general sense of satisfaction with the tool, understanding the barriers to SM use is critical for informing efforts to increase SM adoption and sustained use.

Our analysis also evaluated the distinctions between high- and low-volume SM users to inform how strategies could be employed to increase SM adoption and sustained use within the health care context. User status (high vs. low volume) was not visibly associated with sample characteristics. However, it should be noted that in general educational and income levels as well as eHealth and health literacy levels were higher than usually found in the general Veteran population. This is consistent with existing literature suggesting that eHealth users tend to have higher levels of education, income, and eHealth and health literacy, than the general population (Archer et al., 2011; Cutrona et al., 2013; Dudas and Crocetti 2013; Kim and Nahm 2012). Perceptions of these two groups, sometimes shared, provide clear indications of changes needed to remove barriers and align expectations. Improving ease of use specifically related to navigating the site was identified by most participants as a way to increase uptake and sustained utilization. Barriers such as navigation issues can be addressed through planned system changes.

System changes would support ease of use by improving navigation to the SM tool on MHV, and providing user-requested features, such as formatting tools (e.g., copy/paste option) and pop-up prompts (e.g., automating setting preferences option). Additionally, confusion shared by Veteran participants about the appropriate uses of SM and that their SM are only seen by their primary care physician needs to be addressed. Steps must be taken to inform Veterans about what "Secure" means—for example, a secure system opposed to messaging that only goes to one's primary provider. Such information can adjust individuals' expectations and prevent dissatisfaction related to sharing personal health information with the health care team through SM.

On an interpersonal level, clinicians, staff, and administrators can work together to help inform SM users about the appropriate uses of SM and align expectations to avoid unmet needs and discouragement. Additionally, a proactive approach is recommended to help Veterans overcome basic barriers to SM and MHV use through increased knowledge and skill building. Targeted marketing, education, and skill building can play a critical role in aligning user expectations and providing instruction at the onset of SM use to improve uptake, utilization, and sustained use. Interpersonal barriers such as perceptions of clinician resistance are also a potentially critical barrier to Veterans' sustained SM use. Our study findings echo those of a similar study that found physicians overwhelmingly preferred traditional methods of communication with patients including face-to-face, telephone, and written communication (Hassol et al., 2004). Findings from this previous study indicated physicians were not satisfied with SM because of perceived concern of clinical case overload. However, Lieberman found that physicians were overall satisfied with SM once they became familiar with how it worked (Liederman and Morefield 2003). Findings from our study and other research (Hassol et al., 2004) reporting clinician resistance to SM use should be examined since their adoption of SM will have an effect on patient utilization. These findings indicate that, like patients, clinicians may benefit from SM training, education, and incentive to use SM.

Gathering these data was critical to responding quickly and effectively to support the national implementation and sustained use of SM by Veterans and their clinical care teams. As such, these results and other data collected throughout the system are currently informing system-wide presentations for leadership and clinical team members. Additionally, the development of an interactive game-motivated multimedia instructional web-based application for Veterans and VA employees to support increased awareness, adoption, and skilled use of SM and MHV is currently under way.

The methodology used in this study, particularly the user-testing combined with other qualitative methods, is increasingly being used in the field of anthropology. This study represents an effective application of this methodological approach to a patient-centered evaluation of an electronic health resource within a large health care system, providing a comprehensive framework for future studies designed to evaluate electronic resources and understand patient experiences in a changing health care culture. Multiple datasets allowed the research team to compare Veterans' reported perspectives and experiences with objective SM data sources, providing a more thorough understanding of users' experiences when using SM. For example, learning that Veterans are using SM to communicate with their health care team about sensitive health care topics such as ED and STDs is very important for cultivating a health care culture that allows Veterans to discuss these sensitive health topics in a venue that is comfortable for them. By allowing confidentiality and relative anonymity, SM facilitates the broaching of topics that Veterans might otherwise feel less comfortable discussing in person or by phone. This mixed-methods study provided a rich comprehensive dataset that had depth and breadth to provide a thorough understanding of Veterans' experiences using SM within the health care context.

Though this study provided valuable data, limitations should be noted when interpreting findings. The sample size is comparable to other qualitative mixed-methods studies (Guest et al., 2006), however sample size for qualitative studies such as ours limits generalizability to the general Veteran patient population. This is particularly true in this study due to the relatively high levels of education and health literacy of this sample.

However, this sample was purposively recruited to represent the perspective of VA SM users and saturation of data was reached. Recommendations for future research include the selective recruitment of participants who stand to most benefit from SM utilization (e.g., mental health or chronic health conditions) to strengthen understanding of patients' meaningful use of SM. Future studies may also benefit from collecting retrospective SM data, rather than prospective to ensure SMs are not censored by SM users.

From a methodological data collection perspective, though the use of controlled user tasks allowed the evaluation of users' abilities to complete tasks, using discrete tasks did not allow users to navigate and operate the system as they would in their natural environment. Thus, limited data were gleaned about users' overall experiences when practically using SM. In addition, though the SM content review was conducted longitudinally for a three-month time frame, due to long periods of time in which patients do not interact with their health care team, future studies should collect secondary SM data for a longer time frame (e.g., six months to a year). Collectively, these recommendations support a progression in the field of study in evaluating electronic health resources. As health care systems continue to transform to new models of care, in part through the use of electronic health tools such as SM, it is imperative to examine the phenomena from the patients' perspective and leverage their role as active informants in the evaluation process. This anthropological approach will facilitate a better understanding of their experiences and thereby create the opportunity to foster a patient-centered health care culture.

NOTE

Acknowledgments. The development of this manuscript was supported by the Department of Veterans Affairs, Veterans Health Administration, Office of Research and Development, Health Services Research and Development Service, and National eHealth Quality Enhancement Research Initiative (QUERI) Coordinating Center (RRP 11–397). Stephanie Shimada's efforts were supported by a VA HSR&D Career Development Award (CDA 10–210). Other contributing agencies include the HSR&D and RR&D Center of Innovation for Disability and Rehabilitation Research at the James A. Haley Veterans Hospital, the Center for Healthcare Organization and Implementation Research (CHOIR) at the Edith Nourse Rogers Memorial VA Hospital, the Department of Health Policy and Management in Boston University School of Public Health, the Department of Quantitative Health Sciences at the University of Massachusetts Medical School, the Center for Organization, Leadership and Management Research in the VA Boston Healthcare System, and the VA New England Health Care System. The contents of this manuscript do not represent the views of the Department of Veterans Affairs or the U.S. Government.

REFERENCES CITED

Albrecht, Gary L., Ray Fitzpatrick, and Susan Scrimshaw
  2003 Handbook of Social Studies in Health and Medicine. London: Sage Publications.
Anderson, Robert Thomas
  1996 Magic, Science, and Health: The Aims and Achievements of Medical Anthropology. Fort Worth: Harcourt Brace College Publishers.
Andreassen, Hege K., Marianne Trondsen, Per Egil Kummervold, Deede Gammon, and Per Hjortdahl
  2006 Patients Who Use E-Mediated Communication with Their Doctor: New Constructions of Trust in the Patient-Doctor Relationship. Qualitative Health Research 16(2):238–248.

Archer, N., U. Fevrier-Thomas, C. Lokker, K. A. McKibbon, and S. E. Straus
    2011 Personal Health Records: A Scoping Review. Journal of the American Medical Informatics Association 18(4): 515–522.

Baer, Hans A., Merrill Singer, and Ida Susser
    2003 Medical Anthropology and the World System. Westport: Praeger.

Bunz, Ulla
    2004 The Computer-Email-Web (CEW) Fluency Scale-Development and Validation. International Journal of Human-Computer Interaction 17(4):479–506.

Chew Lisa D., Joan M. Griffin, Melissa R. Partin, Siamak Noorbaloochi, Joseph P. Grill, Annamay Snyder, Katharine A. Bradley, Sean M. Nugent, Alisha D. Baines and Michelle VanRyn.
    2008 Validation of Screening Questions for Limited Health Literacy in a Large VA Outpatient Population. Journal of General Internal Medicine 23(5):561–566.

Committee on Quality of Health Care in America, Institute of Medicine
    2001 Crossing the Quality Chasm: A New Health System for the 21st Century. Washington: The National Academies Press.

Cutrona Sarah L., Douglas W. Roblin, Joann L. Wagner, Bridget Gaglio, Andrew E. Williams, Rosalie Torres Stone, Terry S. Field, and Kathleen M. Mazor.
    2013 Adult Willingness to Use Email and Social Media for Peer-to-Peer Cancer Screening Communication: Quantitative Interview Study. JMIR Research Protocols 2(2):e52.

Davis T. C., M. A. Crouch, S. W. Long, R. H. Jackson, P. Bates, R. B. George, and L. E. Bairnsfather.
    1991 Rapid Assessment of Literacy Levels of Adult Primary Care Patients. Family Medicine 23(6): 433–435.

Dudas, Robert Arthur, and Michael Crocetti
    2013 Pediatric Caregiver Attitudes toward Email Communication: Survey in an Urban Primary Care Setting. Journal of Medical Internet Research 15(10):e228.

Glanz, Karen, Barbara K. Rimer and K Viswanath
    2008 Health Behavior and Health Education: Theory, Research, and Practice (4th edition). San Francisco: Jossey-Bass.

Guest, Greg, Arwen Bunce, and Laura Johnson
    2006 How Many Interviews Are Enough? Field Methods 18(1):59–82.

Harris, Lynne T., Sebastien J. Haneuse, Diane P. Martin, and James D. Ralston
    2009 Diabetes Quality of Care and Outpatient Utilization Associated with Electronic Patient-Provider Messaging: A Cross-Sectional Analysis. Diabetes Care 32(7):1182–1187.

Hassol Andrea, James M. Walker, David Kidder, Kim Rokita, DavidYoung, Steven Pierdon, Deborah Deitz, Sarah Kuck, Eduardo Ortiz.
    2004 Patient Experiences and Attitudes about Access to a Patient Electronic Health Care Record and Linked Web Messaging. Journal of the American Medical Informatics Association 11(6): 505–513.

Haun, Jolie, Virginia J. Noland Dodd, J. Graham-Pole, BA. Rienzo, and P. Donaldson
    2009 Testing a Health Literacy Screening Tool: Implications for Utilization of a BRIEF Health Literacy Indicator. Federal Practitioner 26(12):24–31.

HealthIT.gov n.d.,
    Providers & Professionals, New Stage 2 Core and Menu Objectives for EPs. http://www.healthit.gov/providers-professionals/new-stage-2-core-and-menu-objectives-eps, accessed July 25, 2013.

Houston, Thomas K., Daniel Z. Sands, Mollie W. Jenckes, and Daniel E. Ford
    2004 Experiences of Patients Who Were Early Adopters of Electronic Communication with Their Physician: Satisfaction, Benefits, and Concerns. The American Journal of Managed Care 10(9): 601–608.

Kim, K., and E. Nahm
    2012 Benefits of and Barriers to the Use of Personal Health Records (PHR) for Health Management among Adults. Online Journal of Nursing Informatics 16(3):1–9.

Liederman, Eric M., and Catrina S. Morefield
    2003 Web Messaging: A New Tool for Patient-Physician Communication. Journal of the American Medical Informatics Association 10(3):260–270.

Mathieson, Kieran

1991 Predicting User Intentions: Comparing the Technology Acceptance Model with the Theory of Planned Behavior. Information Systems Research 2(3):173–191.

Norman, Cameron D., and Harvey A. Skinner

2006 eHEALS: The eHealth Literacy Scale. Journal of Medical Internet Research 8(4):e27.

Philipsen, Gerry

1992 Speaking Culturally: Explorations in Social Communication. State University of New York Press, Albany.

Roter, Debra L., Susan Larson, Daniel Z. Sands, Daniel E. Ford, and Thomas Houston

2008 Can E-Mail Messages between Patients and Physicians Be Patient-Centered? Health Communication 23(1):80–86.

Shimada, Stephanie L., Timothy P. Hogan, Sowmya R. Rao, Jeroan J. Allison, Ann L. Quill, Hua Feng, BarrettD. Phillips, Kim M. Nazi, Susan T. Haidary, Thomas K. Houston.

2013 Patient-Provider Secure Messaging in VA: Variations in Adoption and Association with Urgent Care Utilization. Medical Care 51:S21–S28.

Strauss, Anselm C., and Juliet M. Corbin

1998 Basics of Qualitative Research: Techniques and Procedures for Developing Grounded Theory (2nd edition). Sage Publications, Inc. Thousand Oaks, California.

Zhou, Yi Y., Terhilda Garrido, Homer L. Chin, Andrew M. Wiesenthal, and Louise L. Liang

2007 Patient Access to an Electronic Health Record with Secure Messaging: Impact on Primary Care Utilization. The American Journal of Managed Care 13(7):418–424.

Zhou, Yi Yvonne, Michael H. Kanter, Jian J. Wang, and Terhilda Garrido

2010 Improved Quality at Kaiser Permanente through E-Mail between Physicians and Patients. Health Affairs 29(7):1370–1375.

EMPOWERING VETERANS WITH PTSD IN THE RECOVERY ERA: ADVANCING DIALOGUE AND INTEGRATING SERVICES

ERIN P. FINLEY
South Texas Veterans Health Care System

As highly effective treatments for posttraumatic stress disorder (PTSD) become increasingly available, how will the VA (Department of Veterans Affairs) and other public institutions navigate complex questions around appropriate services for Veterans with PTSD? This and related questions will be examined in this article in light of epidemiological, clinical, and ethnographic data on combat PTSD in the 21st century. [Veterans, PTSD, recovery, stakeholders]

INTRODUCTION

In February of 2013, I found myself riding in an elevator at the main Department of Veterans Affairs (VA) hospital in Reno, Nevada. A young man stepped in, very thin and wearing an Operation Iraqi Freedom (OIF) baseball hat over longish dark hair. A worn G. I. Joe t-shirt hung limply over his slightly hunched shoulders. He was accompanied by a black Labrador puppy wearing a vest that said, "PTSD [Post-traumatic stress disorder] Service Dog," although it was unclear if the dog was a trained service dog, as he hitched and fidgeted and spun nervously in circles as the elevator climbed to the next floor.[1] The young man looked sheepishly over at my companion and me several times as he tried to settle his dog, and when the elevator reached the next floor, he ducked his head out the door, tugged on the leash, and was gone.

Across the venues of my work and life over the past decade, I have had the opportunity to meet hundreds of recent Veterans, and yet, in the months since that day in Reno, I have thought often of this young man with whom I exchanged no more than a slight smile and a nod. He has, for reasons I will explain later, begun to serve as a symbol for me of enormous questions facing the VA and the United States more broadly. In the dozen years since the attacks of September 11, 2001, the United States has deployed more than two million service members as part of Operations Enduring Freedom (OEF, Afghanistan), OIF (Iraq), and New Dawn (OND, Iraq; Cohen et al., 2010). The prolonged nature of these conflicts, which have stretched the armed forces to the limit in terms of financial and human resources, has taken a heavy toll on military men and women, as well as on their families and communities. More than 800,000 OEF/OIF/OND Veterans had been seen at Department of VA health care facilities as of mid-2012, exhibiting high

ANNALS OF ANTHROPOLOGICAL PRACTICE 37.2, pp. 75–91. ISSN: 2153-957X. © 2014 by the American Anthropological Association. DOI:10.1111/napa.12028

rates of musculoskeletal (56.7 percent), mental (52.8 percent), nervous system/sensory (44.8 percent), digestive (36.0 percent), and respiratory disorders (26.3 percent, 2012). More than 50,000 service members have been wounded in action (Department of Defense 2013), many with life-altering injuries, while problems related to the impact of multiple and extended deployments on Veterans' psychosocial and family functioning continue to be a major source of concern (MacDermid-Wadsworth et al., 2013; Sayers et al., 2009). Yet even among such a heavy burden of injury and illness, PTSD has retained its prominence as one of the so-called "signature injuries" of these wars (Tanielian and Jaycox 2008), and as undoubtedly the most sustaining symbol of the wars' aftermath in media and other public discussions.

In truth, combat-related PTSD presents an enormous problem for American Veterans and service members. Prevalence rates among OEF/OIF/OND Veterans are frequently cited as reaching between 13 and 20 percent (Institute of Medicine 2012), and PTSD symptoms are linked with significant personal and family suffering (Meis et al., 2010; Monson et al., 2009), functional impairment (Smith et al., 2005), poorer physical and mental health overall (Taft et al., 1999), substance abuse (Kilpatrick et al., 2003), and increased risk of homelessness (Carlson et al., 2013) and suicide (Pompili et al., 2013). Meanwhile, at a national level, the costs of caring for those with PTSD continue to rise; by 2004, the United States was already spending $4.3 billion annually just on disability compensation for Veterans with PTSD (Frueh et al., 2007), and the number of Veterans applying for service-related compensation for PTSD has since skyrocketed (McNally and Frueh 2013).

Despite this ominous picture, the last decade has seen considerable progress toward changing the clinical view of PTSD from that of a chronic illness to one for which there is excellent hope of recovery. There is a rapidly growing body of literature demonstrating the efficacy of evidence-based psychotherapies such as prolonged exposure (PE) therapy and cognitive processing therapy (CPT) in reducing PTSD symptom levels to below the threshold for a diagnosis (Chard 2005; Chard et al., 2012; Eftekhari et al., 2013; Foa et al., 2005; Goodson et al., 2013; Rauch et al., 2009; Resick et al., 2002), and the Department of Defense (DoD) and VA have developed evidence-based guidelines for providing recovery-oriented treatments to all service members and Veterans (Management of Post-traumatic Stress Working Group 2010). The VA, meanwhile, has invested in a top-to-bottom infrastructure renovation aimed at making the evidence-based psychotherapies available at every VA facility nationwide, training thousands of providers, appointing local coordinators to advocate for the new treatments, and reworking clinic schedules to allow for the longer and more frequent treatment sessions required (Karlin et al., 2010). A growing variety of additional research increasingly supports the efficacy and effectiveness of alternative and adjunctive treatments, including eye-movement desensitization and reprocessing (EMDR) therapy (Russell 2008; Taylor et al., 2003), mindfulness and meditation (Kearney et al., 2013; King et al., 2013), and web-based interventions (Brief et al., 2013), thus offering Veterans and their providers a broader range of treatment options to consider.

And yet tough questions remain for the VA and the United States more generally as we move into a post–Iraq and Afghanistan era. First of all, commonly cited rates of combat-related PTSD among U.S. Veterans stand out as somewhere between two and six times higher than reported in any other national military around the world, raising important concerns regarding U.S. efforts to prevent, diagnose, and manage PTSD among its military and Veteran populations. Second, as the VA works to develop a universally accessible and patient-centered infrastructure for treating combat PTSD, a number of questions arise around the problem of determining what, ultimately, is best for Veterans with PTSD. For example, what treatments should be made available? Is it appropriate to consider PTSD a "curable" disorder? And what integrated system of treatment and financial and other benefits is best capable of helping the greatest number of Veterans to achieve full recovery and the highest possible quality of life? Finally, returning to the underlying theme of this volume, what role can anthropologists play in empowering U.S. Veterans and the institutions that serve them to have an informed, participative, and productive dialogue toward building a better national program for those with PTSD? In the remainder of this article, I consider each of these questions and their implications for Veterans living with combat PTSD in post-Iraq/Afghanistan America.

American Vulnerability?

Several recent articles have examined the prevalence of combat-related PTSD across studies conducted among U.S. and non-U.S. Veterans and reported striking heterogeneity. Richardson et al.'s (2010) review of the international literature found that, while studies of combat-related PTSD among U.S. Iraq Veterans reported rates between 4 and 17 percent, comparable studies conducted among Iraq Veterans from the United Kingdom (UK) found rates of only between 3 and 6 percent. Sundin et al. (2010) have identified similar trends, and both articles provide substantive insight into factors that may help to explain these discrepancies, including troops' varying exposure to combat and length and frequency of deployments (see also Buckman et al., 2011), as well as variation in assessment of PTSD and study sampling strategies. Although studies conducted in both U.S. and non-U.S. settings have relied upon a broad array of study designs, one key problem appears to be the use of self-report measures to assess the likely presence of PTSD, often without taking into account functional impairment related to symptoms, which is essential to a PTSD diagnosis under criteria outlined in fourth or later editions of the *Diagnostic and Statistical Manual of Mental Disorders* (Richardson et al., 2010). Studies comparing diagnoses based on self-report with those made using clinical interviews have reported that self-report–based diagnoses may overestimate PTSD prevalence by as much as 40 to 50 percent (Engelhard et al., 2007; Ruggiero et al., 2006). In addition, studies themselves may be conducted among a general military population or on more limited subpopulations, for example, among service members with higher levels of combat exposure, or reservists as opposed to active duty soldiers.

Interestingly, a recent comparison of the findings of two prospective cohort studies among U.K. and U.S. military personnel that used similar designs and assessment measures found an overall PTSD prevalence among deployed combat troops of approximately seven percent among the U.K. sample and 7.6 percent among the U.S. sample. This suggests that identified rates may be more similar than different when study methodology is held constant (Pinder et al., 2012; Smith et al., 2008; Sundin et al., 2010). However, Richardson et al. (2010) rightly caution that the literature on PTSD is so vast and so frequently contradictory that researchers can take away nearly any message from a review of the data. Similarly, members of the media can make almost any claim from the data, and commonly cite PTSD rates of as high as 20 to 35 percent among Veterans of Iraq and Afghanistan (e.g., Alvarez 2008; Reno 2012).

This degree of disparity in the data raises a series of questions. Are we capturing only a fraction of the true prevalence of Veterans' PTSD, or greatly overdiagnosing the disorder? Leaning in either direction (and perhaps in both) would have considerable implications for addressing the needs and well-being of those with the diagnosis. It also returns us to the question of whether we are, as has been repeatedly claimed, medicalizing social, moral, or spiritual problems inseparable from war, to no one's benefit (Dobbs 2009; Tick 2005; Young 1995).

At the same time, it is striking that PTSD, by 2012, had become the third-most frequent cause for receiving disability benefits among U.S. Veterans, with some 7.8 percent of all OEF/OIF/OND Veterans already receiving VA disability for PTSD, and claims pending for nearly as many more (McNally and Frueh 2013). If at first glance these numbers seem concordant with the seven percent rates listed above, it is worth noting that those were rates of PTSD observed among *combat troops*, while the 7.8 percent (and growing) number applies to the entire population of OEF/OIF/OND Veterans, not merely those who were combat-exposed. Service-related PTSD can and does occur for reasons other than combat, such as military sexual trauma (Maguen et al., 2012; Mattocks et al., 2012), and there is some evidence of delayed-onset PTSD in a minority of war Veterans (Horesh et al., 2013). Even so, rates of compensation for PTSD increased by 79.5 percent between 1999 and 2004, while rates for all other health problems increased by only 12.2 percent (Frueh et al., 2007), a notable discrepancy.

More troublingly, compensation seeking has been linked to worrisome patterns in care seeking. Veterans awarded service-connected compensation for PTSD can be given a rating of between 0 and 100 percent disability, with benefits awarded commensurate to the level of disability (up to more than $3,000/month of untaxed income). A report by the VA Office of the Inspector General found that the average patient seeking PTSD-related compensation continued to seek treatment, reporting progressively more severe symptoms and functional impairment over time, until a 100 percent rating was awarded, at which time there was an 82 percent reduction in mental health visits (Frueh et al., 2007). There was no corresponding drop in visits for physical health care. Not only does this suggest that PTSD compensation is not currently associated with recovery, but this pattern of steadily worsening symptoms seems to contradict much of the wider research on PTSD, which typically reports a gradual reduction in symptom severity over time (Roy-Byrne et al., 2004; Yehuda et al., 2009). For example, Harvey et al. (2012) found in a cohort study of United Kingdom reservists that rates of probable PTSD fell slightly from

6.3 percent at approximately 16 months post deployment to 5.1 percent at approximately five years post deployment. Shlosberg and Strous (2005) found that, among 1,323 Israeli soldiers injured in the Yom Kippur War, only 19 still retained an active PTSD diagnosis and significant clinical symptoms some 32 years later.

These findings point to a troubling question for which there is, at this time, very little answer: to what extent do current disability policies for Veterans with PTSD support and/or hinder Veterans' recovery from PTSD? This question was memorably raised by David Dobbs (2009) in a controversial article in *Scientific American*, and has elsewhere been queried by clinicians and researchers worried by patterns they were seeing among Veterans in treatment, who often expressed concern that documentation of treatment gains might result in reduced disability benefits (Frueh et al., 2007; McNally and Frueh 2013). Although a few studies have attempted to understand whether compensation status is linked to treatment outcome (Belsher et al., 2012; Monson et al., 2006; Schnurr et al., 2007), the literature in this area is weak and difficult to interpret, not least because researchers may find it difficult to identify a significant number of Veterans who are *not* seeking compensation to serve as a control group.

There is vastly more to be said on the issues of identifying accurate rates of PTSD and the benefits and pitfalls of compensating Veterans for PTSD-related disability, but the central point is this: very high rates of PTSD diagnosis and the need to promote wellness for those with PTSD without disincentivizing recovery raise enormous problems for a VA seeking to provide high-quality, patient-centered, and recovery-oriented health care for Veterans. These concerns highlight the essential tension between providing Veterans with the health care and compensation that are promised as part of the nation's social contract with its armed forces (perhaps best summarized in the VA-ubiquitous phrase, "serving those who served"), while also creating a system that is functional, sustainable, and provides programs and services that support Veterans in achieving the highest possible quality of life.

Serving Those Who Served?

Among the many physical and mental health care needs that VA providers and facilities address, PTSD may be the illness that best illustrates VA's position as a national health care system whose mandate to serve Veterans is enacted amid (1) the shifting politics of Veterans as high-status consumers; (2) the ethical, institutional, and professional demands of health care provision more generally; and (3) the challenges of facing annual budget approval from a dynamic and unpredictable national Congress. Thus, even in an era when PTSD and the well-being of recent Veterans are considered high-priority issues, and when the body of knowledge on treatment has evolved to a point where there is general clinical consensus that PTSD is treatable (Institute of Medicine 2007), uncertainty remains regarding how best to provide PTSD treatment within a Veteran-oriented system of care.

For example, as I noted above, the VA has invested considerable resources in a multicomponent program to make evidence-based psychotherapies for PTSD available at every VA facility across the nation. These efforts have focused in particular on training providers to offer the two treatments widely considered to have the strongest evidence for their effectiveness: PE and CPT (Chard et al., 2012; Karlin et al., 2010). These treatments have been repeatedly demonstrated to be effective in reducing symptoms across a variety of Veteran and civilian populations, including Veterans of all eras (Chard et al., 2010; Monson et al., 2006), women as well as men (Monson et al., 2006; Schnurr et al., 2007), and among survivors of sexual trauma as well as combat (Monson et al., 2006; Schnurr et al., 2007). Moreover, they have been shown to reduce symptom-related distress so significantly that as many as 67 percent of those who complete treatment no longer meet criteria for a PTSD diagnosis (Bradley et al., 2005).

Even so, the VA has faced an uphill battle in establishing these treatments as the national standard of care. Providers trained in disparate psychological traditions have at times been reluctant to adopt the new treatments, despite strong evidence supporting their effectiveness and sustained training in their use (Finley 2011). Studies have found that significant numbers of Veterans drop out of these treatments prematurely (Chard et al., 2010; Erbes et al., 2009; Garcia et al., 2011), for reasons that include a lack of confidence in their effectiveness and discomfort with the treatments themselves, both of which require engaging with traumatic memories in a manner that can be challenging for those with PTSD (Finley 2011). Responding to the perceived need to provide a range of treatments more broadly acceptable to Veterans and providers alike, VAs across the nation have made a variety of other programs available, including yoga, art therapy, music therapy, and so on, often touted as alternative or adjunctive to pharmacology or psychotherapy. The growth and variety of available programs within VA is only exceeded by the proliferation of therapeutic options in community-based settings, as described by Hautzinger and Scandlyn (2013).

And yet, for all the attention paid to treatment options for PTSD within VA, and to the attempt to redesign the VA's PTSD program as recovery-oriented (by using EBPs to help Veterans get better) and patient-centered (by providing a variety of therapeutic options), there has been little to no public discussion regarding how best to integrate treatment planning with disability benefits in order to provide comprehensive support for long-term recovery and well-being across the life span. Moreover, while Veterans with PTSD who demonstrate significant recovery may theoretically be reevaluated for reduced benefits, there is little information available on how frequently this happens, or following what criteria. Perhaps more worryingly, it is difficult to imagine any public forum where an open and multilateral discussion of ways to refine the current system could take place. Because of their unique status as national heroes to whom a profound debt is owed, U.S. Veterans have proven to be remarkably powerful health-care consumers. As McNally and Frueh (2013) point out, any perceived challenge to the current system, particularly one that reexamines the role of disability benefits, is likely to be rapidly dismissed as "anti-Veteran." Administrators and clinicians at all levels of VA have at times been subject to congressional rebuke for perceived failures to serve Veterans' treatment and/or compensation needs (Finley 2011), and most VA clinicians in day-to-day practice are familiar with the scenario of Veterans unhappy with some element of their care offering to "call my Congressman." It speaks to the relatively protected status of Veterans that, despite a deep and lingering economic recession and animated national debate regarding the federal debt, VA healthcare and disability services are almost never referred to as "entitlement programs" or targeted for cuts, as Medicaid, Medicare, and Social Security regularly are.

Moving from "Stakeholders" to "What is at Stake?"

It is an open question whether Veterans' status will continue to remain so protected as the wars in Iraq and Afghanistan fade into the past. Given this, it seems more urgent than ever to work toward a system that meaningfully integrates benefits and services for Veterans with widely varying levels of illness, disability, and need, as well as skills, resources, and strengths. Veterans themselves must be at the center of any such discussion, and must include those who are deeply disabled as well as those who consider themselves recovered. Clinicians, who daily observe the spectrum of what both "disability" and "recovery" may realistically mean, and researchers, whose work continues to evolve the range of available treatments and services, should also be vital participants, as should administrators and operational leaders representing both health care and benefits arms of the VA (the Veterans Health Administration [VHA] and Veterans Benefits Administration [VBA], respectively). But while the last decade has seen growing interest in health services research that incorporates qualitative methodology and multiple stakeholder perspectives (e.g., McInnes et al., 2012), there remains significant need for the nuanced methods and perspectives offered by anthropology in beginning to tackle such difficult issues.

Although anthropologists have in recent years become increasingly prominent members of research teams across VA, it is in spaces of great uncertainty where their insights may be of greatest value. This is in part because anthropology as a discipline may be unsurpassed in integrating an appreciation for the macro and the micro, and in viewing how political economic structures and processes directly impact the subjective texture of human experience. Anthropology has developed a repertoire of theoretical lenses, such as those of critical medical anthropology, which can be of enormous utility in helping to view complex problems from multiple perspectives and levels simultaneously (e.g., Biehl 2005; Good 1994; Luhrmann 2000). Anthropologists are also skilled in articulating tensions that others may take for granted, and in seeking understanding of the basis for these tensions in questions of *what is at stake* for all those involved, a key question informed by phenomenology (Good 1994; Schutz 1970) and not quite captured in the term "stakeholders."

As an anthropologist, I find myself approaching the central question here, namely, how the VA should structure diagnosis, compensation, and treatment for PTSD in order to support the best clinical outcomes and highest quality of life for OEF/OIF/OND Veterans, with a view to what is at stake for the young man in that Reno elevator. As we never spoke, I can write only of what I saw in him and why, and attempt to explain why he provides an image that resonates so powerfully in relation to these larger questions.

First and most obviously, there is his youth. OEF/OIF/OND Veterans on the whole stand out as older than prior eras of Veterans, in large part because the military's reliance on an All-Volunteer Force has resulted in efforts to encourage men and women to adopt longer periods of service, and because so many of those deployed have been members of the National Guard or Reserves, who are on average older than their active-duty counterparts (Pugh et al., 2014). Even so, if this young man was roughly 25 years old, he stands to be receiving VA services for another 50 years, and so the quality and impact of those services acquires enormous potential for shaping his health and well-being across the life course.

Second, there was his OIF hat. Whether or not he served in Iraq, as his hat would suggest, and it is worth noting that a significant number of those considered to have "deployed in support of OEF/OIF" have never been to Iraq or Afghanistan or other combat zone, instead deploying to a facility within or outside the United States for operation-related training or other purposes, the fact that he has adopted this hat suggests that it has meaning for him. In wearing it, he is presenting himself as at the very least *aligned with* those who served in Iraq. This raises questions of identity, of how he sees himself and how he would wish to be seen.

His dog, too, wore a symbol, a vest indicating that he is a service dog for PTSD, although his awkward behavior in the elevator suggested a more complex story. Meanwhile, even the question of whether service dogs are appropriate for Veterans with PTSD has been a growing point of controversy within VA. Veterans can seek out formally trained service dogs, although vests identifying an animal as a PTSD service dog are also available for purchase online. Advocates argue that service dogs provide love and emotional support to Veterans, and that this can aid in reducing symptoms of anxiety, panic, hypervigilance, and so forth (Yount et al., 2012). On the other hand, clinicians who treat PTSD have raised concerns that having a service dog for PTSD may inhibit recovery by reducing a Veteran's opportunity to regain a sense of mastery over environments and situations that provoke anxiety. Faced with such disparate views, the VHA has invested in ongoing research to establish whether either formally trained service dogs (who receive official training and may legally accompany the Veteran into any site under the Americans with Disabilities Act) or companion dogs (who may or may not receive any training and are typically only welcome where pets are normally allowed) are associated with health or psychosocial benefits for Veterans with PTSD. With this controversy as a backdrop, I am left to wonder about the half-grown puppy huddled in the elevator, his oversized feet clacking on the slippery floor. Did his presence indicate something about his owner's tenuous feeling of safety out in the world, his desire to identify as a Veteran with PTSD, and/or something altogether different and unknowable at so many months' remove?

But it was the young man's bearing and body language, which conveyed such vulnerability and uncertainty, that were perhaps most striking. His cartoon G. I. Joe shirt referenced a child's view of war in a manner that seemed unutterably poignant on his slim shoulders. As he stepped out of the elevator, he seemed poised on a threshold from which he could move in any of a number of directions. Presuming he does have PTSD, some of these relate to his choices and experiences as a patient: Will he undergo one of the evidence-based psychotherapies? Will he benefit from them? Will he refuse psychotherapy in favor of medication or other therapy, attempt multiple complementary therapies, or reject mental health treatment altogether? Will he receive disability compensation for PTSD, and what impact will this financial benefit, or the lack of it, have on his life choices and trajectory? Another set of questions relate to what identity he will take on in the days to come. Will he present himself as an Iraq Veteran with PTSD in venues outside the VA hospital? Will he identify in some primary way as a Veteran with PTSD, and if so, how will he view his own potential for recovery? Will he identify himself in other ways as well, perhaps as a college student, or as a man with a career or a family, and how will he go about integrating these distinct pieces of his identity? In navigating the course of his treatment and his life, what choices will he make around his PTSD, and what will be the consequences of those choices?

Elemental as these questions are, they highlight some of the classic insights of medical anthropology, including illness narratives and identity (Kleinman 1988) and the meaning response (also known as the placebo effect). Daniel Moerman (2002) defined the meaning response as "the psychological and physiological effects of *meaning* in the treatment of illness," and evidence has shown that the impact of meaning can operate in either a positive or negative direction. In other words, those given a reason to expect they will get better very often do get better (placebo), while those given reason to believe they will experience increased sickness or distress over time often do get worse (nocebo), even in the absence of any pathology (Hahn 1998; Moerman 2002).

Hahn (1998) points out that such expectations "are largely learned from the cultural environment," and certainly, the current cultural environment in the United States conveys a number of ideas about PTSD. Most of these gained traction in the years following the Vietnam war when PTSD was first formalized as a clinical diagnosis, when effective treatments were not available, and when a visible minority of struggling Vietnam Veterans became the public face of a war with a devastating psychological legacy (Michalowski and Dubisch 2001; Young 1995). Images of the chronically disabled Veteran with PTSD became prominent in film (e.g., *Rambo*, *Born on the Fourth of July*) and other media, and PTSD became part of a larger public narrative around how Vietnam Veterans had been failed by their country, first in being sent to an unjust war and later in being left abandoned and unsupported in their efforts to survive the emotional aftermath (Michalowski and Dubisch 2001; Young 1995).

Although excellent psychotherapeutic and pharmacological treatments for PTSD are now available and many Veterans receiving care at VA go on to recover from the disorder, this change has occurred only within the past few years, and little seems to have yet shifted in the cultural narrative around PTSD. Media portrayals of the illness typically focus on the most severe cases or on the failures that occur in care, rather than on the promise of new treatments and increased access.[2] Therefore, while the available cultural narratives would seem to have significant potential for promoting nocebo effects among returning Veterans at risk for PTSD, there seems relatively little momentum in the direction of placebo. Without articulating it in quite these terms, the military has reflected this insight in a number of education and psychosocial skills-building programs aimed at normalizing postdeployment distress and readjustment (e.g., Saltzman et al., 2011), attempting in so doing to reduce stigma and increase care seeking. The VA, with similar intent, has created a series of videos in which Veterans with PTSD describe their experiences of treatment and recovery (http://www.ptsd.va.gov/apps/AboutFace/), although it is not clear how widely these have been viewed. But neither effort seems to have done much to change public perspectives on PTSD, not least because many Veterans do not trust either the military or VA to serve as impartial sources for information about PTSD.

Meanwhile, Bellamy (1997) has noted that financial compensation for illness-related disability may itself function as a form of nocebo. In contrast to others who speak more cynically of active malingering (e.g., McNally and Frueh 2013), Bellamy argues that cases in which medical outcomes are worse among those who stand to benefit financially from remaining ill represent a complex combination of "suggestion, somatization, and rationalization." Here again the layered meanings of PTSD, and of the military service that led to it, are important, particularly in shaping the potential for suggestion. For while study after study make it clear that, for many Veterans, stigma against having a mental illness or seeking mental health treatment remains a very real barrier to seeking the help they need (e.g., Finley 2011; Hoge et al., 2004; Stecker and Fortney 2011), PTSD may also be associated with a war heroism that some may find seductive or reassuring. This may be particularly the case in an era of economic struggle when fewer employment options are available for the working and middle class (Hautzinger and Scandlyn 2013; McNally and Frueh 2013), and when those that do exist typically offer little in the way of social status. One can contrast the current range of economic opportunities for recent Veterans with those available in the years following World War II, when manufacturing and other industries provided stable careers that paid sufficient wage to support a family on a single earner's paycheck. So it is that issues of social relations, economic viability and status, identity, meaning, history, and culturally informed notions of illness are all essential pieces of understanding PTSD for this generation of American Veterans. So, too, a diagnosis of PTSD may be deeply stigmatized in some settings while offering the identity of a nobly wounded warrior, with the added promise of financial compensation, in others. All this must be taken into account when attempting to build a system of services and benefits that supports the best possible quality of life for the greatest number of those living with the disorder.

Advancing the Dialogue

In developing a better understanding of the diverse needs of Veterans with PTSD, it is helpful to consider a model for supporting mental health recovery first proposed by Jacobson and Greenley (2001). Drawing on Estroff's (1989) work on identity among the mentally ill, they note that recovery requires reclaiming an identity that includes "illness as only a part of the self, not as a definition of the whole," and also requires gaining a sense of control accomplished by finding ways to successfully reduce symptoms or related distress. They identify hope, empowerment, and re-establishing connection as important components of recovery that are centered within the individual. In looking at relevant system-level factors, they focus on the following three: (1) establishing basic human rights for the mentally ill; (2) supporting a positive culture of healing, which they emphasize should support collaborative patient–provider relations; and (3) providing recovery-oriented services. Their overall model, in leaving room for the importance of identity, in emphasizing patient empowerment and control, and in situating these tasks within a larger system that is itself continuing to evolve, may provide a useful framework for ethnographic research that can aid in imagining what trajectories of recovery can/might look like for Veterans with PTSD, and in better understanding what supports must be in place in order to facilitate them.

At the same time, more structurally focused queries also have great potential. In his 2009 article, Dobbs described Australia's system of stepped compensation for Veterans with PTSD, which provides initial benefits that support the Veteran during a period of treatment and recovery and are gradually reduced over time as the Veteran regains the ability to function as an active citizen. Such examples would suggest there is room for cross-national comparisons with other systems of structuring compensation and treatment, and to investigate whether such systems are associated with differential trajectories of symptoms, distress, and quality of life for Veterans over time. It seems likely, however, that such systems, differential outcomes or no, may also be situated within different sets of orienting cultural assumptions regarding the impact and duration of PTSD and its potential for recovery, and thus any such comparisons will be most productive if conducted with an ethnographic eye. Similarly, as the American VA continues to work to establish universal access to evidence-based psychotherapies and to more effectively track the outcomes of Veterans who have received them, it will be important to observe how any changes in the current system of benefits are implemented, and with what downstream effects.

In short, understanding the individual needs of Veterans such as the young man in the elevator, and the ways these needs intersect with larger structures of national policy and health care, will raise questions that anthropology has a key role to play in answering. Following a model like that provided by Jacobson and Greenley (2001), which incorporates classic anthropological insights and recognizes the importance of both micro- and macrolevel factors, the question of how best to serve our Veterans with PTSD is likely to require a multipronged approach. This should include in-depth interviewing around subjective experiences of identity, empowerment, hope, interactions with providers and the VA system more broadly, and connection with both others in the social world and with valued life goals. At the same time, there is significant need for detailed cross-national comparison of systems of care and compensation, which should examine patient outcomes and quality of life over time, while also using ethnography to inform understanding of sources of variation.

With so much at stake for Veterans and the structures intended to serve them, finding answers to the question of how to build a more coordinated and recovery-oriented system will be an effortful process. But the costs of failing to do so, for our nation, for the young man in the elevator, and for an entire generation of men and women who have served in wartime at great personal risk and sacrifice, are simply too high to ignore.

NOTES

Acknowledgements. This material is based upon work supported by the Department of Veterans Affairs, Veterans Health Administration, Office of Research and Development. The views expressed in this article are those of the author and do not necessarily reflect the position or policy of the Department of Veterans Affairs or the United States government.

1. As the quality of training programs for VA service dogs also varies, the dog may also have been the recipient of poor training.

2. This coverage has had important positive consequences in urging much-needed improvements to the quality and accessibility of PTSD treatment services across VA and the military; however, it has also done much to perpetuate stigma around PTSD while doing little to improve awareness of available treatments.

REFERENCES CITED

Alvarez, Lizette
  2008 Nearly a Fifth of War Veterans Report Mental Disorders, A Private Study Finds. The New York Times, April 18. http://www.nytimes.com/2008/04/18/us/18vets.html, accessed March 15, 2014.
Bellamy, Ray
  1997 Compensation Neurosis: Financial Reward for Illness as Nocebo. Clinical Orthopaedics and Related Research 336:94–106.
Belsher, Bradley E., Quyen Q. Tiet, Donn W. Garvert, and Craig S. Rosen
  2012 Compensation and Treatment: Disability Benefits and Outcomes of U.S. Veterans Receiving Residential PTSD Treatment. Journal of Traumatic Stress 25(5):494–502.
Biehl, Joao
  2005 Vita: Life in a Zone of Social Abandonment. Berkeley: University of California Press.
Bradley, Rebekah, Jamelle Greene, Eric Russ, Lissa Dutra, and Drew Westen
  2005 A Multidimensional Meta-Analysis of Psychotherapy for PTSD. American Journal of Psychiatry 162(2):214–227.
Brief, Deborah J., Amy Rubin, Terence M. Keane, Justin L. Enggasser, Monica Roy, Eric Helmuth, John Hermos, Mark Lachowicz, Denis Rybin, and David Rosenbloom
  2013 Web Intervention for OEF/OIF Veterans with Problem Drinking and PTSD Symptoms: A Randomized Clinical Trial. Journal of Consulting and Clinical Psychology 81(5):890–900.
Buckman, Joshua E. J., Josefin Sundin, Talya Greene, Nicola T. Fear, Christopher Dandeker, Neil Greenberg, and Simon Wessely
  2011 The Impact of Deployment Length on the Health and Well-Being of Military Personnel: A Systematic Review of the Literature. Occupational Environmental Medicine 68(1):69–76.
Carlson, Eve B., Donn W. Garvert, Kathryn S. Macia, Josef I. Ruzek, and Thomas A. Burling
  2013 Traumatic Stressor Exposure and Post-Traumatic Symptoms in Homeless Veterans. Military Medicine 178(9):970–973.
Chard, Kathleen M.
  2005 An Evaluation of Cognitive Processing Therapy for the Treatment of Posttraumatic Stress Disorder Related to Childhood Sexual Abuse. Journal of Consulting and Clinical Psychology 73(5): 965–971.
Chard, Kathleen M., Elizabeth G. Ricksecker, Ellen T. Healy, Bradley E. Karlin, and Patricia A. Resick
  2012 Dissemination and Experience with Cognitive Processing Therapy. Journal of Rehabilitation Research & Development 49(5):667–678.
Chard, Kathleen M., Jeremiah A. Schumm, Gina P. Owens, and Sara M. Cottingham
  2010 A Comparison of OEF and OIF Veterans and Vietnam Veterans Receiving Cognitive Processing Therapy. Journal of Traumatic Stress 23(1):25–32.
Cohen, Beth E., Kris Gima, Daniel Bertenthal, Sue Kim, Charles R. Marmar, and Karen H. Seal
  2010 Mental Health Diagnoses and Utilization of VA Non-Mental Health Medical Services among Returning Iraq and Afghanistan Veterans. Journal of General Internal Medicine 25(1):18–24.
Department of Defense
  2013 OEF/OIF/OND U.S. Casualty Status. www.defense.gov/news/casualty.pdf, accessed October 8, 2013. [Database updated daily.]

Dobbs, David
  2009 Soldiers' Stress: What Doctors Get Wrong about PTSD. Scientific American, April 2009. http://www.scientificamerican.com/article/post-traumatic-stress-trap/, accessed March 15, 2014.

Eftekhari, Afsoon, Josef I. Ruzek, Jill J. Crowley, Craig S. Rosen, Mark A. Greenbaum, and Bradley E. Karlin
  2013 Effectiveness of National Implementation of Prolonged Exposure Therapy in Veterans Affairs Care. JAMA Psychiatry 70(9):949–955.

Engelhard, Iris M., Marcel A. van den Hout, J. O. S. Weerts, Arnoud Arntz, Joup J. C. M. Hox, and Richard J. McNally
  2007 Deployment-Related Stress and Trauma in Dutch Soldiers Returning from Iraq: Prospective Study. British Journal of Psychiatry 191(2):140–145.

Erbes, Christopher R., Kyle T. Curry, and Jenna Leskela
  2009 Treatment Presentation and Adherence of Iraq/Afghanistan Era Veterans in Outpatient Care for Posttraumatic Stress Disorder. Psychological Services 6(3):175–183.

Estroff, Sue E.
  1989 Self, Identity, and Subjective Experiences of Schizophrenia: In Search of the Subject. Schizophrenia Bulletin 15(2):189–196.

Finley, Erin P.
  2011 Fields of Combat: Understanding PTSD among Veterans of Iraq and Afghanistan. Ithaca, NY: Cornell University Press.

Foa, Edna B., Elizabeth A. Hembree, Shawn P. Cahill, Sheila A. M. Rauch, David S. Riggs, Norah C. Feeny, and Elna Yadin
  2005 Randomized Trial of Prolonged Exposure for Posttraumatic Stress Disorder with and without Cognitive Restructuring: Outcome at Academic and Community Clinics. Journal of Consulting and Clinical Psychology 73(5):953–964.

Frueh, B. Christopher, Anouk L. Grubaugh, Jon D. Elhai, and Todd C. Buckley
  2007 U.S. Department of Veterans Affairs Disability Policies for Posttraumatic Stress Disorder: Administrative Trends and Implications for Treatment, Rehabilitation, and Research. American Journal of Public Health 97(12):2143–2150.

Garcia, Hector A., Lance P. Kelley, Timothy O. Rentz, and Shuko Lee
  2011 Pretreatment Predictors of Dropout from Cognitive Behavioral Therapy for PTSD in Iraq and Afghanistan War Veterans. Psychological Services 8(1):1–11.

Good, Byron J.
  1994 Medicine, Rationality, and Experience: An Anthropological Perspective. Cambridge: Cambridge University Press.

Goodson, Jason T., Carin M. Lefkowitz, Amy W. Helstrom, and Michael J. Gawrysiak
  2013 Outcomes of Prolonged Exposure Therapy for Veterans with Posttraumatic Stress Disorder. Journal of Traumatic Stress 26(4):419–425.

Hahn, Robert A.
  1998 The Nocebo Phenomenon: Concept, Evidence, and Implications for Public Health. In Understanding and Applying Medical Anthropology. P. J. Brown, ed. Pp. 138–143. Mountain View, CA: Mayfield Publishing Company.

Harvey, Samuel B., Stephani L. Hatch, Margaret Jones, Lisa Hull, Norman Jones, Neil Greenberg, Christopher Dandeker, Nicola T. Fear, and Simon Wessely
  2012 The Long-Term Consequences of Military Deployment: A 5-Year Cohort Study of United Kingdom Reservists Deployed to Iraq in 2003. American Journal of Epidemiology 176(12):1177–1184.

Hautzinger, Sarah, and Jean N. Scandlyn
  2013 Beyond Post-Traumatic Stress: Homefront Struggles with the Wars on Terror. Walnut Creek, CA: Left Coast Press.

Hoge, Charles W., Carl A. Castro, Stephen C. Messer, Dennis McGurk, Dave I. Cotting, and Robert L. Koffman
  2004 Combat Duty in Iraq and Afghanistan, Mental Health Problems, and Barriers to Care. New England Journal of Medicine 351(1):13–22.

Horesh, Danny, Zahava Solomon, Giora Keinan, and Tsachi Ein-Dor
  2013 The Clinical Picture of Late-Onset PTSD: A 20-Year Longitudinal Study of Israeli War Veterans. Psychiatry Research 208(3):265–273.
Institute of Medicine
  2007 Treatment of PTSD: An Assessment of the Evidence; report released October 17, 2007 by the Institute of Medicine, Washington, D.C., available online at www.iom.edu/Reports/2007/Treatment-of-PTSD-An-Assessment-of-The-Evidence.aspx
Institute of Medicine (IOM)
  2012 Treatment for Posttraumatic Stress Disorder in Military and Veteran Populations: Initial Assessment. Washington, D.C.: Institute of Medicine.
Jacobson, Nora, and Dianne Greenley
  2001 What is Recovery? A Conceptual Model and Explication. Psychiatric Services 52(4):482–485.
Karlin, Bradley E., Josef I. Ruzek, Kathleen M. Chard, Afsoon Eftekhari, Candice Monson, Elizabeth A. Hembree, Patricia A. Resick, and Edna B. Foa
  2010 Dissemination of Evidence-Based Psychological Treatments for Posttraumatic Stress Disorder in the Veterans Health Administration. Journal of Traumatic Stress 23(6):663–673.
Kearney, David J., Carol A. Malte, Carolyn McManus, Michelle E. Martinez, Ben Felleman, and Tracy L. Simpson
  2013 Loving-Kindness Meditation for Posttraumatic Stress Disorder: A Pilot Study. Journal of Traumatic Stress 26(4):426–434.
Kilpatrick, Dean G., Kenneth J. Ruggiero, Ron Acierno, Benjamin E. Saunders, Heidi S. Resnick, and Connie L. Best
  2003 Violence and Risk of PTSD, Major Depression, Substance Abuse/Dependence, and Comorbidity: Results from the National Survey of Adolescents. Journal of Consulting and Clinical Psychology 71(4):692–700.
King, Anthony P., Thane M. Erickson, Nicholas D. Giardino, Todd Favorite, Sheila A. M. Rauch, Elizabeth Robinson, Madhur Kulkarni, and Israel Liberzon
  2013 A Pilot Study of Group Mindfulness-Based Cognitive Therapy (MBCT) for Combat Veterans with Posttraumatic Stress Disorder (PTSD). Depression and Anxiety 30(7):638–645.
Kleinman, Arthur
  1988 The Illness Narratives. New York: Basic Books.
Luhrmann, T. N.
  2000 Of Two Minds: An Anthropologist Looks at American Psychiatry. New York: Vintage Books.
MacDermid-Wadsworth, Shelley, Patricia Lester, C. Marini, Stephen Cozza, Jo Sornborger, Thomas Strouse, and William Beardslee
  2013 Approaching Family-Focused Systems of Care for Military and Veteran Families. Military Behavioral Health 1(1):31–40.
Maguen, Shira, Beth Cohen, Li Ren, Jeane Bosch, Rachel Kimerling, and Karen Seal
  2012 Gender Differences in Military Sexual Trauma and Mental Health Diagnoses among Iraq and Afghanistan Veterans with Posttraumatic Stress Disorder. Womens Health Issues 22(1): e61–e66.
Management of Post-traumatic Stress Working Group
  2010 VA/DoD Clinical Practice Guidelines for the Management of Post-traumatic Stress. Washington, DC: Management of Post-traumatic Stress Working Group, Office of Performance and Quality, VA, Quality Management Directorate, U.S. Army MEDCOM.
Mattocks, Kristin M., Sally G. Haskell, Erin E. Krebs, Amy C. Justice, Elizabeth M. Yano, and Cynthia Brandt
  2012 Women at War: Understanding How Women Veterans Cope with Combat and Military Sexual Trauma. Social Science & Medicine 74(4):537–545.
McInnes, Elizabeth, Sandy Middleton, Glenn Gardner, Mary Haines, Maggie Haertsch, Christine L. Paul, and Peter Castaldi
  2012 A Qualitative Study of Stakeholder Views of the Conditions for and Outcomes of Successful Clinical Networks. BMC Health Services Research 12(1):49–61.

McNally, Richard J., and B. Christopher Frueh

    2013 Why Are Iraq and Afghanistan War Veterans Seeking PTSD Disability Compensation at Unprecedented Rates? Journal of Anxiety Disorders 27(5):520–526.

Meis, Laura A., Robin A. Barry, Shannon M. Kehle, Christopher R. Erbes, and Melissa A. Polusny

    2010 Relationship Adjustment, PTSD Symptoms, and Treatment Utilization among Coupled National Guard Soldiers Deployed to Iraq. Journal of Family Psychology 24(5):560–567.

Michalowski, Raymond, and Jill Dubisch

    2001 Run for the Wall: Remembering Vietnam on a Motorcycle Pilgrimage. New Brunswick, NJ: Rutgers University Press.

Moerman, Daniel E.

    2002 Meaning, Medicine, and the 'Placebo Effect'. Cambridge: Cambridge University Press.

Monson, Candice M., Paula P. Schnurr, Patricia A. Resick, Matthew J. Friedman, Yinong Young-Xu, and Susan P. Stevens

    2006 Cognitive Processing Therapy for Veterans with Military-Related Posttraumatic Stress Disorder. Journal of Consulting and Clinical Psychology 74(5):898–907.

Monson, Candice, Casey T. Taft, and Steffany J. Fredman

    2009 Military-Related PTSD and Intimate Relationships: From Description to Theory-Driven Research and Intervention Development. Clinical Psychology Review 29(8):707–714.

Pinder, Richard J., Neil Greenberg, Edward J. Boyko, Gary D. Gackstetter, Tomoko I. Hooper, Dominic Murphy, Margaret A. K. Ryan, Besa Smith, Tyler C. Smith, Timothy S. Wells, and Simon Wessely

    2012 Profile of Two Cohorts: U.K. and U.S. Prospective Studies of Military Health. International Journal of Epidemiology 41(5):1272–1282.

Pompili, Maurizio, Leo Sher, Gianluca Serafini, Alberto Forte, Marco Innamorati, Giovanni Dominici, David Lester, Mario Amore, and Paulo Girardi

    2013 Posttraumatic Stress Disorder and Suicide Risk among Veterans: A Literature Review. Journal of Nervous and Mental Disease 201(9):802–812.

Pugh, Mary Jo V., Erin P. Finley, Laurel A. Copeland, Chen Pin Wang, Polly H. Noel, Megan Amuan, Helen Parsons, Margaret Wells, Barbara Elizondo, and Jacqueline A. Pugh

    2014 Complex Comorbidity Clusters in OEF/OIF Veterans: Beyond the Polytrauma Clinical Triad. Medical Care 52(2):172–181.

Rauch, Sheila A. M., Erin Defever, Todd Favorite, Anne Duroe, and Cecily Garrity

    2009 Prolonged Exposure for PTSD in a Veterans Health Administration PTSD Clinic. Journal of Traumatic Stress 22(1):60–64.

Reno, Jamie

    2012 Nearly 30% of Vets Treated by VA Have PTSD. The Daily Beast, October 21. http://www.thedailybeast.com/articles/2012/10/21/nearly-30-of-vets-treated-by-v-a-have-ptsd.html, accessed March 15, 2014.

Resick, Patricia A., Pallavi Nishith, Terri L. Weaver, Millie C. Astin, and Catherine A. Feuer

    2002 A Comparison of Cognitive-Processing Therapy with Prolonged Exposure and a Waiting Condition for the Treatment of Chronic Posttraumatic Stress Disorder in Female Rape Victims. Journal of Consulting and Clinical Psychology 70(4):867–879.

Richardson, Lisa K., B. Christopher Frueh, and Ron Acierno

    2010 Prevalence Estimates of Combat-Related PTSD: Critical Review. Australian and New Zealand Journal of Psychiatry 44(1):4–19.

Roy-Byrne, Peter P., Lester Arguelles, Mary Ellen Vitek, Jack Goldberg, Terry M. Keane, William R. True, and Roger K. Pitman

    2004 Persistence and Change of PTSD Symptomatology: A Longitudinal Co-Twin Control Analysis of the Vietnam Era Twin Registry. Social Psychiatry and Psychiatric Epidemiology 39(9): 684–685.

Ruggiero, Kenneth J., Alyssa A. Rheingold, Heidi S. Resnick, Dean G.Kilpatrick, and Sandra Galea

    2006 Comparison of Two Widely Used PTSD-Screening Instruments: Implications for Public Mental Health Planning. Journal of Traumatic Stress 19(5):699–707.

Russell, Mark C.

2008 Scientific Resistance to Research, Training, and Utilization of Eye Movement Desensitization and Re-processing (EMDR) Therapy in Treating Post-War Disorders. Social Science & Medicine 67(11):1737–1746.

Saltzman, William, Patricia Lester, William Beardslee, Christopher M. Layne, Kirsten Woodhead, and William P. Nash

2011 Mechanisms of Risk and Resilience in Military Families: Theoretical and Empirical Basis of a Family-Focused Resilience Enhancement Program. Clinical Child and Family Psychology Review 14(3):213–230.

Sayers, Steven L., Victoria A. Farrow, Jennifer Ross, and David W. Oslin

2009 Family Problems among Recently Returned Military Veterans Referred for a Mental Health Evaluation. Journal of Clinical Psychiatry 70(2):163–170.

Schnurr, Paula P., Matthew J. Friedman, Charles C. Engel, Edna B. Foa, M. Tracie Shea, Bruce K. Chow, Patricia A. Resick, Veronica Thurston, Susan M. Orsillo, Rodney Haug, Carole Turner, and Nancy Bernardy

2007 Cognitive Behavioral Therapy for Posttraumatic Stress Disorder in Women. JAMA 297(8):820–830.

Schutz, Alfred

1970 On Phenomenology and Social Relations: Selected Writings. Chicago: University of Chicago Press.

Shlosberg, Arie, and Rael D. Strous

2005 Long-Term Follow-up (32 Years) of PTSD in Israeli Yom Kippur War Veterans. Journal of Nervous and Mental Disease 193(10):693–696.

Smith, Tyler C., Margaret A. K. Ryan, Deborah L. Wingard, Donald J. Slymen, James F. Sallis, and Donna Kritz-Silverstein

2008 New Onset and Persistent Symptoms of Post-Traumatic Stress Disorder Self-Reported after Deployment and Combat Exposures: Prospective Population Based US Military Cohort Study. British Medical Journal 336(7640):366–371.

Smith, Mark W., Paula P. Schnurr, and Robert A. Rosenheck

2005 Employment Outcomes and PTSD Symptom Severity. Mental Health Services Research 7(2):89–101.

Stecker, Tracy, and John Fortney

2011 Barriers to Mental Health Treatment Engagement among Veterans. In Caring for Veterans with Deployment-related Stress Disorders: Iraq, Afghanistan, and Beyond. J. I. Ruzek, P. P. Schnurr, J. J. Vasterling, and M. J. Friedman, eds. Pp. 243–259. Washington, DC: American Psychological Association.

Sundin, Josefin, Nicola T. Fear, Amy Iversen, Roberto J. Rona, and Simon Wessely

2010 PTSD after Deployment to Iraq: Conflicting Rates, Conflicting Claims. Psychological Medicine 40(3):367–382.

Taft, Casey T., Amy S. Stern, Lynda A. King, and Daniel W. King

1999 Modeling Physical Health and Functional Health Status: The Role of Combat Exposure, Posttraumatic Stress Disorder, and Personal Resource Attributes. Journal of Traumatic Stress 12(1):3–23.

Tanielian, Terri, and Lisa H. Jaycox

2008 Invisible Wounds of War: Psychological and Cognitive Injuries, Their Consequences, and Services to Assist Recovery. Santa Monica, CA: RAND Corporation.

Taylor, Steven, Dana S. Thordarson, Louise Maxfield, Ingrid C. Federoff, Karina Lovell, and John Ogrodniczuk

2003 Comparative Efficacy, Speed, and Adverse Effects of Three PTSD Treatments: Exposure Therapy, EMDR, and Relaxation Training. Journal of Consulting and Clinical Psychology 71(2):330–338.

Tick, Edward

2005 War and the Soul: Healing Our Nation's Veterans for Post-traumatic Stress Disorder. Wheaton, IL: Quest Books.

Yehuda, Rachel, Schmeidler J, Labinsky E, Bell A, Morris A, Zemelman S, and Grossman RA

2009 Ten-Year Follow-up Study of PTSD Diagnosis, Symptom Severity and Psychosocial Indices in Aging Holocaust Survivors. Acta Psychiatr Scand 119(1):25–34.

Young, Allan

 1995 The Harmony of Illusions: Inventing Post-Traumatic Stress Disorder. Princeton, NJ: Princeton
       University Press.

Yount, Rick A., Meg D. Olmert, and Mary R. Lee

 2012 Service Dog Training Program for Treatment of Posttraumatic Stress in Service Members. US Army
       Medical Department Journal, Apr-Jun:63–69.

GENDERED SOCIAL ROOTS OF HOMELESSNESS AMONG WOMEN VETERANS

ALISON B. HAMILTON
VA Health Services Research & Development Center for the Study of Healthcare Innovation, Implementation and Policy; VA Greater Los Angeles Healthcare System; University of California Los Angeles

DONNA L. WASHINGTON
VA Health Services Research & Development Center for the Study of Healthcare Innovation, Implementation and Policy; VA Greater Los Angeles Healthcare System; University of California Los Angeles

JESSICA L. ZUCHOWSKI
VA Health Services Research & Development Center for the Study of Healthcare Innovation, Implementation and Policy; VA Greater Los Angeles Healthcare System

Homelessness is one of the most challenging issues facing U.S. Veterans and those who serve Veterans. While the overall number of homeless Veterans is declining, the number of homeless women Veterans is increasing, with little clarity as to why. In previous work, we have examined pathways to homelessness among women Veterans, with a focus on proximal pathways, that is, how women perceived themselves to have become homeless at the time of the study. In this paper, we dig deeper into the roots of homelessness, specifically into the social institutional roots of homelessness. We examine women's focus group conversations about entering and experiencing the military, particularly with regard to the common occurrence of sexual violence and trauma before and during military service. Drawing on anthropological concepts, we conceptualize trauma at both an individual level as embodied in women's lived experiences, as well as at a collective, gendered level. Gendered traumatic experiences can accumulate over time, creating or reinforcing vulnerable pathways. For women Veterans, gender and the military are both social institutions that may act in combination to create gendered social roots of homelessness that are particular to women, and that may be relevant to the gender difference in prevalence of homelessness among Veterans. [women Veterans, homelessness, gender, trauma, qualitative]

INTRODUCTION

There are currently over 2.2 million women Veterans in the United States, comprising approximately 10 percent of the Veteran population (National Center for Veterans Analysis and Statistics 2013). The Veterans Administration (VA) projects that the proportion of women Veterans will continue to grow, despite an overall decline in the Veteran population. Within the next 10 years, the population of women Veterans will increase to almost 2.5 million, or 13 percent of all Veterans.

ANNALS OF ANTHROPOLOGICAL PRACTICE 37.2, pp. 92–107. ISSN: 2153-957X. © 2014 by the American Anthropological Association. DOI:10.1111/napa.12033

One of the most challenging issues facing U.S. Veterans is homelessness. Veterans comprise a disproportionate fraction of the nation's homeless population, with an estimated one of every four homeless people having served in the military (Perl 2013). While the overall number of homeless Veterans is declining, the number of homeless women Veterans is increasing (U.S. Interagency Council on Homelessness 2010). In fact, the number of homeless female Veterans has increased 140 percent in recent years (U.S. Government Accountability Office 2011). Women Veterans are four times more likely than non-Veteran women to experience homelessness (Gamache et al., 2003). In November 2009, the Secretary of Veterans Affairs (VA) pledged to end homelessness among Veterans by 2015, and numerous federal resources were dedicated to meet this challenge.

Those who are homeless on any given night represent only a fraction of a larger at-risk population. In a prior study of risk factors for homelessness among women Veterans, we found that homeless women Veterans experienced multiple cycles in and out of homelessness over their lifetimes (Washington et al., 2010). Vulnerable Veterans generally do not come to the attention of homelessness services until their homelessness becomes imminent. However, the elimination of Veteran homelessness requires preventing those at risk from reaching this state as well as addressing risk factors as soon as they are identified.

The percentage of homeless women Veterans is expected to increase as the percentage of female Veterans increases (Balshem et al., 2011). Factors associated with homelessness may be present before, during, and after military service. For example, sexual assault may precede military service, and occur during and after military service. Multiple studies have found that women Veterans report incidents of sexual assault that exceed rates reported in the general population (Suris and Lind 2008). Military sexual trauma (MST)[1] has been linked to posttraumatic stress disorder (PTSD), depression, alcohol and drug abuse, disrupted social networks, and employment difficulties (Murdoch et al., 2006). These factors can increase the difficulty with which women Veterans readjust to civilian life and contribute to pathways to homelessness (Hamilton et al., 2011). In this paper, we endeavor to more deeply analyze why women Veterans seem to be at particular risk for homelessness: why is homelessness increasing among women, but not men? We will first describe what is known about risk factors for and pathways into homelessness, and then we will "dig deeper" into the roots of homelessness, particularly into the institutional roots of homelessness as embodied in women Veterans who face both gender and military institutional struggles.

RISK FACTORS FOR HOMELESSNESS AMONG WOMEN VETERANS

In prior research, we conducted a case–control study of homeless and housed women Veterans to identify independent risk factors for homelessness (Washington et al., 2010). Characteristics associated with homelessness were unemployment, disability, poor overall health, screening positive for anxiety disorder or PTSD, and a history of MST. Protective factors were being a college graduate or married. Homeless women Veterans also had a high prevalence of mental health disorders. Serious mental illness (SMI), which is present in a sizable minority of homeless women Veterans (with 36 percent screening positive for psychotic symptoms in the prior four weeks), was associated with more chronic (rather than transient) homelessness.

As noted above, homeless women Veterans reported a homelessness history characterized by frequent cycles in and out of homelessness, suggesting that this group arises from a much larger population of marginally housed at-risk women (Eyrich-Garg et al., 2008). Indeed we found that a sizable proportion of our housed controls had risk factors for homelessness. Many of these women may have been homeless in the past, and may become homeless in the future.

PATHWAYS INTO HOMELESSNESS FOR WOMEN VETERANS

Multiple studies have focused on the mental health of homeless women and formerly homeless women (Austin et al., 2008; Padgett et al., 2006; Wenzel et al., 2009). However, few have addressed how women came to be homeless (Belcher et al., 2001). Most literature on risk factors for homelessness points to childhood adversity, substance abuse, and other mental health problems as major antecedents (Belcher et al., 2001; Martijn and Sharpe 2006; Wenzel et al., 2009). This literature tends to focus on isolating independent, individual-level risk factors, with less attention to how risk factors interplay and accumulate over the life course to result in homelessness (Lehman et al., 2007; van den Bree et al., 2009). We conducted a qualitative study of homeless women Veterans to examine their pathways to homelessness (Hamilton et al., 2011). With a grounded understanding of the interconnected roots of homelessness, we suggested that it would be possible to identify critical junctures where intervention—and even prevention—are possible.

Participants in focus groups (described further below) with women Veterans experiencing homelessness associated their homelessness with one or more of five primary "roots," or initiators: (1) premilitary adversity (including violence, abuse, unstable housing); (2) military trauma and substance use; (3) postmilitary interpersonal violence, abuse, and termination of intimate relationships; (4) postmilitary mental illness, substance abuse, and medical issues; and (5) unemployment. Criminal justice involvement was a subsidiary factor, meaning that it was not as commonly noted as a root of homelessness, but it was a root for a subgroup of women. Contextual factors promoted the pathway toward homelessness. They included a survivor instinct prior to military service that promoted entry into the military; lack of social support and resources; a sense of isolation; a pronounced sense of independence that inhibited care-seeking; and access barriers to medical, mental health, and social services. These contextual factors variably contributed to unmet needs, prolonged vulnerability, and homelessness. Roots, subsidiary, and contextual factors were highly interconnected, often with several being relevant for one individual (see Figure 1).

MOVING DEEPER INTO THE ROOTS OF HOMELESSNESS: THE VOLATILE INTERSECTION OF GENDER AND THE MILITARY AS SOCIAL INSTITUTIONS

In the present analysis, we examine more distal experiences that women related to their pathways to homelessness. In particular, we focus on women's experiences at the

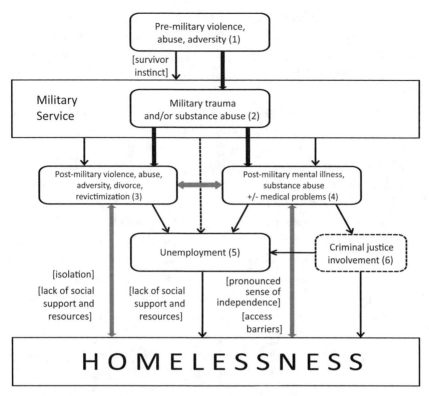

FIGURE 1. Web of homelessness vulnerability described by women veterans experiencing homelessness. (Hamilton et al., 2011)

intersection of gender and the military, both of which we conceptualize as social institutions. As articulated by Martin (2004), social institutions have a number of core features. They are *profoundly social*; they *endure across time and space, entail recurring social practices, constrain and facilitate behaviors and actions*; they have *social positions and relations* characterized by particular expectations, rules/norms, and procedures; they are *constituted and reconstituted by embodied agents*; they are *internalized by group members* as identities and displayed as personalities; they have a *legitimating ideology*; they are *inconsistent, contradictory, and rife with conflict*; they *continuously change*; they are organized in accordance with and *permeated by power*; and finally, *institutions and individuals mutually constitute each other*, that is, they are not separable into macro and micro phenomena (Martin 2004:1256–1258, italics added). Martin notes that some have argued that changes in gender over time have "unsettled" social institutions such as the family, the military, and religion, that is, institutions that had historically legitimized women's subordination. Herbert's (1998) work highlights the ways in which gender and the military intersect, with women's actions in the military creating and re-creating notions of what it means to be a woman in a male-dominated institution. Masculine ideology is asserted both subtly and overtly, unconsciously and consciously (see Burke 2005), with sexual harassment and assault being some of the more severe manifestations of the ideology. Similarly, Segal (1999) characterized the military as a "gender-defining institution," that is, an

institution that functionally defines gender roles and norms, historically against a hegemonic masculinity. As such, the military "constructs" gender, and within that context,
servicewomen construct their gender identity, engaging in "gendering strategies" (Weinstein and D'Amico 1999:5) based on their circumstances, personalities, and a variety of
other factors.

In this paper, we examine homeless women Veterans' (1) reasons for entering the
military, and (2) experiences of being women in the military. We argue that their gendered
experiences as women entering and existing in a male-dominated institution produced
vulnerability to homelessness, and may continue to produce this vulnerability well past
discharge from the military. We do not mean to suggest that all women entering the
military will experience this vulnerability to homelessness, but rather to examine these
distal trajectories into homelessness for women Veterans who have already experienced
homelessness, and who tend to have multiple historical risk factors for homelessness.
Future studies should examine resilience and "hardiness" (see, e.g., Ajdukovic et al., 2013;
Heckman and Clay 2005; Vogt et al., 2008) among women Veterans.

Narratives presented below are derived from a study among women Veterans experiencing homelessness (Washington et al., 2010) that examined risk factors for homelessness
via survey methods, and pathways to homelessness via focus group methods. Twenty-
nine women participated in focus groups in which they discussed why they entered the
military, what they experienced in the military, why they became homeless, and what
services they had sought for their physical and mental health and social service needs. The
average age of participants was 48, ranging from 32 to 68 years. There was an average of
10 years between age at military discharge (mean = 26) to age at first homelessness (mean
= 36). Additional information about methods and sample can be found in Hamilton
et al. (2011, 2012).

REFLECTIONS ON REASONS FOR ENTERING THE MILITARY

Women were systematically asked why they entered the military, and their responses
clustered into three main themes: most described joined the military to escape, some
joined because of family expectations (e.g., other family members had served or were
still serving), and some joined because they were seeking a career, travel opportunities,
or "something to do."

In two of the three focus groups, so many women were agreeing with one another
about joining the military to escape that the moderator asked for a show of hands to
assess how many shared this experience: in one focus group, six of ten raised their hands,
and in another group, seven of 12 raised their hands. One participant explained that she
became pregnant at age 17, was kicked out of her house and went to live with her aunt
and uncle. Her uncle molested her, and she had an abortion. She said, "I think that
that has contributed to a lot of my ups and downs in life of not being able to get over
the homelessness and being molested and then having to abort my child to go back to
the living conditions." The moderator asked her when she went into the military, and
she responded, "I went into the military when I was like 28, 29. I went in late and I

actually ran to the military because of my lifestyle that was going on." Similarly, another participant who had experienced severe domestic violence explained, "I was tired and just determined . . . It was either that or die. I just thought I was going to die so I ran to the military to 'become' something." Another woman said that she "didn't go into the military for a heroic thing"; she was on the run from her drug-using partner who had threatened to kill her. These experiences of running away from abuse into the military were prominent in the focus group narratives:

> I escaped from my husband [who was abusive] into the military.
> I went in to escape abusive family life. I needed to get away.
> My reality was fucked up prior to going in . . . and my escape was to get out of whatever reality . . . just get into the Army. I had to take that trauma into the Service . . . I was just trying to get away from what I was doing, to get away and then I entered this madness and then all of a sudden I woke up with a moment of clarity and said, 'What the fuck am I in? I'm in the Army.'

A participant related her decision to enter the military to wanting to escape from her environment, a tough neighborhood with a heavy gang presence: "I wanted to get off the streets because there were gangs and things and I didn't want to become involved in all that. I saw at an early age people getting shot . . . I was like, let me get off the streets. I didn't want to become a victim of that so I entered the military when I came out of high school."

Other women did not specifically describe adverse premilitary experiences but rather described pressures to join due to their military family members and to an overall lack of sense of direction. For example, one woman said, "I was just kind of not going anywhere with my life and didn't really know what I wanted to do, and I had an older brother that had joined, so I went ahead and joined up also . . . I joined when I was 23." Some women described wanting to belong to "something": "I wanted to be part of something, part of a family, part of a group, part of something that really *means* something and that accepts you." They also noted the "respect" that they thought they would get by "putting on the uniform."

Women's expectations for what would be gained from entering the military—escaping, finding a family, being accepted—were not typically realized:

> My decision to go in was I wanted a career to make something of myself, to put the 20 years in and retire out. And it didn't turn out that way. I was harassed, sexually, non-sexually. I did not feel a part of the family. I felt very pushed out, pushed away. And the harassment that I had gone through was so severe [that now] I have anxiety, even more depression, major PTSD. I have a lot of physical and emotional and mental problems now. If I could do it all over again I would have either got out, gone into another branch, or just switched to other units. My experience was not good.
> I too share that same reason for coming in as a matter of fact. I remember as clear as yesterday crying on the bus, praying Father, what am I going to do? How can I get myself out of this mess? Familial as well as environmental. And there was a magazine next to me [that] said "$30,000 for your college education" and the real travesty of the whole deal is

that . . . I'm still not finished with school, because life kept showing up. It wasn't enough of an escape in actuality.

Women's explanations of why they entered the military illuminate some of the expectations they had of the military as an institution to which they could turn for escape, safety, and opportunity. In other words, some of the social characteristics of the military institution held appeal for women, for example, the institution's legitimating ideology of protection and its predictability with regard to rules and norms—order—in contrast to the lack of order that many women were experiencing premilitary.

These findings regarding women's premilitary circumstances are consistent with studies of predeployment health and of the relationship between adverse childhood experiences and homelessness. For example, Carter-Visscher et al. (2010) examined predeployment gender differences in stressors and mental health among U.S. National Guard troops poised for Operation Iraqi Freedom deployment, and found that men and women did not differ in PTSD symptom severity, but women endorsed significantly more depression symptoms, and screened positive for moderate or greater depression at 13 percent, more than twice the 5 percent rate for men. Women were more likely than men to endorse having a parent with a substance use disorder, having a history of emotional mistreatment, and both childhood and adult sexual assault. Women scored lower than men on preparedness for deployment and perceived unit social support.

Furthermore, there are established relationships between adverse childhood experiences and adult homelessness. Tsai et al. (2011) found that among Veterans in supported housing, those with "relatively numerous childhood problems" were significantly younger when they were first homeless and had worse drug use before entry into supported housing than other participants. In another study of homeless Veterans, Tsai and Rosenheck (2013) found that 40 percent reported childhood abuse, a higher prevalence of childhood problems compared to published samples of nonhomeless Veterans.

In a study of 581 homeless women Veterans enrolled in a Homeless Women Veterans Program, Tsai et al. (2012) found that almost all participants endorsed multiple types and episodes of traumatic events. The most common types of trauma were having someone close experience a serious or life-threatening illness (82 percent) and rape (67 percent). Nearly all participants (99 percent) endorsed at least one trauma item; only three participants endorsed no trauma item. Participants reported being exposed to a mean of 7.40 (SD = 3.14) different types of trauma and a median of 31 total events (M = 50.96, SD = 54.84). Among those who reported rape, 32 percent reported the trauma was inflicted by a family member; 42 percent reported that it occurred in the military. Among those who reported that somebody touched them or made them touch somebody, 39 percent reported it was a family member and 39 percent reported that it occurred in the military. Tsai et al. (2012a) note that the categories of trauma are likely to differ between homeless male and female Veterans due to the different types of exposures encountered by men and women. They suggest that the most salient difference may be exposure to sexual trauma, which is consistent with findings of gender differences in homelessness, with homeless women having higher rates of adult lifetime sexual assault

(62 percent for homeless women compared to 53 percent for homeless men (Kim et al., 2010; Stermac and Paradis 2001), and higher rates of past-year sexual assault (9 percent for homeless women compared to 1 percent for homeless men (Kushel et al., 2003).

BEING A WOMAN IN THE MILITARY

Women's discussions about life in the military centered on challenges associated with being women. Given that the focus groups were conducted with women Veterans experiencing homelessness, adversity—and particularly, trauma—was a prevalent theme. In all of the focus groups in our study, participants conversed about reporting, or attempting to report, MST, which a majority of women had experienced. In one group, sexual abuse and harassment was referred to as "pandemic," but very underreported: "When rapes happened, nobody told." Rapes were swept "under the carpet." (Discussions are quoted at length due to frequent mentions of gendered aspects of their experiences.)

Woman 4:	Once [sexual harassment] gets recorded, all of a sudden you have a personality disorder—Borderline Personality Disorder, Possible Borderline Personality Disorder. I have seen it for 14 months because I had a possible Borderline Personality Disorder, which was diagnosed to me about two months after reporting that I had my trainer banging on my door demanding we make out or else my EPRs [Enlisted Performance Reports] were going to be altered.
Moderator:	How many of you had that experience where after you reported sexual harassment of some sort and wound up getting some sort of a label like that? I see 6 women [out of 10] nodding.
Woman 5:	While in the military or out?
Moderator:	Just labeled in the military and actually even out, once you exited the military after that at some point you wound up getting that label. Anyone else? Afterwards? I see 4 women.
Several women at once:	Both.
Moderator:	But in terms of in the military itself though, after you had reported it I think that there were seven of you that said you reported it and then . . .
Woman 10:	The biggest thing that I experienced with that—and I had a whole bunch of experiences—the biggest thing was that they all had that old boy mentality. They stuck together.
Several women talking:	They stuck together. Even the ones that didn't have any rank, the ones that rank lower than me . . . Exactly.
Moderator:	OK, who did?
Several women talking:	Stuck by the side of the perpetrator. The men. And there were women that were with them.
Woman 2:	. . . You know today on your job if sexual harassment comes up, you are out of there. I mean you can't even put the pen down good before you are out of there. You know what I'm saying? And even more so it should be that way. I know you can't change the military but it is an issue. I'm sure that there are so many women that have been put in a position where they

have had sexual assaults or rapes or did things that they didn't want to do because they were scare tactics were put up against them.

Moderator: Woman 4, you're nodding your head yes about that.

Woman 4: [The harassment] got swept under the rug. And everybody knew about it in the shop. I didn't say a word but all of a sudden all the guys . . . [I was] the only female out of 180 men in my shop. And I had the highest grades in my class. I was a really good mechanic. All of a sudden they put me to work in the snack bar. I was doing "women's work." They would even refer to it as that. They put me to work doing admin stuff instead of working on the engine. I had the highest grade in my class through tech school. I did extra homework and stuff. I was a good mechanic. And so then they finally, it got me so depressed that I finally went to a psychiatrist and the first day I said I don't think this is for me, boom, I was out. And there's nothing you can do about it.

A woman in another focus group described her experience of harassment, with participants strongly resonating with her story:

Woman 5: In the military I had a lot of harassment and everything. Mine got worse in 1983 when I went to [a new base]. I was the first female to invade that company. It was all male.

Moderator: You used the word "invade."

Several women talking: Yeah. You feel you don't belong in these jobs. Yeah.

Woman 5: I was the only one in that company that was qualified to work on any fixed wing or rotary wing aircraft that the Army had. So the First Sergeant wanted me to be training and I refused. And the Platoon Sergeant didn't want me in the Platoon because I was female. So that was two strikes against me there. So afterwards the First Sergeant tried to make me his little darling. And that wouldn't work so he would stand up there in formation and everything and said I'm going to tame you yet . . . . [several women agreeing] . . . [he gave me] the most guard duty in the company as an E6. OK? Every day he put me on guard duty but I would always make sure my uniform would be so sharp you could stand it up on the floor . . . [**Participants**: That's right, that's right.] . . . So the platoon, the Battalion Commander wouldn't let me pull the guard duty. I would just be on stand-by. So when the First Sergeant found out I didn't pull the guard duty . . . he said come go out to the parking lot . . . He pushed me up against the truck and tore my shirt open. By that time I ran across the parking lot and went back into the building. I told the Battalion Commander, they didn't do nothing about it. [**Participants**: They don't care.] . . . That evening I had sent my runner in to clean the Commander's office. He was sitting in there drunk, trying to rape another specialist in there. [**Participants**: I believe it.] So he kept on, and he kept on and he kept on. He just kept trumping charges up on me that didn't even make no sense. Until finally I told them, I said, "I tell you what, it's time for me to ETS [Expiration Term of Service]. I know one thing you can't stop." . . . When it was time for me to go before the Board to get out, over half of my medical records had been destroyed. [**Participants**: Destroyed.] . . . They kept denying [my service connection]. They said they didn't have no evidence. But then when they turned around and gave me my service connection, it was from all the evidence in the military.

One woman whose case was being reviewed for PTSD-related service connection said that she was told, "It's just your word against his . . . If you didn't tell anybody, there's no evidence, nobody cares." When she got out of the military, she said, "I just felt like a failure . . . It was a disaster." Similarly, a woman in another group said that she had been turned down nine times for disability because she never told anybody about being sexually assaulted. She said she had experienced "sex by coercion" as well as "a couple of forced rapes and stuff." She explained, "It's like that. You're like chattel in there. And they just kind of look out and figure out which one they want to do. And you get done." She did not "want to deal with the rapes" when she got home and worked instead on getting off of drugs.

These narratives about being isolated, singled out, silenced, and assaulted because of being female were pervasive throughout the focus groups. The terminology women used is indicative of the ways in which their gender was constructed by the institution (e.g., labeling a woman who had reported harassment with Borderline Personality Disorder, a highly gendered diagnosis) and by the women themselves (e.g., staying silent about harassment/assault, going to extra effort to be the smartest, to have the best-pressed uniform, et cetera), as well as the ways in which the institutions were embodied. Women indeed seemed to use multiple "gendering strategies" (Weinstein and D'Amico 1999) to cope with the struggles they experienced, often being the only female among hundreds of men.

Military sexual assault (MST) against servicewomen has received a substantial amount of attention in the lay press and in research, particularly on women Veterans. Prevalence of MST is difficult to ascertain due to substantial variation in data collection methods and sample compositions (Suris and Lind 2008). In a large female military cohort study, LeardMann et al. (2013) found that of the 13,262 participants, 1,362 (10.3 percent) reported at least one sexual stressor in the three years since entry into the study. Sexual stressors included sexual harassment (reported by 80 percent), sexual assault (8.9 percent), and both sexual harassment and assault (11.2 percent). Women who deployed and reported combat experiences were twice as likely to report sexual harassment and to report both sexual harassment and sexual assault compared with nondeployers. Female service members who reported prior sexual stressors were nearly three times as likely to report recent sexual assault and more than four times as likely to report recent sexual harassment or both sexual stressors compared with those who did not report prior assault.

As noted above, many women had entered the military to escape from violence and abuse. Some connected these premilitary experiences to their victimization in the military. One woman described her experience of her drill sergeant fondling her, which was "a pretty good trauma," after being "abused as a child": "I left from one abuse, from childhood abuse, to husband abuse, from husband abuse to military abuse." After this disclosure, the moderator asked how many participants had abusive situations as children: eight of 12 acknowledged child abuse, and then seven of 12 acknowledged abuse as adults, premilitary.

Given the compelling evidence of MST as an act of gender-specific violence, it seems relevant to consider MST as a form of gender-based violence, that is, any act "that results in, or is likely to result in, physical, sexual or psychological harm or suffering to women, including threats of such acts, coercion or arbitrary deprivation of liberty, whether occurring in public or in private life" (United Nations [UN] Declaration on the Elimination of Violence Against Women [VAW] adopted by the General Assembly [GA] in 1993). Notably, the definition of gender-based violence includes acts or threats "by men *or male-dominated institutions*" (italics added), and it includes violence "perpetuated by the state through policies or the actions of agents of the state such as the police, military or immigration authorities." Some would argue that violence is not only perpetrated at an institutional level but is also experienced at a collective level when it is directed at a group, such as women. As Henry (2006:391) noted regarding violence during wartime, "Individual bodies can become idioms through which expressions of deeply personal and social trauma become manifest . . . Bodies do not simply express trauma; they are a place where identity and meaning can be actively reconfigured into socially and personally acceptable ways for understanding, coping, and creatively managing trauma."

Several women said that their acknowledgement of MST did not occur until several years after military discharge. For example, one woman was asked by a mental health provider if she had ever been sexually assaulted and she said no: "But I got this giant history! Just the very nature of what we went through is a delayed thing. I didn't know! I thought I was in the wrong place at the wrong time and I wasn't a good kid and didn't cooperate." This exemplifies the self-blame that many women expressed, perhaps in part due to the lack of or negative attention paid to their reports, when they reported. Moreover, it exemplifies the often latent nature of traumatic expression, which has been demonstrated even at the biologic level (e.g., Viola et al., 2014).

However, a few women in other groups stated that they had not experienced MST. A younger woman noted, "I've never had any bad experiences with men in the military. Never. Very professional, very. Nothing like that happened to me, ever." Another participant asked her when she entered the military, and she said "'97," to which other respondents replied, "Yeah, that's why." "They got tired of writing checks." We believe that women were referring to MST-related lawsuits that had been won or settled against the military.

Several participants related their experiences of MST to their eventual homelessness, as we described in a prior publication (Hamilton et al., 2011). In one group, all ten women agreed that MST and homelessness fit "hand in hand," along with "low self-esteem and no relationships." One woman expressed that MST could end a military career, and furthermore, one's self-esteem. This connection highlights the way in which some women view the institution as having failed them. Several participants agreed:

Woman 4: Once [sexual assault] happens, you can't consider the military a career... You have to get out and then you get out and you don't feel like you can do anything or that you did something wrong. [**Participant**: That's why I got out.]

Woman 10: If you can't make it in the military, you can't make it nowhere. That's that they tell you. They brainwash you. And then when you get out, the first thing you do is whatever you used to do before you got in there which was drugs. That's why I went straight back to drugs... [**Several participants**: Right.] And one more quick thing. Everybody is raising their hand about sexual assault and Woman 3 isn't raising her hand there. Hers is a physical assault. Same thing—*she had the same thing because she's a woman.* And it's the same thing, it still happens that it was not a sexual issue. I think hers is just as important. [**Several participants**: Also there's verbal abuse too...]

In these narratives of military sexual assault and its aftermath, we see further exemplars of the intersection between the social institutions of gender and the military. Gendered social positions and relations abounded, with women being very clear about their subordinate positions and vulnerability due to their female gender in a predominantly male institution. Furthermore, gender and the military were "constituted and reconstituted by embodied agents" (Martin 2004), that is, women's bodies constituting a "site" for the enactment of male power as well as the means through which these gendered dynamics are lived. Drawing on embodiment theory, Lyon and Barbalet (1994) note that bodies are "institution-making." Servicewomen's bodies seem to be institution-perpetuating as well as acting, in some cases, to tolerate injustices as par for the course in a male-dominated institution. Women's experiences in and of the military institution indeed cannot be separated into micro and macro phenomena, for their experiences were to some extent defined by the legitimating institution but also by those who enacted their power, as well as by women's own histories that served as a backdrop to their entry into the military institution.

The challenge is that women's traumatic experiences in the military seem to become lodged in their bodies, identities, and life courses after leaving the military. As noted, several women described not becoming aware of the trauma's impact until several years after discharge. This is not inconsistent with scientific findings about trauma, which indicate that traumas accumulate over the life course and are associated with a host of physical and mental health problems, as well as homelessness (Padgett et al., 2012). Similar to our findings, Mattocks et al. (2012) found that women Veterans identified stressful military experiences and postdeployment reintegration problems as major stressors. In their individual interviews, women described combat experiences, MST, and separation from family as stressful military experiences. Interestingly, women in their study identified several "behavioral avoidance" coping strategies which mainly related to their bodies, including binging and purging, over-exercising, and prescription drug abuse (as well as compulsive spending).

DISCUSSION

We contend that there is something unique and specific to women's experiences at the intersection of gender and the military that makes their homelessness, and vulnerability to homelessness, different from men's experiences, and this may contribute to the increase in homelessness among women Veterans specifically. Women's more distal experiences and decisions can play a prominent role in the development of vulnerability. In other words, some women Veterans seem to have accumulated adverse experiences *as women* over time that reinforce vulnerable pathways, which for all Veterans, included pathways through military experience. The gendered social roots of homelessness have been noted by others. For example, Tessler et al. (2001) found that perceived pathways into homelessness were socially structured along gender lines. Male participants cited loss of a job, discharge from an institution, mental health problems, and alcohol or drug problems as the main reasons for being homeless. In contrast, female participants cited eviction, interpersonal conflict, and someone no longer able or willing to help. Tsai et al. (2012) also examined gender differences among homeless Veterans, and found that women especially viewed homelessness as arising out of breakdowns in interpersonal relations. Thus, we would agree with Green (1998:4) that "power, history, and gender operate through embodied subjectivity and concrete bodily activity." For women Veterans, gender and the military are both social institutions that act in combination to create gendered social roots of homelessness that are particular to women. As suggested by Connell (2011) and Cheney et al. (this volume), we need to consider these institutions as relational and productive of potentially adverse health and psychosocial consequences for women.

NOTE

Acknowledgements. This study was funded by the Department of Health and Human Services Office on Women's Health (contract number 04–04-PO-36011) and the Department of Veterans Affairs, Women Veterans Health Strategic Healthcare Group. Dr. Washington was an Advanced Research Career Development Awardee of the Veterans Affairs Health Services Research and Development (HSR&D) Service (number RCD-00–017) at the time of this study. Dr. Hamilton was an investigator with the Implementation Research Institute (IRI), at the George Warren Brown School of Social Work, Washington University, St. Louis, through an award from the National Institute of Mental Health (R25 MH080916–01A2) and VA HSR&D QUERI. The views expressed within are solely those of the authors, and do not necessarily represent the views of the U.S. Department of Veterans Affairs or of the Department of Health and Human Services.

1. The definition of MST used by the VA is given by U.S. Code (1720D of Title 38). It is "psychological trauma, which in the judgment of a VA mental health professional, resulted from a physical assault of a sexual nature, battery of a sexual nature, or sexual harassment which occurred while the Veteran was serving on active duty or active duty for training." Sexual harassment is further defined as "repeated, unsolicited verbal or physical contact of a sexual nature which is threatening in character." (http://www.ptsd.va.gov/public/pages/military-sexual-trauma-general.asp)

REFERENCES CITED

Ajdukovic, Dean, Dea Ajdukovic, Marija Bogic, Tanja Franciskovic, Gian Maria Galeazzi, Abdulah Kucukalic, Dusica Lecic-Tosevski, Matthias Schützwohl, and Stefan Priebe
   2013   Recovery From Posttraumatic Stress Symptoms: A Qualitative Study of Attributions in Survivors of War. PLoS ONE 8(8):e70579.

Austin, Erika L., Ronald Andersen, and Lillian Gelberg
  2008 Ethnic Differences in the Correlates of Mental Distress Among Homeless Women. Women's Health Issues 18(1):26–34.
Balshem, Howard, Vivian Christensen, Anais Tuepker, and Devan Kansagara
  2011 A Critical Review of the Literature Regarding Homelessness Among Veterans. VA-ESP Project #05–225. http://www.hsrd.research.va.gov/publications/esp/homelessness.pdf/, accessed January 6, 2014.
Belcher, John R., Jeanie A. Greene, Catherine McAlpine, and Kim Ball
  2001 Considering Pathways into Homelessness: Mothers, Addictions, and Trauma. Journal of Addictions Nursing 13(3–4):199–208.
Burke, Carol
  2005 Camp All-American, Hanoi Jane, and the High-and-Tight: Gender, Folklore, and Changing Military Culture. Boston: Beacon Press.
Carter-Visscher, Robin, Melissa A. Polusny, Maureen Murdoch, Paul Thuras, Christopher R. Erbes, and Shannon M. Kehle
  2010 Predeployment Gender Differences in Stressors and Mental Health Among U.S. National Guard Troops Poised for Operation Iraqi Freedom Deployment. Journal of Traumatic Stress 23(1):78–85.
Connell, Raewyn
  2011 Gender, Health and Theory: Conceptualizing the Issue, in Local and World Perspective. Social Science & Medicine 74(11):1675–1683.
Eyrich-Garg, Karin M., John S. Cacciola, Deni Carise, Kevin G. Lynch, and A. Thomas McLellan
  2008 Individual Characteristics of the Literally Homeless, Marginally Housed, and Impoverished in a U.S. Substance Abuse Treatment-Seeking Sample. Social Psychiatry and Psychiatric Epidemiology 43(10):831–842.
Gamache, Gail, Robert Rosenheck, and Richard Tessler
  2003 Overrepresentation of Women Veterans Among Homeless Women. American Journal of Public Health 93(7):1132–1136.
Green, Linda
  1998 Lived Lives and Social Suffering: Problems and Concerns in Medical Anthropology. Medical Anthropology Quarterly 12(1):3–7.
Hamilton, Alison B., Ines Poza, and Donna L. Washington
  2011 "Homelessness and Trauma Go Hand-in-Hand": Pathways to Homelessness Among Women Veterans. Women's Health Issues 21(4):S203–S209.
Hamilton, Alison B., Ines Poza, Vivian Hines, and Donna L. Washington
  2012 Barriers to Psychosocial Services Among Homeless Women Veterans. Journal of Social Work Practice in the Addictions 12(1):52–68.
Heckman, Carolyn J., and Daniel L. Clay
  2005 Hardiness, History of Abuse and Women's Health. Journal of Health Psychology 10(6):767–777.
Henry, Doug
  2006 Violence and the Body: Somatic Expressions of Trauma and Vulnerability during War. Medical Anthropology Quarterly 20(3):379–398.
Herbert, Melissa S.
  1998 Camouflage Isn't Only for Combat: Gender, Sexuality, and Women in the Military. New York: New York University Press.
Kim, Mimi M., Julian D. Ford, Daniel L. Howard, and Daniel W. Bradford
  2010 Assessing Trauma, Substance Abuse, and Mental Health in a Sample of Homeless Men. Health and Social Work 35:39–48.
Kushel, Margo B., Jennifer L. Evans, Jennifer L., Sharon Perry, Marjorie J. Robertson, and Andrew R. Moss
  2003 No Door to Lock: Victimization Among Homeless and Marginally Housed Persons. Archives of Internal Medicine 163:2492–2499.
LeardMann, Cynthia A., Amanda Pietrucha, Kathryn M. Magruder, Besa Smith, Maureen Murdoch, Isabel G. Jacobson, Margaret A.K. Ryan, Gary Gackstetter, Tyler C. Smith, and the Millennium Cohort Study Team
  2013 Combat Deployment is Associated with Sexual Harassment or Sexual Assault in a Large, Female Military Cohort. Women's Health Issues 23(4):e215–e223.

Lehmann, Erika R., Christiana M. Drake, Philip H. Kass, and Sara B. Nichols
    2007 Risk Factors for First-Time Homelessness in Low-Income Women. American Journal of Orthopsychiatry 77(1):20–28.

Lyon, Margot L., and Jack M. Barbalet
    1994 Society's Body: Emotion and the "Somatization" of Social Theory. *In* Embodiment and Experience: The Existential Ground of Culture and Self. Thomas Csordas, ed. Pp. 48–68. Cambridge, MA: Cambridge University Press.

Martijn, Claudine, and Louise Sharpe
    2006 Pathways to Youth Homelessness. Social Science & Medicine 62(1):1–12.

Martin, Patricia Yancey
    2004 Gender as Social Institution. Social Forces 82(4):1249–1273.

Mattocks, Kristin M., Sally G. Haskell, Erin E. Krebs, Amy C. Justice, Elizabeth M. Yano, and Cynthia Brandt
    2012 Women at War: Understanding How Women Veterans Cope with Combat and Military Sexual Trauma. Social Science & Medicine 74(4):537–545.

Murdoch, Maureen, Arlene Bradley, Susan H. Mather, Robert E. Klein, Carole L. Turner, and Elizabeth M. Yano
    2006 Women and War: What Physicians Should Know. Journal of General Internal Medicine 21(S3):S5–S10.

National Center for Veterans Analysis and Statistics
    2013 http://www.va.gov/VETDATA/Veteran_Population.asp/, accessed December 20, 2013.

Padgett, Deborah K., Bikki Tran Smith, Benjamin F. Henwood, and Emmy Tiderington
    2012 Life Course Adversity in the Lives of Formerly Homeless Persons with Serious Mental Illness: Context and Meaning. American Journal of Orthopsychiatry 82(3):421–430.

Perl, Libby
    2013 Veterans and Homelessness. Congressional Research Service. http://www.fas.org/sgp/crs/misc/RL34024.pdf/, accessed January 6, 2014.

Segal, Mady Wechsler
    1999 Gender and the Military. *In* Handbook of the Sociology of Gender. Janet Saltzman Chafetz, ed. Pp. 563–581. New York: Kluwer Academic/Plenum Publishers.
    2008 Military Sexual Trauma: A Review of Prevalence and Associated Health Consequences in Veterans. Trauma, Violence, & Abuse 9(4):250–269.

Stermac, Lana, and E.K. Paradis
    2001 Homeless women and victimization: Abuse and mental health history among homeless rape survivors. Resources for Feminist Research 28:65–81.

Tessler, Richard, Robert Rosenheck, and Gail Gamache
    2001 Gender Differences in Self-Reported Reasons for Homelessness. Journal of Social Distress and the Homeless 10(3):243–254.

Tsai, Jack, Ellen L. Edens, and Robert A. Rosenheck
    2011 A Typology of Childhood Problems among Chronically Homeless Adults and its Association with Housing and Clinical Outcomes. Journal of Health Care for the Poor and Underserved 22(3):853–870.

Tsai, Jack, Robert H. Pietrzak, and Robert A. Rosenheck
    2013 Homeless Veterans Who Served in Iraq and Afghanistan: Gender Differences, Combat Exposure, and Comparisons with Previous Cohorts of Homeless Veterans. Administration and Policy in Mental Health and Mental Health Services Research 40(5):400–405.

Tsai, Jack, Robert A. Rosenheck, Suzanne E. Decker, Rani A. Desai, and Ilan Harpaz-Rotem
    2012 Trauma Experience among Homeless Female Veterans: Correlates and Impact on Housing, Clinical, and Psychosocial Outcomes. Journal of Traumatic Stress 25(6):624–632.

U.S. Government Accountability Office
    2011 Homeless Women Veterans: Actions Needed to Ensure Safe and Appropriate Housing (GAO-12-182). http://gao.gov/assets/590/587334.pdf, accessed June 17, 2014.

U.S. Interagency Council on Homelessness
  2010 Opening Doors: Federal Strategic Plan to Prevent and End Homelessness. http://usich.gov/
       PDF/OpeningDoors_2010_FSPPreventEndHomeless.pdf/, accessed January 6, 2014.
Van den Bree, Marianne B., Katherine Shelton, Adrian Bonner, Sebastian Moss, Hollie Thomas, and Pamela
       J. Taylor
  2009 A Longitudinal Population-Based Study of Factors in Adolescence Predicting Homelessness in Young
       Adulthood. Journal of Adolescent Health 45(6):571–578.
Viola, Thiago Wendt, Saulo Gantes Tractenberg, Mateus Luz Levandowski, Júlio Carlos Pezzi, Moisés Evandro
       Bauer, Antonio Lúcio Teixeira, and Rodrigo Grassi-Oliveira
  2014 Neurotrophic Factors in Women with Crack Cocaine Dependence During Early Abstinence: The
       Role of Early Life Stress. Journal of Psychiatry & Neuroscience 39(3):206–214.
Vogt, Dawn S., Shireen L. Rizvi, Jillian C. Shipherd, and Patricia A. Resick
  2008 Longitudinal Investigation of Reciprocal Relationship Between Stress Reactions and Hardiness.
       Personality and Social Psychology Bulletin 34(1):61–73.
Washington, Donna L., Elizabeth M. Yano, James McGuire, Vivian Hines, Martin Lee, and Gelberg Lillian
  2010 Risk Factors for Homelessness Among Women Veterans. Journal of Health Care for the Poor and
       Underserved 21(1):82–91.
Weinstein, Laurie Lee, and Francine D'Amico
  1999 Introduction. In Gender Camouflage: Women and the U.S. Military. Francine D'Amico and Laurie
       Lee Weinstein, eds. Pp. 1–14. New York: NYU Press.
Wenzel, Suzanne, Harold D. Green, Jr., Joan S. Tucker, Daniela Golinelli, David P. Kennedy, Gery Ryan,
       and Annie Zhou
  2009 The Social Context of Homeless Women's Alcohol and Drug Use. Drug and Alcohol Dependence
       105(1):16–23.

"YOU NEVER HEARD JESUS SAY TO MAKE SURE YOU TAKE TIME OUT FOR YOURSELF": MILITARY CHAPLAINS AND THE STIGMA OF MENTAL ILLNESS

Karen Besterman-Dahan
HSR&D Center of Innovation on Disability and Rehabilitation Research (CINDRR), James A. Haley Veterans' Hospital, Tampa, FL

Jason D. Lind
HSR&D Center of Innovation on Disability and Rehabilitation Research (CINDRR), James A. Haley Veterans' Hospital, Tampa, FL

Theresa Crocker
HSR&D Center of Innovation on Disability and Rehabilitation Research (CINDRR), James A. Haley Veterans' Hospital, Tampa, FL

The wars in Iraq and Afghanistan have taken a toll on military chaplains (MCs) who often return from deployment with high levels of stress, yet are expected to counsel on a daily basis without decompression of their own, potentially exacerbating any personal trauma. MC with posttraumatic stress disorder (PTSD) who have had deployments abridged due to their positive PTSD screen have reported shame due to leaving service members in their unit in danger while they went to safety. Many MCs report compassion fatigue, PTSD, reintegration issues, and adverse effects to their personal energy, motivation, and mental and spiritual well-being postdeployment, related to stressors from deployment and combat exposure. Only 23–40 percent of Operation Enduring Freedom/Operation Iraqi Freedom/Operation New Dawn (OEF/OIF/OND) service members with a psychiatric disorder seek mental health care, citing stigma as a primary barrier. For MCs, stigma is compounded by a culture in which military health care providers, including MCs, are encouraged to deny their own needs to provide the necessary support to beneficiaries. This paper reviews a pilot study, which explored the impact of operational stress on the psychosocial health and reintegration of MCs, focusing on findings related to mental health and stigma within the military chaplaincy. [military, reintegration, stigma, mental illness]

It disturbed me to no end to hear that there were chaplains getting so burnt out that there were even chaplains that had committed suicide... And that is terrifying to me, that it could get to that point. That's unnerving not because we're supposed to have all the answers, but because we are supposed to be the glimmer of hope when it seems hopeless, and how bad does it get before a chaplain decides it's hopeless too? And just like it's a struggle for soldiers for them to feel that they have the permission to admit they need help or to show emotion, I mean that's got to be true for chaplains too, and our culture is not always open to that either. (National Guard Chaplain)

ANNALS OF ANTHROPOLOGICAL PRACTICE 37.2, pp. 108–129. ISSN: 2153-957X. © 2014 by the American Anthropological Association. DOI:10.1111/napa.12032

All branches of the U.S. military designate chaplains to provide for the religious and spiritual support of military members and their families and to ensure the constitutional right of every military member to freely exercise their religion of choice. Stateside, military chaplains (MCs) have long been a care provider for service members who are dealing with mental health issues, including issues such as reintegration, posttraumatic stress disorder (PTSD), and suicidality (Army 2012; Bonner et al., 2013). MCs are also a critical component of behavioral health (BH) and spiritual support in combat operations, coordinating with leadership and health personnel in suicide prevention and combat and operational stress control. They may be embedded with deployed or nondeployed service members, and have a broad variety of tasks such as monitoring soldiers for signs of stress, and counseling struggling service members and their families at home and while deployed (Abruzzese 2008). Although they are noncombatants, they undergo military training for battlefield skills, including combat survivability and first aid.

MCs play a key role in suicide prevention training, regularly conduct critical event debriefing, and routinely identify soldiers at risk for combat and operational stress reactions (Office of the Surgeon, Multi-National Force, Iraq, Office of the Command Surgeon, Office of the Surgeon, and United States Army Medical Command 2008). A recent study revealed that 36 percent of service members who committed suicide in Iraq in 2007 had met with a chaplain 30 days prior to the event (Office of the Surgeon Multi-National Force-Iraq and Office of the Surgeon General 2008). In 2010, the VA and Department of Defense (DoD) launched an Integrated Mental Health Strategy (IMHS) 2010 paper with a key component focusing on roles for chaplains in the mental health care needs of Veterans and service members. Furthermore, a 2010 DoD Task Force on the Prevention of Suicide report cited chaplains as critical to suicide prevention in the military (Berman et al., 2010). In fact, service members have reported seeking BH care from chaplains at rates similar to those reported for BH personnel (Besterman-Dahan, Barnett et al., 2012; Office of the Surgeon, Multi-National Force, Iraq, Office of the Command Surgeon, Office of the Surgeon, and United States Army Medical Command 2008).

The wars in Iraq and Afghanistan have taken a toll on MCs. Deployed chaplains are each responsible for the spiritual support of up to 1,500 soldiers. Upon return from deployment, many report combat-related stress concerns such as compassion fatigue, PTSD, and reintegration issues (Abruzzese 2008). Unit Ministry Teams (UMTs) personnel have noted adverse effects to their personal energy, motivation, and mental and spiritual well-being related to stressors from deployment and combat (Mental Health Advisory Team-II 2005). Similarly, a recent study of Canadian MCs found high levels of burnout and twice the risk of developing depression and anxiety disorders as other Canadian military personnel (Auld 2010). Furthermore, due to the lack of Uniformed Services Employment and Reemployment Rights Act (USERRA) job protection, deployed Reserve Component (RC) chaplains returning from tours have been found to be at high risk for job loss (Army Chaplain Corps 2009), compounding deployment stress and reintegration issues. Concerns over the mental and physical health of military care providers, including chaplains, treating the physical, spiritual, and mental health of traumatized service members are an emerging issue. Although deployed MCs may return from deployment with increased levels of stress, they are often expected to counsel and minister on a daily basis without decompression of their own, thus potentially exacerbating any personal trauma and stress they might be experiencing (Hayes 2009). Despite the stressors experienced by MCs, there is general stigma against mental illness and health seeking in the Armed Forces (Ursano et al., 2012). In fact, stigma associated with psychological health has changed very little in over a decade despite massive education and screening campaigns in every branch of the military (Dingfelder 2009; Ursano et al., 2012). This is compounded by a culture in which military health care providers, including MCs, are encouraged to deny their own needs to provide the necessary support to beneficiaries (Gates et al., 2010). Before reviewing results of a pilot study that explored the impact of operational stress on the psychosocial health and reintegration of MC, focusing on ways in which stigma operates, it is pertinent to first consider various theoretical frameworks of stigma and place it within various contexts—which overlap in the case of MCs—including health care providers, the military, and military health care providers.

Theoretical Frameworks

Stigma can be understood as an overarching term that includes problems of knowledge (ignorance), attitudes (prejudice), and behaviors (discrimination), which work synergistically to fuel social exclusion (Thornicroft et al., 2007). The definition of the concept of stigma has been noted to be vague and variable (Link and Phelan 2001). Typically it refers to Goffman's description of an "attribute that is deeply discrediting"; those who became associated with a stigmatized condition are reduced "from a whole and usual person to a tainted, discounted one," and the stigmatized are perceived to have a "spoiled identity" (Goffman 1963). Goffman's concept of stigma focuses on the individual impact of the stigma and the processes by which it is internalized and shapes individual behaviors (Kleinman and Hall-Clifford 2009). This is evident in models such as that of Corrigan and Watson, where stigma's primary impact is seen on the individual's emotional response and self-esteem (Corrigan and Watson 2002; Yang et al., 2007).

Link and Phelan (2001) note that stigma research has had an individualistic focus on the perceptions of individuals and the consequences of such perceptions for microlevel interactions, instead of sources and consequences of pervasive, socially shaped exclusion and discrimination. In contrast to "stigma," "discrimination" focuses the attention of research to those who do the discriminating rather than to the people who are the recipients of it, leading to a different understanding of where responsibility lies as well as different solutions (Sayce 1998). To that end, newer models of stigma consider the social processes that occur within the sociocultural environment and effects that can be seen within the individual. For example, Link and Phelan include a component of structural discrimination in their model of stigma, allowing for the identification of how various forms of power (social, economic, political) shape the distribution of stigma within a social environment (Link and Phelan 2001, 2006).

A critical challenge in stigma research is the use of theories that are uninformed by the lived experience of the people being studied, resulting in a misunderstanding of the experience of the stigmatized and the perpetuation of unsubstantiated assumptions (Kleinman et al., 1995; Link and Phelan 2001). One response to this challenge has been within the field of anthropology, where research has focused on understanding stigma as embedded in the moral experience and lives of sufferers, drawing from the concepts of the social dimensions of illness, social suffering, and violence and trauma (Yang et al., 2007). By considering the lived experience in a local world, that place where something is at stake such as status, money, life chances, jobs, or relationships, the stigmatized is understood to be a person with a moral status determined by their local social world and maintained by meeting social obligations and norms (Kleinman and Hall-Clifford 2009; Yang et al., 2007). Those that have or are associated with stigmatized conditions are unable to meet those requirements. Stigma is thus hypothesized to "threaten the loss or diminution of what is most at stake, or actually diminishes or destroys that lived value . . . engagements and responses over what matters most to participants in a local social world shape the lived experience of stigma for both sufferers and responders or observers" (Yang et al., 2007). An important caveat is that the stigmatized and those who stigmatize are interconnected through local social networks. While stigma may share features across contexts, it uniquely affects lives in local contexts. In other words, across cultures the meanings, practices, and outcomes of stigma differ. By focusing on moral experience, the behaviors of both the stigmatized and those doing the stigmatizing can be understood as responses to what is at stake and what is threatened (Yang et al., 2007).

Stigma and Mental Illness

It is estimated that 19.6–24.8 percent of adults over the age of 18 have any mental illness excluding substance use disorders (Bagalman and Napali 2014); however, only 38.2 percent of adults with any mental illness have received mental health services in the last year (Substance Abuse and Mental Health Services Administration 2012). While 50 percent cited cost as the main barrier to receiving mental health care, 35 percent of the reasons cited related to stigma, including concerns over confidentiality, fear of being committed or taking medication, not wanting others to find out, fear of neighbors having negative opinion, and concerns over negative effect on job (Substance Abuse and Mental Health Services Administration 2012). Corrigan notes that both public and self-stigma affect an individual's decision to seek treatment (Corrigan 2004). Public stigma is the perception held by society that an individual is socially unacceptable. Self-stigma is the perception held by the individual that he or she is socially unacceptable, leading to a reduction in self-worth that may be compounded if that person seeks psychological help. Thus, negative perceptions in society toward those who seek psychological services may be internalized and lead people to perceive themselves as inferior, inadequate, or weak. People higher in self-stigma may not seek mental health services in order to maintain a positive image of themselves (Vogel et al., 2007).

Overall, mental illness stigma has been found to have a significant effect on life chances influencing not only health care access but also employment, housing, and personal relationships. Thus, stigma acts as an invisible burden, compounding the symptoms of the illness itself. Some studies have found the stigma of mental illness to be more debilitating to overcome than the mental illness itself (Wallace 2012). Thornicroft (2008) notes that in addition to the universal phenomenon of rejection and avoidance of people with mental illness and the reluctance to be perceived as mentally ill, most cultures have little accurate and useful knowledge about mental illness. Stigmatization of people with mental illness has been found wherever it is studied, contributing to barriers to social inclusion and health care treatment. Stigma associated with mental illness includes attributions of dangerousness, incompetency, and generalized "badness"; furthermore, an inverse relationship between stigma and treatment seeking, adherence and continuation has been found (Kim et al., 2011). The consequences of psychiatric stigma have been found to be consistent across communities including negative labeling, discrimination in family and work settings, treatment avoidance, negative health outcomes, poor self-esteem, ostracism, exclusion, violence, and suicide (Shrivastava et al., 2012).

Health Care Providers

While stigma related to mental illness is significant in the general public, it has been found to occur at even higher rates in health care providers, including medical students, residents, and practicing physicians, where it has been shown to lead to poor utilization of mental health care resources and treatment, preventive care, as well as self-prescription of medications and suicide (Gold et al., 2012). The stigmatization of physicians with mental illness has been related to three contextual influences in the medical profession, including (1) the transmission of the culture of medicine in medical schools; (2) the attitudes of colleagues at work; and (3) the expectations of health care systems and organizations to physicians suffering from mental illness or substance abuse (Wallace 2012).

Multiple studies of medical students have indicated that they experience increased rates of depression, burnout, mental illness, and suicide risk compared to the general population and mental health has been found to worsen over the course of medical training (Schwenk et al., 2010). Despite seemingly better access, medical students tend to have low utilization of mental health services and may engage in harmful methods of coping (Rosenthal and Okie 2005; Tjia et al., 2005). Stigma associated with mental illness and use of services has been cited as barrier to treatment seeking. In addition to general stigma, concerns over confidentiality and documentation in academic records, and fear that revealing their mental illness will compromise their chances for residency training positions or educational opportunities are reported (Schwenk et al., 2010). Medical students' perceptions of stigma associated with mental illness have been noted to be prevalent in medical school, and continue throughout the medical profession. Avoidance of appropriate help seeking is linked to perceived norms where a mental health problem is seen as a form of weakness with negative implications for successful career progression.

Fewer studies are available related to the mental health issues among practicing physicians, who have been found to have higher suicide rates than the general population (Gold et al., 2012). Studies have also found physicians to be reluctant to disclose and seek treatment for mental illness due to fear of professional sanctions such as negative impact on their medical licensing, which can lead to self-medication and increased suicide risk (Center et al., 2003; Gold et al., 2012; Schwenk et al., 2008). Despite greater access to mental health care, physicians are not any more likely to receive pharmaceutical treatment for mental illness, and have described extreme efforts to protect their confidentiality regarding mental health treatment by seeking care outside of the community, avoiding treatment, self-prescribing, or having a colleague, whom they are not seeing for medical care, prescribe medications (Gold et al., 2012). Thus, physicians' mental health is given low priority in the culture of caregiving despite evidence of increased rates of untreated mental illness and suicide.

Finally it should be noted that while stigma related to mental illness is significant in medical students and physicians, another phenomenon exists, which further stigmatizes mental health care providers. Negative perceptions of mental health care providers are prevalent within the medical field and general public. They are often perceived by other medical professionals to be "different" at best, although more often not "real" doctors at all and often described as "emotionally unstable" and "weird" (Kalra 2012; Nasrallah 2011). Furthermore, the stereotype of the "mad psychiatrist" is prevalent in the Western media, where mental health care providers are often portrayed as incompetent, with tendencies to violate sexual or other ethical boundaries with their patients (Bassiri et al., 2011). Thus, mental health professionals are recipients of stigma both toward the illness they treat and toward the treatment field. This stigmatization has been found to have a significant impact on those who work in the mental health field with wide reaching impact on multiple levels, including individual (job dissatisfaction, isolation), patient care (reluctance to advocate for patients and profession, exacerbating experiences of stigmatization), and organizational (unwillingness of others to collaborate with mental health care providers, perpetuating delayed help seeking by patients) (Bassiri et al., 2011; Persaud 2000).

Military

> [Service members hear] 'We can help!' from the mental health providers, while at the same time being told, 'If you're broke, we'll kick you to the curb,' from the rest of the military community. (Army Chaplain) [Finley 2011:110]

Frequent deployments over the course of two wars spanning over a decade have intensified emotional and psychosocial stress on service members and their families. Approximately one-fifth of service members returning from the Iraq and Afghanistan wars report symptoms of PTSD or major depression, rates that are markedly increased since the start of the wars (Dingfelder 2009). Still, 87 percent of active duty and 73 percent of National Guard service members have not sought care within 12 months after returning from war (Kim et al., 2010). Mental illness stigma has been identified as the main barrier to care (Hooyer 2012), and remains one of the biggest problems facing the DoD and Department of Veterans Affairs when it comes to preventing suicide and other negative events. Independently and in coordinated efforts, every branch of the military is currently fighting the stigma related to seeking mental health services (Dingfelder 2009).

However, as a recent report on stigma and barriers to care by the Forum on Health and National Security noted:

> The stigma associated with psychological health has changed little since the start of the war despite massive education and screening campaigns. It is conceivable that the stigmatization process as a means of differentiating "in" and "out" groups plays such a central role in maintaining performance that changing the culture will continue to be a long-term goal. [Ursano et al., 2012:3]

Service members can be said to suffer mental illness stigma disproportionately due to the military culture, wherein mental illness and help seeking is in direct opposition to military values of psychological toughness, resilience, collective responsibility, and group loyalty (Britt et al., 2008; Hoge et al., 2004). Acknowledging a problem, particularly related to mental health, is often perceived as admitting weakness or failure (Army 2012). In this context, mental illness can be viewed as cowardice, or a character flaw, resulting in social exclusion. Thus, service members get caught between the dual messages of the destigmatizing efforts of official military policy, which has increased accessibility to evaluation and treatment, and the culture of military life, which places priority on completing the larger mission above the well-being of any one individual (Finley 2011). Barriers to service members attaining mental health care include embarrassment about treatment, fear of being perceived as weak or being treated differently by unit leadership, and concern that members of their unit will have less confidence in them (Hoge et al., 2004; Kim et al., 2010). Additionally, there are fears of demotion, discharge, loss of security clearance, and benefits (Gutmann and Lutz 2010). There is merit to these concerns; 39 percent of service members who were referred by their commanders and 3 percent who self-referred for mental health treatment have been found to experience a negative career impact (Rowan and Campise 2006). In addition, Hooyer (2012) notes cases of service members who sought mental health treatment, only to be misdiagnosed with mental illnesses related to "preexisting conditions" that predated military service, such as anxiety disorder and personality disorder, and were thus discharged without benefits. These stories influence the help-seeking behaviors of others as they travel through units. Similarities in terms of perceived stigma and barriers to psychological care have been found in service members across militaries of Western nations, including United Kingdom, Australia, New Zealand, and Canada (Gould et al., 2010). Furthermore, stigma related to mental illness and treatment has been found to continue after service members separate from the military (Iversen et al., 2011).

Military Health Care Providers

The impact of military trauma in the current theatres of operation has posed unique stressors for health care providers (Stewart 2009). While there has been a growing body of literature on the impact of the current wars on deployed service members, few studies have examined the impact on health care providers, including MC. Evidence suggests that similar to military combatants, military health care provider exposure to life-threatening situations will increase the probability of negative psychological disorders following these traumatic experiences (Gibbons et al., 2012). In a study of previously deployed health care workers, direct and perceived threats of personal harm were risk factors for PTSD. For health care workers returning from a combat environment, perceived threat of personal harm may be the most predictive factor in determining those with subsequent PTSD (Grieger et al., 2007). The mental health treatment of military service members places unique demands on providers as their patients experience combat stress (Linnerooth et al., 2011). A Mental Health Assessment Team report noted in 2005 that BH was coordinated between BH personnel, UMT (consisting of chaplains and chaplain assistants), and primary care providers. In a survey of BH personnel, 33 percent reported high burnout, 27 percent reported low motivation, 22 percent reported low morale, and 15 percent agreed that the stressors of deployment impaired their BH job (Mental Health Advisory Team-II 2005). The report concluded that

> If our providers are impaired, our ability to intervene early and assist Soldiers with their problems may be degraded. It is vital to understand the processes of provider burnout and compassion fatigue in order to prevent and intervene in order to preserve the care in our caregivers. [Mental Health Advisory Team-II 2005:22]

However, just as military health providers are not immune to the cumulative psychological effects of persistent conflict, they also are not immune to the stigma related to mental illness and treatment within the military. As noted in the final report from the Fort Hood shootings:

> Providers often do not avail themselves of access to support resources similar to those that they supply to our fighting forces . . . Our review suggests a culture that exists in which military healthcare providers are encouraged to deny their own physical, psychological and social needs to provide the necessary support to beneficiaries. [Gates et al., 2010:6]

A recent study found U.S. combat medics experiencing barriers and stigma related to mental health counseling services (Elnitsky et al., 2013). Grieger et al. (2007) noted that while nearly half of those military care providers who met subclinical criteria for PTSD reported at least one mental health consultation for mental health problems postdeployment, none had ongoing treatment. This is concerning given that PTSD symptoms have been found to worsen with the passage of time (Grieger et al., 2007). Gender has also been found a play a role in impacting mental help-seeking behavior of military health care providers, with female officers endorsing the concern that seeking mental health is potentially career damaging, and enlisted female health care personnel less likely to see professional mental health care than their male counterparts (Gibbons et al., 2012).

STUDY

The purpose of this pilot study was to explore the impact of deployment as a chaplain within a combat zone on the psychosocial and health characteristics and reintegration of MCs, specifically those of the Army National Guard (ARNG).

Methods

Methods, recruitment, and instruments are described in detail elsewhere (Besterman-Dahan, Barnett et al., 2012). Briefly, this research utilized in-depth interviews, social network analysis questionnaires, and a cross-sectional, descriptive, online anonymous survey. Following approval by the local Institutional Review Board, 27 MCs were interviewed at regional Chaplain Annual Sustainment Training (CAST) conferences and by telephone. Inclusion criteria included chaplains who were current active members of the ARNG during the time frame of Operation Enduring Freedom (OEF), Operation Iraqi Freedom (OIF), and Operation New Dawn (OND).

Analysis

Interviews and field notes were transcribed into text files and entered into Atlas.ti. Transcripts of the interviews were analyzed using content analysis (Krippendorff 1980; Weber 1990). Initially, team members compared and contrasted perceptions of key findings following interviews. Two investigators reviewed the transcripts to develop an initial list of analysis codes with definitions and examples. After all transcripts were coded, like codes were compared, contrasted, combined, and synthesized into higher level concepts. Points of agreement and discrepancies were discussed and decisions were made jointly to determine whether new categories needed to be added.

Results and Findings

Twenty-seven ARNG chaplains were interviewed for this study, either in person at regional CAST conferences ($n = 23$) or by telephone ($n = 4$). Demographics of the participants can be found in Table 1. Briefly, the majority of the participants were male ($n = 23$), had been deployed ($n = 19$; 18 in a chaplain capacity), and were of a mainline Protestant denomination ($n = 17$). Most ($n = 16$) had ≥ 11 years of military experience; however the majority ($n = 15$) had ≤ 10 years' experience in a chaplain capacity. While a variety of topics were discussed in the interviews, this paper focuses on participants' experiences of stigma and mental health issues.

Context

Before discussing the themes related to mental health and stigma, it is important to provide some context regarding the experiences of the MC. A chaplain shortage occurred among all military branches during the OEF/OIF wars. According to one participant in a leadership position, in 2005 the ARNG was 52 percent filled; at that time, the DoD standards for becoming a chaplain changed so people were able to come in with only distance learning and no congregational experience. Numerous participants suggested that this lack of experience was a potential problem with being able to handle the large, complex caseloads of service members in a pluralistic religious environment, particularly with the additional stressors of frequent deployments, trauma, and combat exposure. Congregational experience exposes chaplains to a variety of traumas, suicides, illness, death, and family issues. Therefore, participants explained, when something tragic happens, an experienced chaplain is able to respond with "how are we gonna organize this chaos and how are we gonna help people respond to it," something chaplains with little,

TABLE 1. Participant Demographics

Variable	Frequency	Percent
Gender		
Male	23	86
Female	4	15
Denomination		
Baptist	9	33
Lutheran	3	11
Protestant (nondenomination)	6	22
Evangelical	3	11
Presbyterian	1	4
Methodist	4	15
Jewish	1	4
Deployed		
Yes—once	13	48
Yes—multiple	6	22
No	8	30
Deployment capacity		
Deployed as chaplain	18	67
Deployed nonchaplain	3	11
Employment		
Unemployed	0	0
Underemployed	6	22
Full-time/active National Guard	14	52
Other	7	26
Military experience		
0–5 years	7	26
6–10 years	3	11
11–15 years	3	11
16–20 years	6	22
21–30 years	7	26
Missing	1	4
Prior military experience nonchaplain capacity		
No	20	74
Yes	7	26
Chaplain/pastoral experience		
0–5 years	12	44
6–10 years	3	11
11–15 years	2	7
16–20 years	4	15
21–30 years	5	19
Missing	1	4

if any, congregational experience "are unable to do." Participants reported that MCs were being deployed on average every two to three years. Lack of congregational experience coupled with frequent deployments likely converged, contributing to the findings which follow.

Participants relayed many of their responsibilities, both when deployed and stateside, in terms of being on call and counseling both service members and families, which could occur at any time of the day or night. One chaplain noted the importance of situational awareness, "what's going on outside the compound as well as within; [having] the ability to do ministry 24/7." Deployed chaplains also describe their roles working with service members, from blessing convoys before they go out, to praying with the wounded and over the fallen, and counseling soldiers for the many personal issues that come up. One participant noted that he averaged "5.8 counseling sessions a day, seven days a week. And it burned me out badly." Similarly, stateside MC "put out fires all the time as a chaplain," working with service member families and with soldiers who just returned and/or are about to be deployed. Participants described being on call all the time, in order to deal with a crisis whenever it came up "so it's not a matter of being nine to five and we're done, it's the phone could ring in the middle of the night or five in the morning or whatever." Other responsibilities for stateside MC include casualty and death notifications, where the chaplain accompanies the notifying officer to deliver the news of a death or serious injury to next of kin.

While specifics of combat exposure are discussed in detail elsewhere (Besterman-Dahan, Barnett et al., 2012), participants described their experiences during deployment. Exposures ranged from incoming rounds at the bases where they were stationed to volunteering to go "outside the wire"—the relative safe zones of the camp base or forward operating base in a warzone—to visit service members that were geographically distant. Some volunteered to do this in order to increase credibility and relationships with soldiers, others to "know what the combat soldier experiences outside the wire." Participants also described being caught in roadside bomb attacks of their vehicles and of their base, seeing "bodies cut literally in half." Many spoke of being exposed to "mass casualties" [more than three people wounded or killed] including those from their own unit, civilians and the enemy. They also described being an integral part of assisting with the wounded and dying, being in the operating room during surgeries, and praying over the dead. Several relayed stories of hearing loss, traumatic brain injury, and other injuries from combat exposure, in some cases due to proximity of the blasts to their chapels. In one instance a participant was asked to bear witness to the unearthing of a mass grave of two hundred bodies, "woman and children were just lined up gunned down, bodies being unearthed, children still holding their mothers."

Numerous participants reported being underemployed or unemployed upon return from deployment, often as a result of their deployment. As one participant explained:

> We had six Battalion and one Brigade chaplain in our team, all working together and of those, five of us knew that we were not going home to a guaranteed job, we were not going home to a paid position at a church capacity even though we had left in that capacity.

They described belonging to small congregations and the lack of USERRA protections for their chaplaincy positions, in addition to the hesitancy of congregations to hire an MC who is likely to deploy. Oftentimes chaplains thus came back and were scrambling to find jobs wherever they could, including teaching, electronic retail stores, security, and insurance. Some also were able to become employed fulltime by National Guard, although not always in a chaplain capacity. This issue was not limited to MCs belonging to smaller congregations; several participants who were assigned to congregations by church hierarchies also cited this issue. Indeed, our findings confirm surveys of Army Reserve (USAR) chaplains, 78 percent of whom have deployed at least once, on the impact of military duty on nonmilitary employment, which found a high rate of unemployment after mobilization (Army Chaplain Corps. 2009). Survey respondents noted how churches often do not tolerate long or multiple deployments, the lack of USERRA job protection result, and how local religious leaders employ preferentially for nonmilitary pastors resulting in loss of their church assignment, having their families removed from the rectory during deployment, and marital disintegration as a result of unemployment (Army Chaplain Corps. 2009).

Mental Health: Self-Awareness

> P: I just took my pain and I turned it, you know, I took my pain, turned it inside out, took care of others. That's kind of how I got through it.
> F: Isn't that what a lot of chaplains seem to do?
> P: I think so. I think the ones that survive do.

Given the context and experiences of the ARNG we interviewed, many expressed awareness of the stress and mental health issues of themselves and fellow chaplains. They also described barriers to recognizing the signs early and dealing with it in a timely manner. One common theme was the idea that the chaplain is the "lone ranger" or "superhero" taking care of everyone else except for themselves. Feelings of guilt to take time for self-care and the idea that they should not need assistance were prevalent.

> P: I have to get rid of the superhero mindset and uh . . . . Take off the cape, be willing to uh, solicit help, be it from other chaplains or just from God Himself and you know, God, I'm overwhelmed here, I need your help, I don't know what to do.
> F: Do you think that's something that people, that other chaplains tend to forget?
> P: Yeah I think it's easy to forget. It's real easy to forget. I think it's easy to, not just as a chaplain really I guess, in any sort of pastoral type of role, but it's easy to start to get this type of mindset that you're the fix-it for everybody to start making it about yourself. Being there for everyone, being what they need, and putting a lot of pressure on yourself that I got to keep it together or I can't help anybody else.

This tendency toward being "the lone ranger" is further reinforced by structural issues, including policies and perceived roles and duties of chaplains within both the military and civilian congregations. For example, participants described coming home from deployments and not being offered the same decompression services offered to the other members in their units or being asked to counsel and lead reintegration programs that other returning soldiers were attending. Others relayed not being given time off to decompress between coming home and starting new positions within the National Guard, often having requests for additional time being turned down. For example, one participant described having less than ten days between coming home from a deployment and relocating away from his family to a new full-time National Guard assignment.

Similarly, participants with civilian congregations also relayed not being able to take time off during visits home during or after deployments due to expectations of their civilian congregations or their government employers to immediately work upon return. One MC described this experience on his return from deployment:

> Coming back from Iraq, the, the welcome home when we got back was good, but I was immediately taken away from that and put on OWT status, Operational Warrior Training, where I was an instructor . . . So, while the rest of the group was demobing to go home, I was set aside to, given my new quarters and being told my new responsibilities. Which was fine, but there was no real time to step down from one assignment to the next assignment to the next assignment, you know, kind of deal. Some breathing time in between would have been good.

Another participant relayed the experience of a fellow MC on leave during deployment, and the expectations of his civilian congregation:

> I have talked to chaplains and he's on his 2 weeks R & R to be with his family. His congregation insisted that he preach the two Sundays that he was there and conduct Bible studies, the hell with the family, you're not gonna go off for 2 weeks on vacation with your wife, we want you here to work. I mean the congregations are real bastards about their ownership of the chaplains and they see no connection between what chaplains are learning and the expertise they're gaining for free that can be applied to congregation. All they're worried about is are you conducting that Bible study or are you gonna preach that sermon, are you gonna be there when I call you on the phone. They want a chaplain and they feel that they own you lock, stock and barrel and they have no . . . absolutely zero compassion when it comes to having come home from the war and then God help you if you get activated a second or third time.

Those chaplains who had more military experience, medical experience (e.g., former medic), were older, or had greater congregational experience—in other words, more experience working with people, trauma, and the opportunity to build life experience and resiliency—reflected on the need for chaplains to be self-aware, reaching out for help in order to remain being helpful to others.

> You never heard Jesus say make sure you take time out for yourself. I see his ministry as giving of himself, giving of himself, giving of himself, and yet there were times when he recharged. The times when he would go out by himself to pray and chaplains want to be spiritual, we want to be religious, but for some that doesn't recharge their batteries so you have to, back to the self-awareness, know what it is that will recharge your batteries in order to get that . . . I think that most people, you really have to be intentional about that self-care so knowing yourself to know what are those things that make you recharge your batteries.

Help Seeking and Stigma

> Letting other people take care of you. Some chaplains don't like that. They think that's a sign of weakness and I think for particularly chaplains that are really interested in your career and where your career is going they don't want anyone to think you might have this chink in their armor or this weakness.

Stigma related to mental health and help seeking was discussed in relation to a number of issues. Among the concerns was the consideration that a chaplain may be a high-ranking officer, and how acknowledging that they may be having a mental health problem impacts how others would perceive them in those roles.

> I think I really abused alcohol for a while after I came back. I think it was a form of self-medication, of numbing all the pain because I didn't have time, I couldn't let people see me cry or sad even though I did, but I was the second highest ranking guy on our base. I had soldiers looking up to me and as [I have been told] no matter what you're doing chaplain, soldiers are watching you, always remember that, soldiers... and I am aware of that and so I wanted to model that behavior.

Others relate the stigma to the culture of the military and fear of a negative impact on their career. Some chaplains relayed not wanting to speak with mental health providers within the military or VA due to fear of documentation perceived to potentially harm their career. They also cited barriers of speaking with Vet Center mental health care providers. Even though they knew that at Vet Centers their cases would not be documented, they often know the providers professionally, and were not comfortable being viewed as someone with a mental health problem. Several participants explained that they preferred to speak with other chaplains instead of mental health professionals in order to get a religious perspective on their suffering; however they noted non-MCs did not understand many of their issues. There was a pervasive concern in confiding problems in fellow MCs both of being judged as weak or less able to perform, as well as a lack of confidentiality. These fears were perceived to harm future job opportunities.

> P: I think chaplains are as afraid of admitting that they need to do that as any other Joe. I know one other chaplain, that until I told that individual that I was struggling and that I needed to go get help, and that I was going to get help. Until I did that, that chaplain had never told me, that they had, they themselves had sought out help but they had never acknowledged that to me in any way.
> F: So it's like everybody's secret?
> P: It seems like it. Everybody wants to keep it secret

Key among the fears of being perceived as weak and unable to perform the job is this leading to not being considered fit to be deployed. Participants explained that "nobody can promote unless they deploy. That's just a reality." In other words, doubt about one's ability to perform and be effective in one's role as a chaplain, translates into not be chosen to deploy, stalling one's career. As one participant put it:

> There's a lot of fear of affecting careers by seeking out mental health and I've ran across a little bit of that, a lot of that and then commanders who don't understand counseling and stuff and therapy. It's like the old boy thing, like the John Wayne thing, suck it up and move on. Then a lot of the military, they just don't trust the system.

Other Stigma

In addition to stigma related to recognizing and seeking treatment for mental health issues, there were several other stigmatizing behaviors participants contended with. Two of these related to the role of the MC and gender, both of which are intertwined with understandings of identity, of being a soldier.

As noncombatants, some chaplains describe feeling as though they were considered "less than a soldier," "a waste of time and space" by commanders who are "not chaplain friendly"; told "Okay, well yeah, we'll put up with you, but don't get in the way." Participants relayed situations of not being regarded or respected by their commanders because of not being the preferred denomination (or due to being any religion in some cases). Also noted were commanders not listening to issues the chaplains brought up, or in some cases, reprimanding them for the ways in which they tried to engage the soldiers.

> One [commander] I had didn't really see the need for a chaplain.... Everybody gets a hostile boss occasionally. So you, you deal with them. Dealing with that on top of the combat and then [this] on top of that, you know, it's a little bit much. Since the chaplains are noncombatants, he looked at the position as less than a soldier. There, there was no recognition of, okay gee; I have to learn all the religious requirements and all the military requirements. It didn't matter. You know, "You're noncombatant, you can't carry a weapon, so what do I need you for?" You know, "What are you going to do here?"

This discredited role was reinforced by not offering some MCs returning from deployment the same reintegration programs as other returning soldiers, or worse yet, expecting returning chaplains to lead the reintegration programs, as well as expecting chaplains to start back in their next assignments within as little as a week of returning home.

In addition to grappling with the stigmatizing behaviors toward the chaplain role, female MCs deal with issues related to being female in both the military and in the chaplaincy. As one female participant explained:

> As a woman in the military, obviously we're in the minority. As a woman in the ministry, you're a minority. As a woman in ministry in the military, you're such a small minority, it's ridiculous... such a small cross section and a lot of people just don't know what to do. So they might, have issues about women in the ministry, they might have issues about women in the military, they might have both.

Several of the female participants described being transferred out of units and losing spots for deployment—and thus promotion—because of commanders who feel that their chaplain has to be a man. They described being put down for being emotional and not in "military mindset," so trying to "watch my male counterparts and kind of change myself around to fit." They also spoke of contending with fellow soldiers of lower rank who openly disrespected them because they did not believe in women in ministry and/or military. Thus, already battling the perception of being an outsider and weak, asking for help was especially risky. As one female participant said of her confiding in another chaplain, "I am so afraid of them saying, 'She's weak. She can't handle it.'"

DISCUSSION

As with stigma related to mental illness in other health care providers such as physicians and medical students, our findings suggest that similar contextual influences may be salient with MCs in their mental health care seeking, including structural issues, military culture, and role expectation of self and by others. Both public stigma, the perception held by society that an individual is socially unacceptable, and self-stigma, the perception held by the individual that he or she is socially unacceptable, leading to a reduction in self-worth if a person seeks psychological help (Vogel et al., 2007) clearly seems to be at play in many cases in our study. Particularly as participants relate a "super-hero" or "lone ranger" self-concept with chaplains tending to think they are there to take care of everyone and should not need assistance; as one participant stated "I thought that as a chaplain that I would be okay, my mental health would be okay." This is further exemplified by the pervasive fear the chaplains expressed of being perceived as weak or inferior—either as a chaplain or an officer—and the subsequent negative impact this could have on their career.

While stigma does involve social interactions at the individual level, these interactions take place within broader social contexts in which organizations, institutions, and larger cultural structures shape and influence understandings of what is different and stigmatized (Wallace 2012). Therefore, newer models of stigma must be considered, which include the social processes that occur within the sociocultural environment, with effects seen within the individual, such as how various forms of power (social, economic, political) shape the distribution of stigma within a social environment (Link and Phelan 2001, 2006). In other words, we cannot overstate the agency of the individual seeking treatment, but rather must consider how stigma is embedded in the system in which the ARNG chaplains are operating. Similar to health care providers, our participants deal with stigma related to confidentiality and documentation in records, and with concerns that revealing their mental illness will compromise their chances for career opportunities. Participants mentioned incidents where confidence between chaplains had been broken in relation to discussion of a mental health issue, further setting a tone of mistrust in an environment already competitive for promotions and assignments. Like medical school, the medical profession and the military (Britt et al., 2008; Hoge et al., 2004; Schwenk et al., 2010), avoidance of appropriate help-seeking behavior has been found to start early, and is linked to perceived norms where a mental health problem is seen as a form of weakness with negative implications for successful career progression. Furthermore, as with mental health professionals, MCs—and perhaps particularly females—may fight stereotypes and negative perceptions about their roles being "less than a soldier" and a "waste of time and space." MCs we spoke with were not always given opportunities to participate in reintegration programs like others in their unit. Rather, they were expected to minister and lead reintegration programs directly upon return from deployment—in one case being asked to relocate to a new assignment one week after returning from a deployment in a combat zone. While they are already grappling with overcoming guilt and a "superhero" self-image, these policies convey the message that their emotional pain and stress count less than any other soldier's, or that they should "suck it up and move on" because it is more important to counsel others than to take time for self-care and awareness. For MCs who may already be struggling to feel that they have permission to admit they need help or show emotion, it is reinforced that they really do not need to seek help for their own issues.

Often we heard older, more experienced participants, not necessarily worried about career advancement; explain that it was only through their own experiences that they learned the importance of self-care, and that they now make it a priority to mentor younger chaplains to include strategies for self-care in their routines, whether stateside or during deployment.

> There I am a 45 year old chaplain.... I'm allowed to have emotions, I've had all the counseling classes, I'm a trained professional and yet I struggled coming home. What's happening with the 18 year old, the 20 year old, the 25 year old that doesn't have the life experience, that doesn't have the training that I have, that doesn't have the self-awareness that I have. How do they take everything from there and make sense of it and put it in a place that makes them better people? A lot of chaplains are honestly lone rangers, they're mavericks.

As previously discussed, stigma is embedded in moral experience; thus, stigmatized conditions may threaten what really matters for sufferers in their local world (Yang et al., 2007). For the participants, this included confidentiality, status, and sanctions; these are not mutually exclusive, as some overlap. Because chaplains knew so many of the other chaplains, BH personnel, and Vet Center personnel, there was a mistrust of documentation and perceived potential for backstabbing and judgment, with implications for subsequent jobs or status. This mistrust also extended to other MCs; participants explained that because of the competition over assignments and promotions, chaplains have been known to "eat their own" in order to move ahead. In fact even after interviews at conferences, many participants would come back for assurance that their interviews would be kept in strict confidence. Additionally, MCs spoke of their status as a chaplain and an officer, that they are being looked up to, and "should be able to handle things"—the "super-hero" image—which is threatened with revealing a "weakness" or "flaw'" such as mental illness or the need for help. Finally, wealth and life chances are perceived as being threatened via the fear of being seen as weak, incapable, or having potential career sanctions, illustrating how mental illness stigma is embedded in the system in which the chaplains operate, a concern brought up again and again by participants. This was particularly relevant for female chaplains, already dealing in military and ministry environments, which are predominantly male, with the compounded stress of having to prove themselves, which can potentially have a negative impact on help-seeking behavior for mental health issues (Finley 2011).

RECOMMENDATIONS

This paper describes stigma experienced by ARNG chaplains related to mental health and treatment seeking. While it is well documented that stigma related to mental illness

TABLE 2. Recommendations

Participant recommendations
- Develop self-care components in chaplaincy candidate school and include regular refresher courses.
- Develop a nonpunitive, supportive environment for help seeking—where status and wealth are not threatened.
  - One participant described how he has a commanding officer who is very open about choosing service members for missions who have sought mental health help over those who have not but he thinks should.
  - Other participants relayed how they talk to lower ranking, less experienced chaplains about their own experiences with seeking mental health in order to encourage them.
- Develop a peer mentorship program for more experienced with less experienced chaplains, including specialized programs for women.
- Strongly recommend (they were hesitant to say "mandate") time off during deployment and after deployment for self-care.
  - Minimum time off between assignments coming home from deployments, especially for full-time National Guard.

Recommendations: military chaplaincy training (Schwenk et al., 2010)
- Build on the characteristics of the military chaplaincy, emphasizing professional competence and outstanding performance to reinforce factors in the creation of a culture that promotes professional mental health.
- The effective care of mental illness, the maintenance of mental health and effective emotional function, and care of professional colleagues with mental illness should be taught as part of the ethical and professional responsibility of the outstanding chaplain and become a critical component of the teaching, role modeling, and professional guidance that chaplaincy candidates receive as part of their curriculum in professionalism.

Recommendations: military (Finley 2011)
- Reframe the military's cultural emphasis on toughness and stamina.
  - From an ethos of *grin and bear it* to one aimed at *maintaining optimal fitness.*
- Include positive self-care as part of the stated goal for every service member to support mission readiness and the well-being of the group.
- Antistigma efforts that include communicating an ideal of strength that emphasizes prompt care seeking as a way of remaining fit and ready to meet one's obligations to unit and family.
- Additional research and responsiveness in the needs of female service members, including identity issues, roles, and responsibilities postdeployment, types of social support during and after deployment, and inclusion of families.

and treatment occurs at higher rates in both health care providers and the military, this study contributes to the literature of how this stigma is compounded even further for military behavioral care providers, MCs. This study served to better understand how stigma operates among MCs, and thus where key leverage points may be for change. This is critical to develop effective antistigma intervention that target those stigma processes that threaten what really matters to those stigmatized, as compared to other antistigma interventions that seek to modify public opinions (Yang et al., 2007). Kleinman and Hall-Clifford (2009) have stated that it is critical to focus antistigma interventions on the lived world and to identify actual difficulties that the stigmatized face in order to understand how stigma threatens what is really at stake. This study confirms that stigma associated with psychological health has changed very little in over a decade despite massive education and screening campaigns in every branch of the military (Dingfelder 2009; Ursano et al., 2012) and that it is a salient issue with a little studied population, MCs. Furthermore, a culture has been found to exist in which "military healthcare providers are encouraged to deny their own physical, psychological and social needs to provide the necessary support to beneficiaries" (Gates et al., 2010:6). Findings from this study support this culture, so recommendations (Table 2) focus on structural and systematic changes as opposed to strictly individually focused interventions to support improved treatment seeking. Because the experiences of our participants mirrored those experienced by health care providers and service members, we have compiled, integrated, and built on existing recommendations aimed at transforming professional attitudes and institutional/system-wide policies as well as incorporated suggestions from the participants themselves to address the lived world and actual difficulties faced.

NOTE

Acknowledgments. The development of this manuscript was supported with material and operational support from the RR&D Center of Innovation on Disability and Rehabilitation Research (CINDRR) in Tampa, FL. In addition, this material is based upon work supported by the Department of Veterans Affairs, Veterans Health Administration, Office of Research and Development, and a grant from VHA Rehabilitation Research and Development Grant (RR&D D7800P). The contents of this manuscript do not represent the views of the Department of Veterans Affairs or the U.S. Government.

REFERENCES CITED

Abruzzese, Sarah
    2008 War's Stresses Take Toll on Military's Chaplains—NYTimes.com. http://www.nytimes.com/2008/05/29/washington/29chaplains.html, accessed October 18, 2011.
Army Chaplain Corps
    2009 Survey of Reserve Component Chaplains: Relationships with Civilian Religious Bodies.
U.S. Army
    2012 Army 2020: Generating Health and Discipline in the Force ahead of the Strategic Reset. Washington, DC: U.S. Army.
Auld, Alison
    2010 Can Military Chaplains Suffering Burnout, Compassion Fatigue at High Rates. Toronto: The Globe and Mail. http://www.theglobeandmail.com/news/national/chaplains-burning-out-military-says/article1570994./, accessed November 1, 2013.
Bagalman, Erin, and Angela Napili
    2014 Prevalence of Mental Illness in the United States: Data Sources and Estimates. Congressional Research Service. http://www.fas.org/sgp/crs/misc/R43047.pdf, accessed March 10, 2014.
Bassiri, Mojdeh, Zaza Lyons, and Sean Hood
    2011 Stigmatisation of Psychiatrists: Experiences of Psychiatrists and Psychiatric Registrars in Western Australia. Education Research and Perspectives 38(2):35–44.
Berman, Alan, John Bradley, Bonnie Carroll, Robert G. Certain, Jeffory C. Gabrelcik, Ronald Green, Marjan G. Holloway, David Jobes, Janet Kemp, David Litts, Richard McKeon, Peter Proietto, Philip Volpe, and Aaron Werbel
    2010 The Challenge and the Promise: Strengthening the Force, Preventing Suicide and Saving Lives. Final Report of the Department of Defense Task Force on the Prevention of Suicide by Members of

the Armed Forces. DTIC Document. http://oai.dtic.mil/oai/oai?verb=getRecord&metadataPrefix=html&identifier=ADA529502, accessed November 6, 2013.

Besterman-Dahan, Karen, Scott Barnett, Edward Hickling, Christine Elnitsky, Jason Lind, John Skvoretz, and Nicole Antinori
    2012 Bearing the Burden: Deployment Stress among Army National Guard Chaplains. Journal of Healthcare Chaplaincy 18(3–4):151–168.

Bonner, Laura M., Andy B. Lanto, Cory Bolkan, G. Stennis Watson, Duncan G. Campbell, Edmund F. Chaney, Kara Zivin, and Lisa V. Rubenstein
    2013 Help-Seeking from Clergy and Spiritual Counselors among Veterans with Depression and PTSD in Primary Care. Journal of Religion and Health 52(3):707–718.

Britt, Thomas W., Tiffany M. Greene-Shortridge, Sarah Brink, Quyen B. Nguyen, Jaclyn Rath, Anthony L. Cox, Charles W. Hoge, and Carl Andrew
    2008 Perceived Stigma and Barriers to Care for Psychological Treatment: Implications for Reactions to Stressors in Different Contexts. Journal of Social and Clinical Psychology 27(4):317–335.

Center, Claudia, Miriam Davis, Thomas Detre, Daniel E. Ford, Wendy Hansbrough, Herbert Hendin, John Laszlo, David Litts, John Mann, Peter A. Mansky, Robert Michels, Steven H. Miles, Roy Proujansky, Charles F. Reynolds III, and Morton M. Silverman
    2003 Confronting Depression and Suicide in Physicians. Journal of the American Medical Association 289(23):3161–3166.

Corrigan, Patrick
    2004 How Stigma Interferes with Mental Health Care. American Psychologist 59(7):614–625.

Corrigan, Patrick W., and Amy C. Watson
    2002 The Paradox of Self-Stigma and Mental Illness. Clinical Psychology: Science and Practice 9(1):35–53.

Dingfelder, Sadie F.
    2009 The Military's War on Stigma. Monitor on Psychology 40(6):52.

Elnitsky, Christine A., Paula L. Chapman, Ryan M. Thurman, Barbara L. Pitts, Charles Figley, and Brian Unwin
    2013 Gender Differences in Combat Medic Mental Health Services Utilization, Barriers, and Stigma. Military Medicine 178(7):775–784.

Finley, Erin P.
    2011 Fields of Combat: Understanding PTSD among Veterans of Iraq and Afghanistan. New York: Cornell University Press.

Gates, Robert, Togo West, Vern Clark, and Independent Review Board
    2010 Protecting the Force: Lessons Learned from Fort Hood. Department of Defense. http://www.defense.gov/pubs/pdfs/dod-protectingtheforce-web_security_hr_13jan10.pdf, accessed March 10, 2014.

Gibbons, Susanne, Edward Hickling, and Dorraine Watts
    2012 Combat Stressors and Post-Traumatic Stress in Deployed Military Healthcare Professionals: An Integrative Review. Journal of Advanced Nursing 68(1):3–21.

Goffman, Erving
    1963 Stigma: Notes on a Spoiled Identity. Englewood Cliffs, NJ: Prentice-Hall.

Gold, Katherine J., Ananda Sen, and Thomas L. Schwenk
    2012 Details on Suicide among US Physicians: Data from the National Violent Death Reporting System. General Hospital Psychiatry 35(1):45–49.

Gould, Matthew, Amy Adler, Mark Zamorski, Carl Castro, Natalie Hanily, Nicole Steele, Steve Kearney, and Neil Greenberg
    2010 Do Stigma and Other Perceived Barriers to Mental Health Care Differ across Armed Forces? Journal of the Royal Society of Medicine 103(4):148–156.

Grieger, Thomas A., Tonya T. Kolkow, James L. Spira, and Jennifer S. Morse
    2007 Post-Traumatic Stress Disorder and Depression in Health Care Providers Returning from Deployment to Iraq and Afghanistan. Military Medicine 172(5):451–455.

Gutmann, Matthew C., and Catharine Lutz

    2010 Breaking Ranks: Iraq Veterans Speak out against the War. Berkeley, CA: University of California Press.

Hayes, Martha J.

    2009 Compassion Fatigue in the Military Caregiver. DTIC Document. Carlisle Barracks, PA: Army War College. http://www.dtic.mil/docs/citations/ADA498593, accessed November 1, 2013.

Hoge, Charles W., Carl A. Castro, Stephen C. Messer, Dennis McGurk, Dave I. Cotting, and Robert L. Koffman

    2004 Combat Duty in Iraq and Afghanistan, Mental Health Problems, and Barriers to Care. New England Journal of Medicine 351(1):13–22.

Hooyer, Katinka

    2012 Going AWOL: Alternative Responses to PTSD Stigma in the US Military. Field Notes 4(1):106–128.

Iversen, Amy C., Lauren van Staden, Jamie H. Hughes, Neil Greenberg, Matthew Hotpf, Roberto J. Rona, Graham Thornicroft, Simon Wessely, and Nicola T. Fear

    2011 The Stigma of Mental Health Problems and Other Barriers to Care in the UK Armed Forces. BMC Health Services Research 11(1):31.

Kalra, Gurvinder

    2012 Talking about Stigma towards Mental Health Professionals with Psychiatry Trainees: A Movie Club Approach. Asian Journal of Psychiatry 5(3):266–268.

Kim, Paul, Thomas Britt, Robert P. Klocko, Lyndon A. Riviere, and Amy B. Adler

    2011 Stigma, Negative Attitudes About Treatment, and Utilization of Mental Health Care among Soldiers. Military Psychology 23(1):65–81.

Kim, Paul, Jeffrey Thomas, Joshua Wilk, Carl Castro, and Charles Hoge

    2010 Stigma, Barriers to Care, and Use of Mental Health Services among Active Duty and National Guard Soldiers after Combat. Psychiatric Services 61(6): 582–588.

Kleinman, Arthur, and Rachel Hall-Clifford

    2009 Stigma: A Social, Cultural and Moral Process. Journal of Epidemiology and Community Health 63(6):418–419.

Kleinman, Arthur, Wen-Zhi Wang, Shi-Chuo Li, Xue-Ming Cheng, Xiu-Ying Dai, Kun-Tun Li, and Joan Kleinmen

    1995 The Social Course of Epilepsy: Chronic Illness as Social Experience in Interior China. Social Science & Medicine 40(10):1319–1330.

Krippendorff, Klaus

    1980 Content Analysis. Thousand Oaks, CA: Sage Publications, Inc.

Link, Bruce G., and Jo C Phelan

    2006 Stigma and Its Public Health Implications. Lancet 367(9509):528–529.

———— 2001 Conceptualizing Stigma. Annual Review of Sociology 27:363–385.

Linnerooth, Peter J., Adam J. Mrdjenovich, and Bret A. Moore

    2011 Professional Burnout in Clinical Military Psychologists: Recommendations Before, During, and after Deployment. Professional Psychology: Research and Practice 42(1):87–93.

Mental Health Advisory Team-II

    2005 Behavioral Healthcare System Assessment. Operation Iraqi Freedom (OIF-II) Mental Health Advisory Team (MHAT-II). http://timemilitary.files.wordpress.com/2012/07/2-oif-ii_report-105.pdf, accessed March 10, 2014.

Nasrallah, Henry A.

    2011 Invisible Tattoos: The Stigmata of Psychiatry. Current Psychiatry 10(9):18–19.

Office of the Surgeon Multi-National Force-Iraq and Office of the Surgeon General

    2008 Mental Health Advisory Team V Operation Iraqi Freedom 06–08: Iraq Operation Enduring Freedom 8 (Afghanistan). Washington, DC: US Army Medical Command.

Office of the Surgeon, Multi-National Force, Iraq, Office of the Command Surgeon, Office of the Surgeon, and United States Army Medical Command

    2008 Mental Health Advisory Team (MHAT) V: Operation Iraqi Freedom 06–08: Iraq Operation Enduring Freedom 8: Afghanistan. http://armymedicine.mil/Documents/Redacted1-MHATV-OIF-4-FEB-2008Report.pdf, accessed November 1, 2013.

Persaud, Raj
  2000 Psychiatrists Suffer from Stigma Too. Psychiatric Bulletin 24(8):284–285.
Rosenthal, Julie M., and Susan Okie
  2005 White Coat, Mood Indigo—Depression in Medical School. New England Journal of Medicine 353(11):1085–1088.
Rowan, Anderson B., and Rick L. Campise
  2006 A Multisite Study of Air Force Outpatient Behavioral Health Treatment-Seeking Patterns and Career Impact. Military Medicine 171(11):1123–1127.
Sayce, Liz
  1998 Stigma, Discrimination and Social Exclusion: What's in a Word? Journal of Mental Health 7(4):331–343.
Schwenk, Thomas L., Lindsay Davis, and Leslie A. Wimsatt
  2010 Depression, Stigma, and Suicidal Ideation in Medical Students. Journal of the American Medical Association 304(11):1181–1190.
Schwenk, Thomas L., Daniel W. Gorenflo, and Loretta M. Leja
  2008 A Survey on the Impact of Being Depressed on the Professional Status and Mental Health Care of Physicians. Journal of Clinical Psychiatry 69(4):617–620.
Shrivastava, Amresh, Megan Johnston, and Yves Bureau
  2012 Stigma of Mental Illness-1: Clinical Reflections. Mens Sana Monographs 10(1):70–84.
Stewart, Della W.
  2009 Casualties of War: Compassion Fatigue and Health Care Providers. Medsurg Nursing 18(2):91–94.
Substance Abuse and Mental Health Services Administration
  2012 Rockville, MD: Results from the 2011 National Survey on Drug Use and Health: Summary of National Findings. NSDUH Series H-44, HHS Publication No. (SMA) 12–4713.
Thornicroft, Graham
  2008 Stigma and Discrimination Limit Access to Mental Health Care. Epidemiologia E Psichiatria Sociale 17(1):14–19.
Thornicroft, Graham, Diana Rose, Aliya Kassam, and Norman Sartorius
  2007 Stigma: Ignorance, Prejudice or Discrimination? British Journal of Psychiatry 190(3):192–193.
Tjia, Jennifer, Jane L. Givens, and Judy A. Shea
  2005 Factors Associated with Undertreatment of Medical Student Depression. Journal of American College Health 53(5):219–224.
Ursano, Robert J., Carol S. Fullerton, and Mark C. Brown
  2012 Stigma and Barriers to Care Caring for Those Exposed to War, Disaster and Terrorism. DTIC Document. http://oai.dtic.mil/oai/oai?verb=getRecord&metadataPrefix=html&identifier=ADA562004, accessed October 3, 2013.
Vogel, David L., Nathaniel G. Wade, and Ashley H. Hackler
  2007 Perceived Public Stigma and the Willingness to Seek Counseling: The Mediating Roles of Self-Stigma and Attitudes toward Counseling. Journal of Counseling Psychology 54(1):40–50.
Wallace, Jean E.
  2012 Mental Health and Stigma in the Medical Profession. Health 16(1):3–18.
Weber, Robert P.
  1990 Basic Content Analysis. New York: Sage Publications.
Yang, Lawrence Hsin, Arthur Kleinman, Bruce G. Link, Jo C. Phelan, Sing Le, and Byron Good
  2007 Culture and Stigma: Adding Moral Experience to Stigma Theory. Social Science & Medicine 64(7):1524–1535.

NEGOTIATING DOMAINS OF PATIENT DIGNITY IN VA SPINAL CORD INJURY UNITS: PERSPECTIVES FROM INTERDISCIPLINARY CARE TEAMS AND VETERANS

JASON D. LIND
HSR&D Center of Innovation on Disability and Rehabilitation Research (CINDRR), James A. Haley Veterans' Hospital, Tampa, FL

GAIL POWELL-COPE
HSR&D Center of Innovation on Disability and Rehabilitation Research (CINDRR), James A. Haley Veterans' Hospital, Tampa, FL

MARGEAUX A. CHAVEZ
HSR&D Center of Innovation on Disability and Rehabilitation Research (CINDRR), James A. Haley Veterans' Hospital, Tampa, FL

MARSHA FRASER
HSR&D Center of Innovation on Disability and Rehabilitation Research (CINDRR), James A. Haley Veterans' Hospital, Tampa, FL

JEFFREY HARROW
HSR&D Center of Innovation on Disability and Rehabilitation Research (CINDRR), James A. Haley Veterans' Hospital, Tampa, FL

Patient dignity is a significant concern among inpatient Veterans with spinal cord injuries (SCIs) because they may lack physical control over their bodies and thus rely on others for a variety of specialized needs, including mobility, personal care, wound care, bowel and bladder care, and rehabilitation, among others. This study examines the complexities of providing and negotiating dignified care in the context of interdisciplinary care teams in SCI, and the challenges Veterans with SCI face maintaining dignity in the context of limited independence. Based on a mixed methods approach that included in-depth interviews, observations, and pile sorting at six Veterans Health Administration (VA) SCI units, the goal of this study was to explore ways in which dignity was defined, negotiated, and conferred during patient and provider interactions. Study results have immediate value to VA leadership, VA providers, and Veterans by calling attention to the ways in which the concept of patient dignity can be integrated into clinical practice on SCI units. This study provides a methodological framework to capture complex interactions among interdisciplinary care teams and patients, and offers a significant contribution to our understanding of how patient and provider interactions are

ANNALS OF ANTHROPOLOGICAL PRACTICE 37.2, pp. 130–148. ISSN: 2153-957X. © 2014 by the American Anthropological Association. DOI:10.1111/napa.12027

conferred and negotiated. [patient dignity, spinal cord injury, Veterans, interdisciplinary care teams, pile sort]

INTRODUCTION

The Veterans Health Administration (VA) has the largest network of spinal cord injury (SCI) care in the nation, providing a variety of health care services to over 27,000 Veterans with SCI and related disabilities (Veterans Health Administration 2011). The spinal cord is the main pathway that transmits information between the brain and nerves that lead to muscles, skin, internal organs, and glands. Injury to the spinal cord therefore results in disruption of movement, sensation, and bodily function. The extent of disruption is dependent on location and severity of injury and manifests differently among each individual. In general, paraplegia results from injury to the lower part of the spinal cord, causing paralysis of the lower part of the body including the bowel and bladder. Tetraplegia (sometimes called quadriplegia) results from injury to the spinal cord in the neck area, causing paralysis to the lower body, upper body, and arms (Paralyzed Veterans of America 2001). The VA system of SCI care provides a coordinated lifelong continuum of services for Veterans of all ages. SCI services are delivered through a "hub and spoke" system of care that include 24 regional SCI centers offering primary, surgical, rehabilitation, long-term care, and specialty care from interdisciplinary primary care teams (Veterans Health Administration 2011).

Interdisciplinary care teams have become important to health care management in a number of fields where patients need constant, consistent care, including chronic illness and disability management (Dennis et al., 2008; Hemmelgarn et al., 2007; Kuzma et al., 2008; Wagner et al., 2001). Interdisciplinary care teams in VA SCI units include physicians; nurses; social workers; psychologists; and physical, occupational, and recreational therapists; as well as a variety of other specialists depending on patient needs (i.e., respiratory therapists, wound care specialists, surgeons, and urologists). As noted by Wagner (2000), the role of the interdisciplinary care team is to communicate regularly, and participate in the care of a defined group of patients.

Parallel with interdisciplinary care teams, the VA is implementing patient aligned care teams (PACTs) as an implementation of the patient-centered medical home; an effort to encourage greater patient involvement in their own care. The PACT model provides patient-centered care through collaboration and input from both patient and provider in a manner that promotes quality of life, communication, accountability, education, and respect (Bowen and Schectman 2010). Rubenstein et al. (2004) called on researchers in the VA to set research agendas that incorporate participatory methods, include Veterans' voices, and address intervention strategies that impact quality of care and patient-centered care.

As part of the VA's mission to implement a culture of patient-centered care, patient dignity is a significant concern among inpatient Veterans with SCI because they may lack physical control over their bodies and thus rely on others for a variety of specialized needs, including mobility, personal care, wound care, bowel and bladder care, and rehabilitation, among others. For example, some SCI patients rely on nursing staff to perform bowel and bladder care, grooming, showering, and feeding. Some persons with SCI may need assistance with mobility issues such as in-bed repositioning, and transfers between beds, chairs, and stretchers. The use of technology (i.e., ceiling-mounted lift systems) to assist with mobility can create the potential for unanticipated threats to the dignity of the individual. As a result, we undertook this study to examine the challenges and complexities that spinal cord injured Veterans and SCI staff face negotiating patient dignity.

The purpose of this study was to explore how patient dignity is defined and perceived by both patients and staff, and to identify factors (e.g., patient care handling tasks, equipment, environmental challenges, and SCI staff behavior) that potentially threaten patient dignity with the goal of suggesting ways in which patient dignity can be maintained in VA SCI units. Using an anthropological perspective, this chapter will explore ways in which dignity is defined, negotiated, and conferred at the intersection of patient and provider interaction. Based on this approach, results provide immediate value to VA leadership, VA providers, and Veterans by calling attention to the ways in which the concept of patient dignity is negotiated, and how the construct of maintaining dignity can be integrated into clinical practice on VA SCI units.

Understanding Patient Dignity in the Clinical Setting

Dignity is a complex concept with bioethical (Beckwith 2010), philosophical (Christakis 2007), and practical applications (Coenen et al., 2007; Jacobson 2009; Matiti and Trorey 2008; Woogara 2005). Most commonly, dignity is understood as a feeling of personal worth or a behavior that either commands or confers worth (Haddock 1996). When considered alongside patient care, "dignity is complex and multi-faceted, relating to feelings, control, presentation of self, privacy, and behavior from others" (Baillie 2009:23). Patient dignity is frequently explored within the context of palliative (end of life) and long-term care (Chochinov et al., 2002; Christakis 2007; Doorenbos et al., 2006; Jacobson 2009; Periyakoil et al., 2010). Fewer studies have examined this construct in primary and preventative care (Beach et al., 2005; Hofmann 2002). Although researchers have examined SCI patients' post-injury experiences (Carpenter 1994; Lohne et al., 2010), quality of life (Hammell 2004), and changing perceptions of the self (Chow 2007; Yoshida 1993), only one study has specifically explored their dignity (Lohne et al., 2010).

The construct of dignity is complex and multifaceted. Definitions of dignified care have been derived by synthesizing evidence from multiple actors, including patients, physicians, nurses, and physical therapists (Albers et al., 2011; Baillie 2009; Beach et al., 2005; Chochinov et al., 2002; Christakis 2007; Haddock 1996; Matiti and Trorey 2008; Walsh and Kowanko 2002). These studies make clear distinctions between having dignity (self-worth), giving dignity (ensuring patient autonomy and privacy), and being treated with dignity (respect for persons). Matiti (2002) proposed 11 categories that together maintained patient dignity. For the purpose of this project, we employ a dual definition of dignity that includes "*the dignified self*" and "*dignity of the other*" (Haddock 1996; Jacobson 2007; Nordenfelt and Edgar 2005). The dignified self refers to feelings of self-worth, identity, and a sense of control and autonomy (Haddock 1996; Matiti and Sharman 1999). Dignity of the other is experienced through social interaction; concerning the conveyance of worth onto others in a specific time and place (Jacobson 2007). In this sense, dignity can be "lost or gained, threatened, violated or promoted" (Jacobson 2007:295). We also employ Baillie's (2009) model of how patient dignity is affected by the hospital environment, staff behavior, and patient factors.

Numerous studies have shown that involving patients in decisions (disease self-management) has been associated with improved health outcomes (Greenfield et al., 1985, 1988; Lorig et al., 1999, 2001). Patient–provider communication has also been shown to improve health outcomes. A review of 21 studies of patient–provider communication by Stewart (1995) found a correlation between effective physician–patient communication and improved patient health outcomes. Beach et al. (2005) looked at the relationship between treating patients with dignity and patient reported satisfaction with care. The study concluded the association between treatment with dignity and patients' perceived receipt of quality preventive care was stronger than the association between being involved in decisions and receiving optimal preventive care.

Because the construct of patient dignity is complex, and can vary from one patient population and clinical setting to another, innovative theoretical and methodological frameworks are needed in order to conceptualize and apply concepts of dignity to this clinical context. We used Kleinman's theory of using explanatory models (EMs) to understand and reconcile the different perceptions and needs related to patient dignity between Veterans and SCI staff. In addition, we developed methods from cognitive anthropology because they are able to capture nuanced differences in cultural knowledge among members of different populations. This integrated approach is valuable because it encapsulates the complex variation of knowledge and behavior related to ways in which patient dignity is defined and negotiated, and because findings can be readily applied in the clinical setting.

EMs: Interpreting Illness Experience

Kleinman (1977) argued that applying social science frameworks and methodologies to clinical setting helps improve patient and provider relations and supports more effective treatment practices. Drawing specifically from theories in medical anthropology and his experience as a psychiatrist and an anthropologist, Kleinman developed the EMs approach to reconcile biomedical knowledge about disease and patient understandings of illness within a "clinical reality." Moreover, he posited that EMs and "clinical social science" can help patients and providers negotiate care within the context of the clinical setting (Kleinman et al., 2006). Kleinman goes on to note the relationship between clinically applied anthropology and the EM of illness:

> Each illness episode and each clinical encounter presents the anthropologist who works in medical settings with an occasion to interpret how illness and clinical reality are organized in particular local cultural systems of meanings, norms, and power. We can disclose the significance of illness in a family constellation, demonstrating what the experience of being sick means to the sick person and how that meaning is negotiated . . . [Kleinman 1985: 69]

For the purposes of this study, we used Kleinman's EMs framework for understanding dignity and dignified care within the context of the patient and provider experience at VA SCI units. The strength of this approach is that it can be incorporated immediately in the clinical setting to elicit patient understandings and perceptions of dignified care, identify discrepancies between patient and provider approaches, and help illuminate ways in which patient dignity can be negotiated (Kleinman et al., 2006).

Cognitive anthropology provides a social science framework for understanding patient and provider perceptions of dignified care. It is a way to understand how humans organize the material objects, events, and experiences that make up their world. This approach attempts to understand cognitive categories (or cultural domains) as participants see them, not as we researchers see them (D'Andrade 1995). In this study, ethnography and cultural domain analysis were used to systematically understand how SCI patients and staff perceive and categorize relationships of patient dignity by examining how they subjectively rank items based on their potential to threaten patient dignity, and how they perceive and experience these relationships. This was done using pile sort methodologies that have been employed in a variety of ethnographic research (Copeland 2011; Kennedy et al., 2011; Maiolo et al., 1994; Nyamongo 2002; Roos 1998; Wong 1991) and recently have been recognized for their potential in clinical and rehabilitation settings (Jahrami 2012; Periyakoil et al., 2010).

METHODS

This study employed a mixed-methods approach, including ethnography and cultural domain analysis, within a multiple case study design. A total of 102 participants, including Veteran SCI inpatients ($n = 48$) and SCI staff ($n = 54$), participated in the study. All data were collected at six regional VA SCI centers that provide comprehensive SCI services. The SCI centers represented geographic diversity throughout the United States. The study was approved by local institutional review boards and VA research and development committees, and all participants provided informed consent to participate in the study.

Freelisting is an emic technique used to obtain items in a cultural domain from a group or population (Borgatti 1999). Freelisting was done at the initial SCI center in order to develop cultural domain items for subsequent pile sorting. During interviews, Veterans and staff were asked to make a list of all the patient care tasks, equipment, people, and places they encounter on an average day in the SCI unit. Preliminary freelisting data were collected at the initial SCI center with Veterans ($n = 9$) and SCI staff ($n = 11$).

Pile sorting is a common method used to elicit judgments of similarity among items in a cultural domain (Bernard 1996; Bernard and Ryan 2010; Borgatti 1999). Pile sorts were conducted at the remaining five SCI centers with Veterans ($n = 35$) and SCI staff ($n = 42$). Each participant was given a set of 68 cards and asked to "sort each of the 68 items based on whether it has a high, medium, low or no potential to threaten patient dignity." In most occasions, participants were asked to discuss their reasoning for placing each item in the "high, medium, low or no" categories; these conversations were audio-recorded as part of the face-to-face interviews.

TABLE 1. Research Participants by Research Site

SCI Site	Veteran Participants	Staff Participants	Veteran Interviews	Staff Interviews	Completed Pile Sorts	Completed Freelists
Site no. 1	9	12	9	12	N/A	20
Site no. 2	8	8	8	8	16	N/A
Site no. 3	9	8	9	8	16	N/A
Site no. 4	9	9	9	9	17	N/A
Site no. 5	7	8	7	8	14	N/A
Site no. 6	6	9	6	9	14	N/A
Total	48	54	48	54	77	20

Multidimensional scaling (MDS) was then used to analyze participants' pile sorts. MDS is a statistical method that uses matrix algebra to map cultural domain items to points in two-dimensional space, such that items corresponding to more similar items are placed nearer to each other in the space. Cluster analysis can then be used to group items in the space (Borgatti 1999).

In-depth, face-to-face interviews and demographic surveys were conducted with Veterans ($n = 48$) and SCI staff ($n = 54$). Veterans and staff were asked to talk about their experiences with SCI; to discuss their definitions and personal experiences relating to patient dignity; to talk about what kinds of things can potentially threaten patient dignity; and ways in which patient dignity can be maintained and promoted. Interviews lasted between 20 and 90 minutes. Table 1 show participants by research site and includes the number of participants that completed interviews, freelisting, and pile sorting activities.

Data Analysis

Demographic survey data were organized and analyzed for simple frequencies using SPSS version 21 (SPSS IBM, New York). ATLAS.ti version 7.1 (ATLAS.ti Scientific Software Development, GmbH) was used to analyze face-to-face interviews with Veterans and SCI staff. Constant comparative techniques were used identify themes and domains of patient dignity. Cultural domain analysis, including freelisting, pile sorts, MDS, and hierarchical cluster analysis, was conducted using Visual Anthropac version 1.0 (Analytic Technologies, Lexington, KY).

RESULTS

Results are presented separately by methodological approach. Demographic data revealed that among the 48 Veteran participants, 46 (95.8 percent) were male, 2 (4.6 percent) were female; with a mean age of 60 years (range: 26–87 years). Among Veteran participants, 34 (70 percent) self-identified as white, while 12 (25 percent) self-identified as black, and 2 (4.6 percent) as of Hispanic origin. The mean time since SCI was 14.9 years (range: 5 months to 53 years). At the time of study participation, Veteran participants had been SCI inpatient for a mean of 10.2 months (range: one week to nine years).

TABLE 2. Freelists: Domains and Items of Patient Dignity

People in the SCI Unit	Equipment Used in the SCI Unit	Patient Care Handling Tasks	Places in the SCI Unit
· Physician	· Manual wheelchair	· Bowel care	· Private patient room
· Nurse	· Electric wheelchair	· Dressing	· Bathroom
· Physical therapist	· Ceiling lift	· Bathing	· VA canteen
· Occupational therapist	· Environmental control unit	· Occupational therapy	· Recreational therapy area
· Psychologist	· Slings	· Showering	· Shared patient room
· PVA advocate	· Commode	· Medicating	· Hallways
· Kinesiotherapist	· Specialty bed	· Physical therapy	· VA café (for Vets)
· Family	· Shower chair	· Turning	· Rehabilitation gym
· Volunteers	· Personal computer	· Feeding	· Dining room
· Recreational therapist	· Other lifts	· Wound care	· Patio
· Respiratory therapist	· Assistive technology device	· Transfer to appointment	· Hospital clinics/hospital laboratories
· Chaplain	· Call light	· Grooming	
· Housekeeping	· Ventilator	· Respiratory therapy	
· Food service staff	· Colostomy bag	· Recreational therapy	
· Dietitian	· Catheter	· Skin care	
· Social worker	· Privacy screen	· Bladder care	
· Friends	· Gown	· Transfer to bed	
· Other patients	· TV	· Transfer to shower	
	· Personal phone	· Transfer to chair	
		· Transfer to bathroom	

Among the 54 SCI staff, 28 (51.9 percent) were nurses, 11 (20.4 percent) were physical or occupational therapists, 6 (11 percent) were physicians, 4 (7.4 percent) were nurse managers, 3 (5.6 percent) psychologists, and 2 (3.7 percent) were social workers. Also, 38 (70.4 percent) were female, while 16 (29.6 percent) were male. The average age of SCI staff members was 47 years of age (range: 26–63 years). Additionally, 23 (42.5 percent) SCI staff members self-identified as white, 17 (31.4 percent) self-identified as black, 6 (11.1 percent) self-identified as of Hispanic origin, 4 (7.5 percent) self-identified as Asian, and 4 (7.5 percent) self-identified as "other." In terms of experience working on SCI units, 22 (40.8 percent) reported having 1–5 years of experience, 16 (29.6 percent) having 6–15 years; and 16 (29.6 percent) with 16–21 years or more of experience working on SCI units.

Freelisting

Analysis of the 20 freelists produced 397 unique items, of which 241 (60 percent) were mentioned by just one person. Items that were mentioned by at least 30 percent of participants (N = 68) were chosen for use in the pile sort activity; these items represented four domains of dignity. The list of items is presented in Table 2.

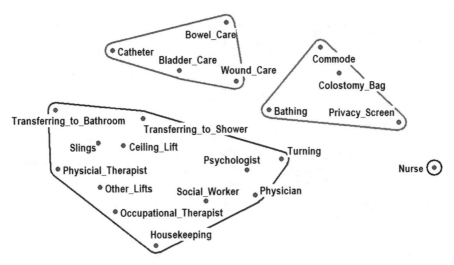

FIGURE 1. Pile sort: Veteran perceived threats to patient dignity.

Pile Sort Results

MDS analysis was used to map the sorted items in two-dimensional space in order to visualize the model. Figure 1 shows an MDS map of Veteran pile sort data that represent perceived threats to patient dignity. To simplify the model, 21 key items, representing patient care tasks, staff, and equipment are represented in the model.

MDS analysis produces a stress factor: the closer the stress is to zero, the more likely the items are not randomly organized; in other words, the higher the likelihood the map represents the actual data. The MDS map in Figure 1 had a stress factor of 0.191, indicating a less than a one-percent chance that the items are not random, or without structure (Sturrock and Rocha 2000). As we move from top to bottom in Figure 1, Veterans categorized items as having a "high" to "medium" potential to threaten dignity on the top; and having a "low" or "no" potential to threaten dignity on the bottom. In the middle of the map, as we move from left to right, the perceived threat to dignity becomes more ambiguous, indicating that Veterans tend to categorize these items randomly (equally having a "high, medium, low, or no" potential to threaten to dignity). Hierarchical cluster analysis (indicated as circled groups in the MDS map) shows how Veterans group the items as being in a similar category related to potential threats to dignity.

In the MDS model in Figure 1, Veterans categorize intimate patient care tasks (e.g., bowel care, bladder care, wound care) and some equipment (catheter) as having the greatest potential to threaten dignity. During interviews, Veterans expressed that these items pose a potential risk to their wellbeing, sense of control, and privacy. Bowel and bladder care were almost always cited as being particularly undignified due to the intimate nature of these tasks.

Other patient care tasks (e.g., transfers, turning, and bathing), along with some equipment (e.g., ceiling lifts, slings, colostomy bag, and commode), were categorized together as having a "medium" to "low" potential to threaten dignity. Interview data

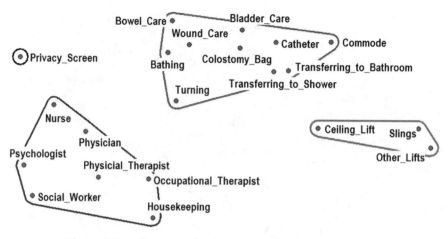

FIGURE 2. Pile sort: SCI staff perceived threats to patient dignity.

suggested that Veterans perceived bathing as a necessity in order to stay clean (something that can promote their sense of dignity) and turning as a necessity to preventing pressure ulcers (bed sores). In general, lift systems, including ceiling lifts and slings, were perceived as having a "low" potential threaten dignity because they are seen as inanimate objects. While some Veterans noted that using slings and lifts could be "uncomfortable," they rarely perceived them to be a threat to dignity. Patient transfers (e.g., transferring to the shower) were generally perceived as posing a slightly higher threat because they involve staff interaction, risk of exposure, and safety concerns. Interview data suggest that Veterans perceive transferring as a necessity for their mobility, noting that transferring in of itself is not a threat to dignity. However, transferring could threaten dignity if staff transferred a patient in an unsafe way, or in a way that they were exposed.

Veterans categorized staff (i.e., psychologist, physician, physical and occupational therapist, social worker, and housekeeping) as having a "low" or "no" potential to threaten patient dignity. Veterans explained that in general, SCI staff do their best to preserve their dignity. While many Veterans had examples of occurrences when they felt staff did something to threaten their dignity, this was usually the exception rather than the norm. The item "nurse" fell into its own group, suggesting an ambiguity; as many Veterans categorized "nurse" as having a high potential to threaten dignity, compared to those who categorized "nurse" as posing "no" threat to dignity. Interview data suggest that Veterans tend to categorize nurses as having the highest potential to threaten patient dignity because they perform intimate tasks like bowel care. On the other hand, Veterans explain that nurses also have the greatest potential to promote patient dignity in the way they protect privacy, autonomy, personhood, and independence while performing these tasks.

Figure 2 shows an MDS map of the SCI staff pile sort data that represent perceived threats to patient dignity. Again, 21 key items, representing patient care tasks, staff, and equipment are represented in the model. The MDS map in Figure 2 had a stress factor of .141, indicating a less than a one-percent chance that the items are not random, or without structure.

As we move from top to bottom in Figure 2, SCI staff categorized more items relating to patient care tasks (i.e., bowel care, bladder care, wound care, and bathing) and equipment (i.e., colostomy bag, catheter, and commode) as potentially posing the highest threat to patient dignity compared to Veterans. Interview data indicate that staff perceives most patient care tasks as potentially threatening to dignity, especially if the task is carried out incorrectly, or poses a safety concern.

Unlike Veterans, SCI staff categorized their fellow staff members (e.g., nurse, physician) as having a "medium" potential to threaten dignity. Interview data indicate that when SCI staff reflect on their own potential to threaten patient dignity, they identified nurses and physicians as potentially posing the greatest threat, because they are perceived as being responsible for direct patient care and medical decisions. Other staff members with moderate patient contact (e.g., psychologist, physical and occupational therapist) are categorized as having a "low" to "medium" threat, while other staff members with minimal contact (social worker and housekeeping) were perceived to pose a "low" or "no" threat to dignity.

In contrast to Veterans, SCI staff perceived safe patient handling equipment (e.g., slings, ceiling lifts, and other lifts) as posing a "medium" threat to dignity. Interview data suggest that staff tend to view safe patient handling equipment and patient care tasks like transfers as an integrated system that can potentially expose or make patients feel uncomfortable or unsafe.

Face-to-Face Interviews

Defining patient dignity

Based on qualitative analysis of transcript data, definitions of dignity between Veterans and SCI staff were similar. Veterans viewed dignity as a function of both how they were treated by staff, and how they felt about themselves. The concept of self-respect and respect for others was prevalent. Veterans often invoked the "golden rule," noting that in order to be respected, one had to show respect to others. Veterans expressed that the way they were addressed (using terms such as Mr. and Sir), the tone of voice, and staff attitude were important in their ability to maintain self-dignity. SCI staff members shared similar views of the importance of showing respect to patients, which included empathizing with patient and addressing them in a respectful manner. The following quotes express these sentiments:

> Respect, I consider it a mutual or reciprocal thing. I try to be respectful of the nursing staff . . . and I expect the same from them. (Veteran)

> For me, dignity is when a person has a very good view of you, the way I carry myself and how other people treat me, if they treat me with respect, I'm a pleasure to be around. I think dignity has a lot to do with that. (Veteran)

Treating them with respect, how you would want to be treated if you were a patient in the hospital. (SCI Staff)

For me, dignity means just show me respect, you know, as a human being and as a person and just, you know, don't treat me as some kind of outsider just because I'm paralyzed. (Veteran)

It's more like honor or respect whether they want to be called sir, ma'am or by their first or last name. (SCI Staff)

Veterans and staff related the concepts of autonomy, self-advocacy, self-reliance, and pride as being strongly associated with dignity. For Veterans, being able to do things on their own (grooming, transfers, bowel care, etc.) without having to rely on staff increased their sense of dignity. Staff echoed these sentiments and added the importance of listening to patients' desires and giving patients choices of how to carry out tasks. SCI staff would often champion concepts of patient self-care management by explaining tasks to patients prior to performing them and providing patients the opportunity to voice their preferences of how tasks are carried out. Providing Veterans with the space to perform tasks on their own was important in maintaining a sense of personal pride and self-reliance. The following quotes express these ideas:

It means doing as much as I can for myself and be as strong as I can for myself and not to just fall in self-pity. (Veteran)

I know what type of care I need and I know how to explain what I need done. Some nurses or CNAs don't like for the patient to dictate what their needs are, but I was always told you should be able to explain what you need. (Veteran)

Give patients choices about how to take care of them, you know. That makes a big difference. They like to give feedback for their own care. And that adds to their feeling of okay, I am in a little bit more control than I could have been. And that makes a difference. (SCI staff)

Making sure you ask the Veteran, but also treating him as a human being. I have patients who have spinal injuries and we should treat them as if they were ourselves. Explain to them what we are doing. Don't just go in there and just start doing stuff and not saying anything to them. All of our patients need to know that we are listening to them and taking care of their needs. (SCI staff)

Yeah, it's degrading when you can't put your own clothes on. It hurts your pride, you know, because you can't. You have to lay there and have to have someone lay me out and then I didn't like it at all that someone had to come in there and physically put my clothes on me every morning. You know, I didn't like that at all. (Veteran)

Another important aspect of dignity for Veterans was privacy of space. Veterans appreciated when staff closed doors to the bathroom, used a privacy screen around the bed, and knocked on the door before entering the room. Staff recognized these activities as important ways to preserve patients' dignity. Staff also emphasized the importance of maintaining confidentiality of protected health information (PHI) in preserving patient dignity. Staff were particularly aware of PHI in situations where patients shared a room.

> Well, make sure when you're lying there naked that somebody pulls the curtain so that everybody walking by doesn't look in. You got visitors and family members walking around, you know. If you go to the shower make sure you're properly covered, things like that. (Veteran)

> Their privacy . . . When they are being dressed or when they're being taken care of they like their privacy around them especially if they share a room with someone. (SCI staff)

> Every person wants their own private space. We have a thing called bowel care and things like that; you don't want a person looking at you while you're having that procedure done on you. (Veteran)

> Sometimes, there are two people in the same room. If you want to do anything or talk to the patient about something medically related, we would like the patient to be alone. We make sure the patient is not with somebody else at the same time. For example, if they have a psychiatric problem and need medication, we don't want to discuss this when somebody else is in the room. (SCI staff)

Threats to Patient Dignity

Veterans and SCI staff identified actions, attitudes, and behaviors that compromise communication, respect, self-worth, self-advocacy, and privacy as the greatest threats to dignity. This quote exemplifies the importance of communication and self-advocacy between patient and SCI staff.

> Sometimes they give you medication. What's this for? An ulcer? I don't have an ulcer. I said, who's the doctor that ordered this? So the doctor comes in the next day and I said, doc, what's the deal on this ulcer pill? I don't have an ulcer. Then the doc says it's a preventive because if you're lying, it helps prevent having an ulcer and heartburn. I says, doc, I thought we had the understanding, don't do anything to me, and don't give me a pill or anything unless we discuss it first. (Veteran)

Much of the discussion around "threats to patient dignity" centered on interactions between patients and staff that played out during patient care tasks, patient care management, and unit organizational functions.

In terms of patient and staff interaction, Veterans noted that SCI staff members can both threaten and promote patient dignity. Veterans identified nurses as having the highest potential to threaten patient dignity because they spend the most time with patients and perform intimate tasks that can pose a risk to a patient's dignity. On the other hand, Veterans identified nurses as having the greatest potential to promote patient dignity, in the way they carry out patient care handling tasks, and the way they protect privacy, autonomy, personhood, and independence while they perform these tasks.

Both Veterans and staff recognized that the manner in which patient handling and mobility tasks were done can threaten or promote patient dignity. Dialogue (i.e., asking questions, listening, and two-way communication) was a critical to the way Veterans perceived whether their dignity was maintained during patient care handling tasks. The following quote exemplifies this notion:

> I don't like to be talked down to. I will not be talked down to. I've been in too many arguments with too many doctors and nurses, especially when I'm right and they're wrong. They think the patient doesn't have any idea what they're talking about and I wind up being right and they wind up being wrong, you know, I don't like to be treated like I'm dumb. (Veteran)

Organizational factors, including scheduling when certain patient care tasks are performed, were critical to Veterans' sense of dignity. Leaving patients waiting for care, or performing tasks outside the normal routine (due to staff shortages) were often perceived as threatening dignity. Therefore, consistency in scheduling care tasks and maintaining continuity of care during shift change were viewed as critical for maintaining dignity.

> Staff could certainly threaten somebody's dignity. I think when we get into our routine for the day making sure that we, maybe it's very comfortable for us to be dealing with the bowel program, but a patient who is lying in stool, it may be very uncomfortable. So I think making sure that that area is approached correctly. (SCI staff)

Negotiating Patient Dignity

We asked Veterans and SCI staff about their perceptions and experiences about what kinds of things they do to ensure that patient dignity is upheld. Both Veterans and SCI staff recognized that the manner in which patient handling and mobility tasks were done can threaten or promote patient dignity. Qualitative analysis revealed that Veterans and SCI staff often negotiate patient care as a way to promote dignity. The act of negotiating patient care was interrelated with and most often revolved around patient care tasks, equipment use, and unit organization. Successful negotiating between Veterans and SCI staff consisted of several elements: (1) clear and open, two-way communication; (2) shared decision making; (3) allowing for expressions of autonomy or personal preference; and (4) explanation of patient care tasks. In negotiating dignified care, a dialogue occurs between patient and staff: patients express questions, needs, and preferences regarding how care tasks are performed; staff acknowledges the patient through listening, questioning, and taking into account patient care and safety protocols.

As discussed earlier, patient dignity often hinges on the way patient care tasks are performed. Some patient care tasks like bowel care, bladder care, and bathing are very intimate and pose the greatest threat to dignity. For these tasks, negotiation between patient and staff is critical in providing dignified care. The following quotes characterize these sentiments:

> They keep me with a female nurse, but one night I was scheduled for a bath and they were shorthanded and they asked me if I wanted a male and I said no, and it was a young kid, you know, and I said no. I prefer a female, and that was the only time they asked and right away they switched with a female nurse and that was fine. (Female Veteran)

I would rather have you listen to me and ask you questions and you ask me questions. We come down to a reasonable solution for the problem, and we act on it and then, it's good for the both of us. (Veteran)

With bowel care you always ask them, "How do you like it?" For their bowel care they will tell you how long it will take and what to do, and usually in 35–40 minutes you come back and check up on them. (SCI staff)

Negotiating patient care also includes preferences about what kind of equipment is suitable for a particular task. Although Veterans did not classify equipment as posing a high threat to their dignity, most felt that being able to negotiate which piece of equipment they prefer gave them a sense of control and autonomy.

As a nurse, you may have your own way of putting a patient in bed. But really I think most of us try to do it the patient's way. You can't use a sling on a patient who says no, I don't like this. So you have to find another sling they are willing to use … find their way of doing it. (SCI staff)

One time I did [bladder care] my way and that way didn't work because this guy had his own type of catheter and it came off, so I had to put him back in bed and redo it all over. If I had done it his way in the beginning I would have been okay. But I made double work for myself. From then on it was no more. (SCI staff)

They tried to put me in a prone shower chair instead of the regular shower chair I was used to. This thing has a screen and they put it over you and strap you to it. It was going right across my back and across the wound. Finally, I just told them, "You're gonna have to get six of the biggest guys you got in here because I'm gonna fight you tooth and nail. I'm not going in that thing ever again." Then they brought in the [regular] shower chair. (Veteran)

Negotiating patient care also includes issues of patient and staff interaction relating to unit organization (i.e., staffing changes, shift changes, and patient care scheduling). Interview data revealed that a principal complaint among Veterans in terms of dignity is the lack of consistency in the way patient care handling tasks are carried out by staff. These inconsistencies need to be negotiated and communicated to patients in order to promote dignity.

Because if you and the patient communicate you can more prioritize your assignments. You know, Mr. Smith wants to get up at 10 o'clock and the other one wants to get up an hour later, then you get the one up first so you don't have a problem. Kind of let them decide on some things you know makes your day go better. And then if you come back, come back at that time and they won't get upset. So it is really important to keep your word with them. (SCI staff)

It seemed like the first shift gets me up and if I go over to the second shift, the second shift don't think, they don't have time to put me in bed, so they say, well you've got to go to bed now at this time, which is a half hour before my time is up which is not benefitting me. I'm trying to stay in the wheelchair as long as I can.

Previous studies that were designed to understand the factors that impact patient dignity in a clinical care setting have highlighted several of the same themes that emerged in our study. Not surprisingly, several studies found that staff play a significant role in how dignity is perceived and conferred in clinical settings (Baillie 2009; Baillie and Gallagher 2012; Brown et al., 2011; Gallagher and Seedhouse 2002; Haddock 1996; Matiti and Trorey 2008). Patient dignity studies commonly focus on nurses because they are they are most involved in daily, intimate patient care tasks (Bailie 2009; Brown et al., 2011; Coenen et al., 2007; Doorenbos et al., 2006). Two studies highlighted the important role that communication between staff and patients can play in promoting patient dignity (Matiti 2002; Matiti and Sharman 1999), such findings are also supported in our study. Similar to Bailie (2009) and Matiti and Trorey (2008), results from our study suggest that patient dignity is strongly promoted through the maintenance of patient privacy and confidentiality. Our results are also similar to several studies that found patients often associate independence and a sense of autonomy with maintaining personal dignity in the clinical palliative care setting (Albers et al., 2011; Chochinov 2002, 2004, 2007; Chochinov et al., 2002; Matiti 2002).

The research methods used to collect domains of patient dignity in VA SCI centers are novel in their approach compared to similar studies of dignity. This study provides a methodological framework that is able to capture complex interactions between inter-disciplinary care teams and patients. It shows that cognitive anthropological methods, notably freelisting and pile sorting techniques that focus on cultural knowledge, are uniquely positioned to understand the complex variation of perceptions and experiences related to ways in which patient dignity is defined and negotiated. While we had initial concerns conducting pile sorting activities with limited mobility patients in a clinical setting, we found that the vast majority of SCI patients were receptive to the method and that it sparked interest in the study and introduced topics of conversations that we would have otherwise been overlooked. Our study suggests that this methodological approach can be integrated into similar clinical and rehabilitation settings.

Until now, the SCI population has received only scant attention in the patient dig-nity literature (Hammell 2004; Lohne et al., 2010). As cited earlier, other clinically based studies of patient dignity have focused on hospital inpatients or patients expe-riencing end-of-life care. This study brings the discussion of dignity to the context of SCI.

In addition, this study offers a significant contribution to our understanding of how patient care is negotiated among interdisciplinary care teams and patients. Results show that, at least in VA SCI units, interdisciplinary care teams demonstrate flexibility in their ability to better address patient needs. These insights coincided with the VA's transition from physician-centered care to adopting a culture of patient-centered care, focusing on placing the patient in a position to participate actively in decisions about their own medical care.

Results of this study can provide immediate value to VA SCI clinics, especially front line staff, by calling attention to the ways in which the concept of patient dignity can be integrated into clinical practice on SCI units. Our findings suggest that SCI staff is cognizant and knowledgeable about threats to patient dignity and how to ameliorate them. However, findings also indicate that in practice, patient dignity is sometimes compromised, and best practices for negotiating care are not always implemented. The challenge is to put dignity promotion into practice with a focus on negotiation, organization, and communication.

This research used Kleinman et al.'s (2006) EMs as a theoretical framework to understanding divergent perceptions of patient dignity. However, the EM can be easily adapted in the clinical setting to collect both patient and staff EMs related to the principal domains of patient dignity: respect for persons, patient autonomy, patient care tasks, equipment use, and SCI unit organization. Equipped with this information, members of interdisciplinary care teams can better understand the perceptions and experiences the patient holds about domains related to dignity. Comparing the patient EM of dignity with the EM of the interdisciplinary care, team can help clinicians identify major discrepancies that may cause problems or issues in protecting patient dignity. Such comparisons help clinicians know which aspects of this EM need clearer explanation and communication with patients. Kleinman et al. (2006:147) explain that "part of the clinical process involves negotiations between these EMs, once they have been made explicit."

On SCI units, EMs of patient dignity can be obtained during patient team meetings or at the bedside through a set of targeted questions and dialogue that identifies areas of conflict that need to be negotiated. Understanding patients' EMs of dignity will enable clinicians to consistently provide dignified care.

NOTE

Acknowledgements. This study was funded in part from VA Central Office with material and operational support from the HSR&D Center of Innovation on Disability and Rehabilitation Research (CINDRR) in Tampa, Florida. In addition, this material is based upon work supported by the Department of Veterans Affairs, Veterans Health Administration, Office of Research and Development. The views expressed in this article are those of the author and do not necessarily reflect the position or policy of the Department of Veterans Affairs or the United States Government.

REFERENCES CITED

Albers, Gwenda, H., Roeline W. Pasman, Mette L. Rurup, Henrica C. W. de Vet, and Bregje D. Onwuteaka-Philipsen
   2011   Analysis of the Construct of Dignity and Content Validity of the Patient Dignity Inventory. Health & Quality of Life Outcomes 9(1):45–53.
Baillie, Lesley
   2009   Patient Dignity in an Acute Hospital Setting: A Case Study. International Journal of Nursing Studies 46(1):23–37.
Baillie, Lesley, and Ann Gallagher
   2012   Raising Awareness of Patient Dignity. Nursing Standard 27(5):44–49.

Beach, Mary Catherine, Jeremy Sugarman, Rachel L. Johnson, Jose J. Arbelaez, Patrick S. Duggan, and Lisa A. Cooper
  2005 Do Patients Treated with Dignity Report Higher Satisfaction, Adherence, and Receipt of Preventive Care? The Annals of Family Medicine 3(4):331–338.
Beckwith, Francis J.
  2010 Dignity Never Been Photographed: Scientific Materialism, Enlightenment Liberalism, and Steven Pinker. Ethics & Medicine 26(2):93–110.
Bernard, Harvey Russell, and Gery W. Ryan
  2010 Analyzing Qualitative Data: Systematic Approaches. Thousand Oaks, CA: Sage Publications, Inc.
Bernard, Russell
  1996 Research Methods in Anthropology: Qualitative and Quantitative Approaches. 2nd edition. Walnut Creek, CA: AltaMira Press.
Borgatti, Stephen P.
  1999 Elicitation Techniques for Cultural Domain Analysis. In The Ethnographic Toolkit. Schensul, Jean and Margaret Weeks, eds. Pp. 115–150. Thousand Oaks, CA: Sage Publishers, Inc.
Bowen, Judith L., and Gordon Schectman
  2010 VA Academic PACT: A Blueprint for Primary Care Redesign in Academic Practice Settings. VA Offices of Primary Care and Academic Affiliations, Academic PACT Workgroup. Washington, DC.
Brown, Hilary, Bridget Johnston, and Ulrika Ostlund
  2011 Identifying Care Actions to Conserve Dignity in End-of-Life Care. British Journal of Community Nursing 16(5):238–245.
Carpenter, Christine
  1994 The Experience of Spinal Cord Injury: The Individual's Perspective—Implications for Rehabilitation Practice. Physical Therapy 74(7):614–629.
Chochinov, Harvey Max
  2002 Dignity-Conserving Care—A New Model for Palliative Care: Helping the Patient Feel Valued. Journal of the American Medical Association 287(17):2253–2260.
———. 2004 Dignity in the Eye of the Beholder. Journal of Clinical Oncology 22(7):1336–1340.
———. 2007 Dignity and the Essence of Medicine: The A, B, C, and D of Dignity Conserving Care. British Medical Journal 335(7612):184–187.
Chochinov, Harvey Max, Thomas Hack, Susan McClement, Linda Kristjanson, and Mike Harlos
  2002 Dignity in the Terminally Ill: A Developing Empirical Model. Social Science & Medicine 54(3):433–443.
Chow, Sherman
  2007 "Either You Conquer It, or It Conquers You": An Applied Anthropological Approach to Veterans with a Spinal Cord Injury. Thesis, Department of Anthropology, University of South Florida. http://scholarcommons.usf.edu/etd/669, accessed March 10, 2014.
Christakis, Nicholas
  2007 The Social Origins of Dignity in Medical Care at the End of Life. In Perspectives on Human Dignity: A Conversation. Jeff Malpas and Norelle Lickiss, eds. Pp. 199–207. The Netherlands: Springer. http://link.springer.com/chapter/10.1007/978--1--4020--6281--0_20, accessed July 18, 2013.
Coenen, Amy, Ardith Z. Doorenbos, and Sarah A. Wilson
  2007 Nursing Interventions to Promote Dignified Dying in Four Countries. Oncology Nursing Forum 34(6):1151–1156.
Copeland, Toni J.
  2011 Poverty, Nutrition, and a Cultural Model of Managing HIV/AIDS Among Women in Nairobi, Kenya. Annals of Anthropological Practice 35(1):81–97.
D'Andrade, Roy G.
  1995 The Development of Cognitive Anthropology. Cambridge, UK: Cambridge University Press.
Dennis, Sarah M., Nicholas Zwar, Rhonda Griffiths, Martin Roland, Iqbal Hasan, Gawaine Powell Davies, and Mark Harris

2008 Chronic Disease Management in Primary Care: From Evidence to Policy. Medical Journal of Australia 188(8):S53–56.

Doorenbos, Ardith Z., Sarah A. Wilson, and Amy Coenen
2006 A Cross-Cultural Analysis of Dignified Dying. Journal of Nursing Scholarship 38(4):352–357.

Gallagher, Ann, and David Seedhouse
2002 Dignity in Care: The Views of Patients and Relatives. Nursing Times 98(43):38–40

Greenfield, Sheldon, Sherrie Kaplan, and John E Ware, Jr.
1985 Expanding Patient Involvement in Care. Effects on Patient Outcomes. Annals of Internal Medicine 102(4):520–528.

Greenfield, Sheldon, Sherrie H. Kaplan, John E. Ware, Jr., Elizabeth M. Yano, and Harrison J. L. Frank
1988 Patients' Participation in Medical Care: Effects on Blood Sugar Control and Quality of Life in Diabetes. Journal of General Internal Medicine 3(5):448–457.

Haddock, Jane
1996 Towards Further Clarification of the Concept "Dignity." Journal of Advanced Nursing 24(5):924–931.

Hammell, K. Whalley
2004 Quality of Life among People with High Spinal Cord Injury Living in the Community. Spinal Cord 42(11):607–620.

Hemmelgarn, Brenda R., Braden J. Manns, Jianguo Zhang, Marcello Tonelli, Scott Klarenbach, Michael Walsh, and Bruce F. Culleton
2007 Association between Multidisciplinary Care and Survival for Elderly Patients with Chronic Kidney Disease. Journal of the American Society of Nephrology 18(3):993–999.

Hofmann, Bjørn
2002 Respect for Patients' Dignity in Primary Health Care: A Critical Appraisal. Scandinavian Journal of Primary Health Care 20(2):88–91.

Jacobson, Nora
2007 Dignity and Health: A Review. Social Science & Medicine 64(2):292–302.
———. 2009 A Taxonomy of Dignity: A Grounded Theory Study. BMC International Health and Human Rights 9:3.

Jahrami, Haitham
2012 Card Sort Methodology: An Objective Measure in Rehabilitation Research. Journal of Rehabilitation Research and Development 49(2):vii–viii.

Kennedy, David P., Harold D. Green, Christopher McCarty, and Joan S. Tucker
2011 Nonexperts' Recognition of Structure in Personal Network Data. Field Methods 23(3):287–306.

Kleinman, Arthur
1977 Lessons from a Clinical Approach to Medical Anthropological Research. Medical Anthropology Newsletter 8(4):11–15.
———. 1985 Interpreting Illness Experience and Clinical Meanings: How I See Clinically Applied Anthropology. Medical Anthropology Quarterly 16(3): 69–71

Kleinman, Arthur, Leon Eisenberg, and Byron Good
2006 Culture, Illness, and Care: Clinical Lessons from Anthropologic and Cross-Cultural Research. Focus: The Journal of Lifelong Learning in Psychiatry 4(1):140–149.

Kuzma, Anne Marie, Yvonne Meli, Catherine Meldrum, Patricia Jellen, Marianne Butler-Lebair, Debra Koczen-Doyle, Peter Rising, Kim Stavrolakes, and Frances Brogan
2008 Multidisciplinary Care of the Patient with Chronic Obstructive Pulmonary Disease. Proceedings of the American Thoracic Society 5(4):567–571.

Lohne, Vibeke, Trygve Aasgaard, Synnøve Caspari, Åshild Slettebø, and Dagfinn Nåden
2010 The Lonely Battle for Dignity: Individuals Struggling with Multiple Sclerosis. Nursing Ethics 17(3):301–311.

Lorig, Kate R., David S. Sobel, Philip L. Ritter, Diana Laurent, and Mary Hobbs
2001 Effect of a Self-Management Program on Patients with Chronic Disease. Effective Clinical Practice 4(6):256–262.

Lorig, Kate R., David S. Sobel, Anita L. Stewart, Byron William Brown, Jr., Albert Bandura, Philip Ritter, Virginia M. Gonzalez, Diana D. Laurent, and Halsted R. Holman

1999 Evidence Suggesting That a Chronic Disease Self-Management Program Can Improve Health Status While Reducing Hospitalization: A Randomized Trial. Medical Care 37(1):5–14.

Maiolo, John R., Miriam M. Young, Edward W. Glazier, Michael A. Downs, and John S. Petterson
1994 Pile Sorts by Phone. Field Methods 6(1):1–2.

Matiti, Milika, and Janet Sharman
1999 Dignity: A Study of Pre-Operative Patients. Nursing Standard 14(13):32–35.

Matiti, Milika R.
2002 Patient Dignity in Nursing: A Phenomenological Study. Ph.D. dissertation, School of Education and Professional Development, University of Huddersfield.

Matiti, Milika R., and Gillian M. Trorey
2008 Patients' Expectations of the Maintenance of Their Dignity. Journal of Clinical Nursing 17(20):2709–2717.

Nordenfelt, Lennart, and Andrew Edgar
2005 The Four Notions of Dignity. Quality in Ageing and Older Adults 6(1):17–12.

Nyamongo, Isaac K.
2002 Assessing Intracultural Variability Statistically Using Data on Malaria Perceptions in Gusii, Kenya. Field Methods 14(2):148–160.

Paralyzed Veterans of America
2001 An Introduction to Spinal Cord Injury: Understanding the Changes. 4th edition. Washington DC: Paralyzed Veterans of America. www.pva.org http://www.pva.org/site/c.ajIRK9NJLcJ2E/b.8907635/k.6A0F/PDFs_For_Your_Health.htm, last accessed December 13, 2013

Periyakoil, Vyjeyanthi S., Arthur M. Noda, and Helena Chmura Kraemer
2010 Assessment of Factors Influencing Preservation of Dignity at Life's End: Creation and the Cross-Cultural Validation of the Preservation of Dignity Card-Sort Tool. Journal of Palliative Medicine 13(5):495–500.

Roos, Gun
1998 Pile Sorting: "Kids Like Candy." In Using Methods in the Field: A Practical Introduction and Casebook. Pp. 97–110. Walnut Creek, CA: AltaMira Press.

Rubenstein, Lisa V., Edmund F. Chaney, and Jeffrey L. Smith
2004 Patient-Centered Care in the VA: A Research Perspective. Forum. Chicago, IL, November 1: 3–8.

Stewart, Moira A.
1995 Effective Physician-Patient Communication and Health Outcomes: A Review. CMAJ: Canadian Medical Association Journal 152(9):1423–1433.

Sturrock, Kenneth, and Jorge Rocha
2000 A Multidimensional Scaling Stress Evaluation Table. Field Methods 12(1):49–60.

Veterans Health Administration
2011 Spinal Cord Injury/Disorders Services: Patient Brochure. Office of Patient Care Services. http://www.sci.va.gov/docs/VA_Spinal_Cord_Injury_Patient_Brochure.pdf, accessed March 10, 2014.

Wagner, Edward H.
2000 The Role of Patient Care Teams in Chronic Disease Management. BMJ: British Medical Journal 320(7234):569–572.

Wagner, Edward H., Brian T. Austin, Connie Davis, Mike Hindmarsh, Judith Schaefer, and Amy Bonomi
2001 Improving Chronic Illness Care: Translating Evidence into Action. Health Affairs 20(6):64–78.

Walsh, Ken, and Inge Kowanko
2002 Nurses' and Patients' Perceptions of Dignity. International Journal of Nursing Practice 8(3):143–151.

Wong, Penelope A.
1991 The Use of the Successive Pile Sort in an Ethnographic Study of a Shelter for Battered Women. http://soar.wichita.edu/handle/10057/1809, accessed December 5, 2013.

Woogara, Jay
2005 Patients' Rights to Privacy and Dignity in the NHS. Nursing Standard 19(18):33–37.

Yoshida, Karen K.
1993 Reshaping of Self: A Pendular Reconstruction of Self and Identity among Adults with Traumatic Spinal Cord Injury. Sociology of Health & Illness 15(2):217–245.

THE INTERSECTIONS OF GENDER AND POWER IN WOMEN VETERANS' EXPERIENCES OF SUBSTANCE USE AND VA CARE

ANN M. CHENEY
Central Arkansas Veterans Healthcare System; Division of Health Services Research, University of Arkansas for Medical Sciences

AUDREY DUNN
Tufts University

BRENDA M. BOOTH
Division of Health Services Research, University of Arkansas for Medical Sciences

LIBBY FRITH
Division of Health Services Research, University of Arkansas for Medical Sciences

GEOFFREY M. CURRAN
HSR&D, Central Arkansas Veterans Healthcare System; Division of Health Services Research, University of Arkansas for Medical Sciences

In this article, we show that the Veterans Health Administration (VA), similar to military organizations, is a gendered organization where women Veterans' experiences are embedded in and shaped by gender inequalities and structures of power. Based on an in-depth analysis of women Veterans' substance use histories and VA treatment seeking experiences, we illustrate how gender power dynamics are (re)produced and maintained through everyday social interactions and organizational practices and processes that render women Veterans both visible and invisible: visible as sexual objects and invisible as suffering subjects. By retelling the illness and treatment experiences of women Veterans with trauma histories and co-occurring substance use and mental health disorders—a highly stigmatized population of Veterans—we highlight the importance of giving voice to their concerns when developing policies and programs to address the unique health care needs of women Veterans. [gender-based violence, gender roles and norms, substance abuse, rape, women Veterans, VA care]

INTRODUCTION

I met Alyssa,[1] a woman Veteran in her early twenties, for the first time at the inpatient substance use treatment center at the local Veterans Health Administration (VA) health care system. She suffered from posttraumatic stress disorder (PTSD), depression, and anxiety and had been using marijuana, ecstasy, and alcohol to "numb out" and stave off nightmares of being kidnapped, raped, stabbed, and hung upside down. Since leaving

---

ANNALS OF ANTHROPOLOGICAL PRACTICE 37.2, pp. 149–171. ISSN: 2153-957X. © 2014 by the American Anthropological Association. DOI:10.1111/napa.12030

the military, she had been in and out of four substance use treatment programs, entering treatment initially to follow her superiors' orders and then to escape homelessness. This time she admitted herself to the substance use inpatient treatment program at the VA to start the process of recovery; it was her third visit to this program.

Sitting on an armchair across from Alyssa in a small room in the VA, I listened as she described the events leading up to her substance abuse. In the first weeks of her deployment overseas, Alyssa was sitting atop a tower patrolling the roads for suspicious activity when a mortar landed nearby. It did not go off, but she believed that the shrapnel from the explosion would have killed her. Alyssa expressed that this was one of the worst experiences during her deployment; the event and the lingering images of death stuck with her and she began drinking on a daily basis during her deployment. This was not the only traumatic experience she confronted while deployed overseas. She identified the second traumatic event: "When I got drunk and woke up and there was a man in my bed and I didn't invite him in there."

Alyssa was raped by a man in her unit notorious for "having violent behavior" and for getting women drunk and "having sex" with them. She blamed herself for the rape and did not report it. "It would be my word against his and the fact that I was getting drunk. So, to *them*, it could have been that I was making it up because I was drunk," she said. As our conversation progressed, Alyssa explained that the "*them*" were male soldiers, commanders, and "higher ups"; servicemen who "protect their own." The feelings of desperation, self-blame, and disempowerment that Alyssa experienced during her military service were not unique to her, but were experienced by other women in our study. As Alyssa's story and those of other women Veterans with similar histories unfold, we will see how alcohol and drugs became a way to cope with the lingering emotional and psychological struggles linked to chronic exposure to gender-based violence.

THEORETICAL FRAMEWORK

In this article, we build on recent trends in the anthropological study of gender-based violence to highlight the complex ways in which violent acts against women are embedded in structures of power. We employ the term gender-based violence to capture "violence that results from culturally specific ideologies of gender roles and norms" (Wies and Haldane 2011:4) to consider how multiple forms of interpersonal violence, including childhood sexual abuse, rape, in-military and postmilitary sexual harassment and sexual assault, and intimate partner violence as well as structural violence (i.e., violence linked to social and economic inequalities), such as racial/ethnic discrimination, homelessness, and poverty, shape the help-seeking behaviors and treatment experiences of women Veterans abusing alcohol and drugs.[2] By situating women Veterans' stories in frameworks of gender and power, our intent is to bring to light women's subjective understandings of trauma exposure as well as show how their suffering is connected to inequalities and violations of human rights that emerge from institutional hierarchies and relations of power (Farmer 2003).

We use Kanter's (1977) theory of tokenism—a framework outlining the processes that unfold between dominants and minorities in skewed groups—to situate women

Veterans' experiences of seeking VA care within broader frameworks of gender and power. We propose that women Veterans in VA care function as what Kanter referred to as "token women"—a term coined to describe the experiences of women (or a solo woman) in a male-dominated environment—and share three common experiences. First, they are highly visible and capture a disproportionate amount of attention from those in dominant positions in VA settings (e.g., male Veterans, providers), and their behaviors are scrutinized and judged. Second, polarization, or in this case the exaggeration of gender differences, creates boundaries between male Veterans (i.e., the dominant group) and women Veterans (i.e., the minority group), reaffirming solidarity among men and fostering a sense of isolation and disconnection among women. Last, assimilation or the encapsulation of women Veterans into stereotypical gender roles distorts women's behaviors and social identities, exaggerating socially undesirable and gender-typed behavioral characteristics (e.g., complaining).

Scholars have shown that tokenism is an especially useful framework for understanding how gender power dynamics place women as soldiers in the military in marginalized and subordinate social positions (Hauser 2011; Yoder et al., 1983). Military organizations are gendered institutions that champion masculine ideologies upholding images of soldiers as aggressive, assertive, and physically strong (Firestone and Harris 2003). Within these contexts, hegemonic masculinity, referring to idealized masculine identities that are constructed in relation to femininity and effeminate characteristics, is valued (Connell 1987). Lacking esteemed masculine characteristics, women are often depicted as innately unsuited for military service and through the gendering process are encouraged to perform more traditional gender roles and identities (Matthews et al., 2009).

Ethnographic work among women in Israeli's Defense Forces (IDFs) offers concrete examples of how the values and norms embedded within military contexts reproduce conventional gender roles, expectations, and identities for both men and women. Hauser (2011) found that "lone girls" in IDF—military women serving on male-dominated bases—served in "female positions," including clerical and administrative work, educational roles (e.g., cultural instructors), and caregiving positions in which they provided emotional and psychological support to men. In addition to holding subordinate social positions, Levin (2010) found that women serving in IDF were expected to perform *either* more traditional gender identities and were expected to act "girly," thus embodying weak gender characteristics or more masculine gender identities and were perceived as "dykish," embodying more masculine characteristics and power.

The concept of being the "lone girl" serving in male-dominated spaces and the dichotomy of "dykish" and "girly" that emerged in Israeli women's narratives resonates with the experiences of women in the United States (U.S.) military. Recent work among U.S. military women highlights that servicewomen deployed to support the wars in Iraq and Afghanistan were among the minority within their units (sometimes they were one of two or three women) and on overseas bases, and as the gender minority they faced a constellation of circumstances that increased their risk for sexual harassment and sexual assault (Cheney et al., n.d.). Furthermore, within the U.S. military contexts women have been desexualized or hypersexualized and have often been gender typed as dykes or whores, embodying an image of woman as either tough and unfeminine and sexually undesirable, or weak and feminine and sexually attractive (Hampf 2004; Herbert 1998). The social positions that women occupy in the military along with their gendered performances places military women—as a collective group—at the margins of military organizations, heightening their vulnerability to sexual harassment and sexual and physical abuse.

While it is evident that the military is a "gendered institution" (Barrett 1996:141) in which stereotypical gender norms and expectations are reenacted in everyday social interactions reproducing systems of dominance and power (Green et al., 2010; Whitworth 2008), little is known about how these processes unfold in VA health care settings. By using Kanter's (1977) work on tokenism as our starting point and drawing on anthropological theories of gender and violence, we show that the VA, similar to other male-dominated spaces, represents a gendered organization where everyday social interactions reproduce and maintain gender inequalities (Stead 2013). Through an in-depth exploration of women Veterans' experiences of seeking VA care, we argue that the gender inequalities that women experience during active duty are mirrored in their experiences of accessing VA substance use treatment settings—male-dominated spaces—and undermine the effectiveness of treatment for women Veterans with trauma histories who are abusing alcohol and drugs.

CARING FOR THE COMPLEX TRAUMA HISTORIES OF WOMEN VETERANS

Anywhere from the 9.5 to 33 percent of women Veterans have been sexually assaulted and/or faced severe and threatening sexual harassment during their military service (Turchik and Wilson 2010). Recent estimates indicate that 15.1 percent of women Veterans experienced sexual victimization while supporting Operation Enduring Freedom (OEF) and Operation Iraqi Freedom (OIF; Kimerling et al., 2010). In the VA health care system, soldiers' experiences of sexual assault, including attempted or completed rape, and sexual harassment during military service are categorized and understood as military sexual trauma (MST).[3] But, women Veteran's trauma histories are complex and even prior to entering the military many have experienced repeated acts of violence against them. In research among women Veterans who served in the Vietnam, post-Vietnam, or Persian Gulf War era, Sadler et al., (2004) found that women Veterans who were repeatedly exposed to violence during their military service reported the highest rates of childhood physical and sexual abuse, premilitary rape, and postmilitary rape. In this same study, Sadler et al. found that a large portion of these women entered the military to escape homes where they had been exposed to violence and abuse. Structural inequalities (e.g., poverty) along with family and psychosocial factors influence women's decisions to enter the military—a male-dominated environment where their risk for exposure to gender-based violence increases, impacting their overall health and well-being.

There are a number of psychological wounds linked to women Veterans' experiences of sexual harassment and assault throughout the lifespan, including, but not limited to, PTSD, depression, eating disorders and disordered eating, and borderline personality disorder (Cheney et al., 2014; Forman-Hoffman et al., 2012; Mott et al., 2012). Rape has also been linked to substance abuse among women Veterans from the post-Vietnam–, Persian Gulf–, and OEF- and OIF-service eras. In a retrospective telephone survey assessing rape history and substance use and mental health problems, Booth et al. (2011) found that one-third of women Veterans met the diagnostic criteria for either abuse or dependence for alcohol or drugs (see the Diagnostic Criteria for Substance Use and Dependence and Alcohol Abuse and Dependence, DSM-IV-TR, American Psychiatric Association, 2000) and half of those women had experienced rape at some point in their lives. Pavao et al. (2013) found in a study among homeless Veterans using VA services that homeless women with histories of MST were more vulnerable to substance use disorders (SUDs) than homeless women without MST histories, and that SUDs were among the most common problems homeless women Veterans with MST faced.

Not surprisingly, women Veterans with exposure to MST represent a significant portion of women using VA substance use and mental health services. In a nationally representative study on the help-seeking behaviors of Veterans accessing VA outpatient mental health care services, investigators found that more than one-third (35.8 percent) of women Veterans reported a history of MST; among those women almost half (43.1 percent) sought care at specialty substance use clinics (Valdez et al., 2011). Unfortunately, this vulnerable population of women Veterans has expressed sentiments of discontent with VA services, perceiving care as largely geared toward men's needs (Kelly et al., 2008).

Sexual trauma is one of many potentially stressful and/or traumatic experiences that women Veterans face, but it is important to note that it does not account for the range of traumatic events some have experienced over the course of their life. Women Veterans have also experienced combat- and deployment-related stress. The recent wars in Iraq and Afghanistan have shown that despite the Department of Defense's policy banning women from serving in military occupational specialties, involving direct ground combat,[4] women have been under enemy fire, experienced mortar/artillery attacks, and witnessed the death and/or serious injury of their comrades (Holmstedt 2007). They have also endured separation from loved ones and chronic exposure to harassment spurred by living and working along male troops during overseas deployments, have struggled with transitioning home and adjusting to life as caregivers and women Veterans, and found difficulty in finding postdeployment health care services (Street et al., 2009). Additionally, women Veterans have been victims of intimate partner violence, and are, in fact, significantly more likely than other women (i.e., nonveteran women) to suffer from partner abuse (Dichter et al., 2011).

THE RESEARCH

This study was based on two years of data collection, from 2011 to 2013, conducted in Arkansas. In 2011, we began an ethnographic study of substance use, help-seeking behaviors, and treatment ideas among former and current members of the Army National Guard, Air Guard, and Reserve forces. In recent decades, members of the National Guard and Reserve (NG/R) forces have increasingly been deployed to support wars abroad, so much so that the number of soldiers deployed to fight the wars in Iraq and Afghanistan has outweighed those sent to support previous conflicts. NG/R soldiers have experienced some of the greatest psychiatric distress; their rates surpass those found among soldiers in the active component of the military (Vogt, Samper et al., 2008). Given that investigators have previously found high rates of PTSD and depression among NG soldiers in areas of the southern U.S. (Stecker et al., 2010), our work set out to explore, in greater detail, the complexities of psychiatric distress and substance abuse among NG/R soldiers.

We used ethnographic and qualitative methods, including participant observation; informal, unstructured interviews; and substance use life-history interviews, to obtain a nuanced understanding of the ways that military and VA culture inform and give meaning to service members' and Veterans' substance use, help-seeking behaviors, and treatment experiences. To date, we have conducted 51 substance use history interviews with service members and Veterans and invited a subsample of them to participate in a longitudinal component of the study, involving in-depth interviews over a span of 18 months. The follow-up interviews have explored changes in substance use in relation to life events and thoughts and attitudes about treatment seeking along with experiences with treatment seeking. We have also used structured diagnostic instruments, the Mini International Neuropsychiatric Interview (MINI) and the SF36V,[5] to assess participants' mental health status. Ultimately, our goal is to build on Veterans' preferences and ideas to develop, in partnership with military personnel and Veterans, intervention and outreach approaches to address substance use in these populations. This research is ongoing.

The study was reviewed by and received full ethical approval from the Central Arkansas Veterans Healthcare System Institutional Review Board prior to the start of the research. In addition, the research was discussed with and approved by local military leaders. All of the service members and Veterans who volunteered to participate in the study were made aware of the purposes of the research and the potential risks and benefits of participation in the study. In addition, we were careful to inform the participants that any information they shared would be confidential, that their names and identities would not be revealed, and that they did not have to participate or could choose to end the interview at any point. We obtained oral consent from service members, Veterans, and VA staff to observe and participate in events for service members and/or Veterans (e.g., yellow-ribbon events) and written consent for individual interviews.

The research involved observational work across a range of activities, including meals, yellow-ribbon events, drill weekends, and predeployment trainings as well as the spaces in and around VA mental health and substance use clinics. We conducted informal and unstructured interviews with military leaders, such as chaplains, officers, and noncommissioned officers, as well as with VA-based clinical staff, chaplains, and patients, all of whom shared their perspectives on issues related to the military culture, gender, Veterans, and substance use.

We also gathered information more formally through semistructured interviews with seven women Veterans. The women were between the ages of 24 and 56, and three were African American and four were Euro-American. They served in diverse service eras, including post-Vietnam, Desert Storm, and OEF, and OIF. Three women were OEF/OIF-era Veterans and had deployed overseas. All were enlisted soldiers and their ranks ranged from E3, including Army Private First Class and Airman First Class, to Staff

Sergeant (status of E6 in the Army and E5 in the Air Force). All had served in either the Army National Guard, Air Guard, or the Reserves and several served in the active component of the military: four served in the Army National Guard, one served in the Air Force Reserves, one served in the Active Component of the Army and Army Reserves, and one served in the Army National Guard and Active Component of the Army.

All of these women struggled with or were continuing to struggle with substance abuse and simultaneously suffered from various forms of psychological distress, including PTSD, anxiety, panic disorder, depression, and/or borderline personality disorder. Most had been homeless at some point during their substance use, and all had accessed the inpatient substance use program at the local VA (sometimes more than once) and several had accessed other in- and outpatient mental health and substance use services (e.g., MST programs, substance use aftercare program). Nearly all of these women (6/7) had been sexually harassed and/or sexually assaulted during military service and several recounted stories of sexual assault occurring in childhood, immediately prior to entering the military, and postmilitary. The one woman who did not experience sexual trauma recounted a story of chronic exposure to intimate partner violence in which she endured emotional and psychological abuse and experienced life-threatening physical abuse. Several women also shared similar stories of intimate partner violence.[6]

In this article, we employ the term *gender-based violence* to capture the breadth of discriminatory and unjust circumstances that women recounted as they retold their substance use and treatment experiences. However, when interpreting women's stories, we use the terms that they used to describe their histories of trauma and violence exposure giving voice to their personal experiences. Furthermore, while women Veterans were at the heart of our analyses to deepen our understanding of how gender power dynamics shape women Veterans' experiences of seeking help for substance use, we have listened to the voices of male service members and Veterans. Medical and feminist anthropologists have increasingly emphasized the value of incorporating men's perspectives in studies that have traditionally been linked to women's experiences. For instance, scholars have drawn attention to how men's reproductive stories broaden understanding of the complex ways gender intersects and informs reproductive practices, choices, and treatments (Inhorn et al., 2009).

In our analyses of our interviews with men, we have paid close attention to their perceptions of and attitudes toward women in the military and the VA, noting references to gender stereotypes and labels (e.g., "butch"), power differentials embedded in gender relations, and experiences of marginality and isolation. The 44 men in the study were between the ages of 23 and 70, and 23 were African American and 21 were Euro-American. They served in diverse service eras, including Vietnam, Korea, Desert Storm, and OEF and OIF. All were enlisted soldiers and their ranks ranged from E3, including Army Private First Class and Airman First Class, to Sergeant 1st Class (status of E7 in the Army). All had served, at one point in their military service, in the Army National Guard, Air Guard, or Reserves. All had histories of substance use and the majority of the men had accessed VA services, such as substance use treatment and/or mental health treatment.

In what follows, we illustrate what can and does happen in the months and years after women leave the military and seek care as Veterans in the VA health care system. In our analysis, we retrace the roots of women Veterans' distress bringing to light how the inequalities they faced as female soldiers in the military are reproduced as women Veterans navigating VA care, fostering a sense of exclusion and marginality. Although we focus on women's experiences at the inpatient substance use clinic at the VA, we have drawn from the narratives of all the women and have included stories of accessing in- and outpatient VA mental health care services to reconstruct a narrative of the gendered clinical environments that women Veterans navigated when seeking care. Our analytic approach was designed to capture and give voice to the experiences of a highly marginalized group of Veterans—women with co-occurring substance use and mental health disorders—as well as illustrate how anthropologically based insights can inform current dialogues and policies related to Veterans at the margins of the VA health care system.

THE (RE)PRODUCTION OF GENDER AND POWER IN VA SETTINGS

Visibility and Invisibility

The VA is a gendered organization where women Veterans, similar to servicewomen in military organizations (Hauser 2011; Levin 2010), oscillated between states of visibility and invisibility: they were visible as sexual objects and invisible as suffering subjects (Scheper-Hughes and Lock 1987). Within this male-dominated environment, gender inequalities present in the military context were reproduced in VA settings, placing women in devalued social positions and at the margins of the VA healthcare system. In discussing the challenges that women Veterans experience when accessing VA care, a male Veteran who served during the Iraq and Afghanistan service era illustrated this point well. This male Veteran's perception of women Veterans was entangled in images of military women as sexual objects:

> I don't like women [Veterans] . . . I will not date a woman in the military because I know how most of them are: A lot of them are straight up whores. I mean they really are, they'll sleep with anything. And some of them would even be married and do it [have sex]. I really don't have a lot of respect for women in the military because of that.

This man's perception of military women and women Veterans was not unique; rather images of women as sexual objects and "whores" were present in other men's discussions of women Veterans in the VA and reproduced in women's renditions of their experiences in VA settings.

The narrative data from both male and female Veterans in the study illuminate what feminist scholars have referred to as "surface and deep (in)visibility" (Lewis and Simpson 2010:64); nuanced terms that capture women's experiences of exclusion and marginality in male-dominated environments offer explanations as to how power is maintained and (re)produced through organizational practices and process that render women invisible.

At first glance, their stories highlight the problems women Veterans experienced as "token women" in male-dominated contexts where they were often the "lone female" and highly visible. Their behaviors (unlike those of men) were scrutinized and judged, their gender identity placed them as different from the typical patient (i.e., male Veteran), and, their actions and comportments were stereotyped and distorted. At a deeper level, their stories reveal the everyday social interactions and clinical practices that contribute to women's invisibility and the reproduction of gender inequalities and relations of power.

The women Veterans in the study talked about being the minority on the VA campus where they were highly visible and captured a disproportionate amount of attention. Several of the women discussed how their underrepresentation in the larger VA hospital, including the hallways, elevators, and grounds of the campus, made them so visible that they felt unsafe. Jessica, a young Euro-American woman in her early thirties who frequented the VA on a weekly basis to seek ongoing buprenorphine treatment for opiate use, explained why:

> You guys don't realize there are a ton of females here. A ton! But they kinda stay low profile. We come to our appointment and we go home. We don't linger, we try not to stand out. Because when we stand out we get raped.

She explained how women's visibility made it especially challenging to seek care: "It's really hard to go through any of these programs, even the domiciliary, as a female because you can't go anywhere without being cat called." She paused, then referred to an incident that occurred while we were walking through the VA hospital: "Or like you saw in that hallway, guys just 'Um, mm, mm.' That's just so rude and disrespectful. I get so sick of it." Jessica, who was raped at age 12, raped during her deployment to Iraq, and then gang raped after leaving the military, carried a silver switchblade in her purse. Despite knowing that weapons were prohibited on VA campus she continued to carry it for self-protection.

The experience of rape, as Jessica pointed out and the other women's narratives will underscore, was a salient concern in the lives of these women Veterans and largely influenced their treatment-seeking behaviors. For instance, when we asked Barb, an African American woman in her mid-forties who endured chronic sexual harassment during her deployments to Iraq, if some Veterans experienced more difficulty with accessing VA care, she replied, "definitely females." Lowering her voice to a whisper she explained why: "They don't want to say anything because I bet you, over 90% of the time it's because they are being raped, some type of rape; that they are being picked on, and being made to seem that they're incompetent."

These narratives underscore the social origins of illness, alerting us to how institutional hierarchies and relations of power foster inequalities and violations of human rights that can dramatically shape health and well-being (Farmer 2003; Kleinman et al., 1997). Jessica experienced chronic exposure to gender-based violence and suffered from PTSD, panic attacks, and anxiety and was hypervigilant in public spaces, including the campus grounds and hallways of the local VA. Her experiences of rape and the chronic struggle with co-occurring substance use and mental health disorders were not unique to her, but experienced by nearly all the women in our study. Additionally, many of the women also experienced poor physical health and suffered from chronic medical conditions (e.g., diabetes, obesity). Their suffering calls attention to how social inequalities and subjective experiences of distress are embodied becoming visible on and through the body (Csordas 1990).

Heightened Visibility as the "Only Female"

Many women indicated that they were either the "only female" or one of two women in the substance use program. Men in the study also indicated that few "females" accessed the inpatient substance use program during the course of their treatment. Men frequently made comments such as "In my class there are no women at all" and "When you go up to 2K [inpatient substance use program] you might see one female, one female," illustrating that women were often the "only female" in the substance use program. Shirley, a Euro-American woman in her mid-fifties who had a history of abusing crystal meth and pain medication, spent part of the 30 days on the inpatient substance use unit as one of two women: "There was one other gal, and she and I were roommates for, about a month or so. I had been there for myself for a time, and then she came in." She then relocated to the local homeless shelter for Veterans in a nearby community where she was the "only female" for nearly three months. "It was just me and forty-three guys," she commented. While Shirley felt comfortable among groups of men and indicated that they "respected" her, there were times when she felt "out of place" and excluded from discussions among the men.

Unlike Shirley, the other women in the study recounted stories of distress, expressing their discomfort in male-dominated VA spaces. Alyssa described how she felt as the "only female" in the inpatient substance use program:

> This is a Veterans hospital so I felt maybe I'd be more comfortable here. But I got here, I was the *only female*. There were men everywhere. They were looking you up and down like they could eat you up.

As one of two or as the "only female" in the program, the women were often isolated and their safety on the unit was a concern; consequently, their rooms were *always* under lock and key. Jessica, who attended the inpatient program, emphasized this point. Making direct eye contact, she said angrily: "They have to put us in a locked room; a room that locks!" She likened the experience to one of extreme confinement, "It feels like we're in a prison."

Women's heightened visibility and isolation on the unit threatened their safety and also made them especially vulnerable to sexual objectification. Norma, a Euro-American woman in her fifties who had been accessing VA services for over 25 years to manage her symptoms of PTSD, borderline-personality disorder, and substance abuse, recounted stories of sexual objectification. She sought treatment in the inpatient substance use program in the early 1990s and returned nearly 20 years later. She described her first experience: "It was the same as it was when I came in 2011. You're a piece of meat, anywhere you go." Explaining the objectification in detail, she reenacted several scenes, as if the men were making the comments at that moment: "'When you gonna invite me over?' 'When you gonna cook for me?' 'Hey babe.'" Pausing for a moment she looked up and whistled: "You're just like meat, they're wanting to conquer [you], cook you up!"

Polarization and the "Unique" Veteran Patient

Women recounted stories of how everyday interactions and clinical practices made women feel different and/or "unique" from male patients, which created boundaries between male and female Veterans. Men also expressed sentiments of difference toward women Veterans, contributing to perceptions of women as the atypical Veteran patient. For instance, when we asked a male Veteran what he thought about receiving treatment in a mixed-gender setting with women Veterans, he commented, "It doesn't bother me . . . it would just be 'Ok, there's a girl here. Whatever.'"

As several of the women indicated, adherence to a dress code was one of the most salient clinical practices that polarized male and female Veterans. Women on the unit, unlike men, were required to adhere to dress codes. Women were not permitted to wear sweatpants, tank tops with spaghetti straps, skirts that hung above the length of their hand, and low-cut shirts. Alyssa, who viewed this practice as degrading and irrelevant to her recovery, illustrated how such rules heightened differences between male and female Veterans:

> The head nurse she tells me I can't wear sweat pants into the meeting, but it's okay for the men to come in there in their basketball shorts and their sweat pants. That's not appropriate! If I'm *not* going to be able to wear my sweat pants around, then it shouldn't be allowed for them to come in here wearing basketball shorts because just as much as you say that you may think that I'm revealing, how much do you think he's revealing in his basketball shorts?

"Every time" the nurse saw her, the nurse pointed to her, noting her attire. She recounted one instance that was especially bothersome: "I'm walking by and I hear her [the nurse's] staff say, 'Is she supposed to have those sweat pants on?'"

Jessica shared similar sentiments and also expressed that staff focused on ensuring that women did not dress "provocatively." She perceived the focus on women's sexuality as unwanted and distracting:

> When you're recovering from drugs and you're really trying to get help, you're not at the top of your game. I mean you're just flat, torn-up. You want to be able to come out of your room in the morning to get a cup of coffee without having to fix your hair or worry about what you're wearing because we're not allowed to come out of our rooms in any night clothes. We have to be wearing normal clothing.

Jessica believed that dress codes and expectations of proper hygiene (e.g., fixing their hair) derailed recovery efforts: "This is why we don't come into these programs because we're made to feel like we're whores."

In narratives like these we see how everyday clinical practices placed women's bodies and sexuality as the focal point of their interactions heightening their visibility in the clinical settings. At the same time, this practice fostered feelings of difference and their struggle with substance abuse became less visible. The organizational practices and processes that shaped women's experiences of visibility and invisibility were also reproduced in other VA settings. The narratives of women Veterans seeking emergency care for post-military rape shed light on the invisibility of women as suffering subjects. Jessica, who sought emergency treatment from the VA after being gang raped, illuminated this point:

> The ambulance called and said that I had been raped and the VA re-routed me to another hospital. . . . they sent me to Jones' Hospital, they dropped the ball on my rape kit . . . when I got here [VA] . . . I did an intake evaluation on [a mental health unit] and that was it. She [the nurse] said, "This is a really unique situation we've never dealt with someone who has just been raped."

Jessica was not hospitalized or immediately connected to a counselor. Rather, they learned that she was already in dialectical behavioral therapy (DBT) and encouraged her to continue with her sessions. But, as she pointed out angrily, "That's not enough. They should have had some kind of inpatient something or other for several weeks. I'm still crazy over it!"

Theresa, a Euro-American woman in her forties who sought VA emergency care after being kidnapped, raped, abused, and threatened to death by two men, shared a similar story: "I went into the VA hospital and I said, 'I need help.' I couldn't stop crying . . . It was either VA or the bridge and jump off it." As she narrated her experience in the emergency room setting, it became evident that her rape, despite having asked staff for help, was not immediately addressed: "They just did the suicide thing and sent me to [inpatient mental health unit]." She believed the rape was overlooked because, as she described, "my pee test was dirty, so it was just, 'She's a drug addict.' . . . They didn't see anything but substance use." Restating the providers' words, she said, "This is a crack head, whore that says she tried to kill herself." Shortly after being admitted for the attempted suicide, she learned about the MST program and asked her providers for more information. "They cuckooed me off," she said. Reenacting the scene as if she were the providers: "You're just suicidal." Her providers did not connect her to care for the rape.

Theresa sought ER care for the gang rape described above in 2009. It was the second rape. Thirty-three years prior her Army recruiter raped her at knifepoint as two men stood by waiting for their "chance" to participate in an attempted gang rape. While she escaped the attempted gang rape, her superiors sexually harassed her throughout her military service and at one point a superior attempted to sexually assault her. The rape, chronic sexual harassment, and attempted assault had destructive psychological effects. Crack became her "slow suicide." But, despite being "cuckooed off" after the gang rape, Theresa fought to get help for the lingering effects of repeat sexual traumas. She eventually "planted" herself in the PTSD clinic where she located a provider who she said "turned my world around." For the first time she stopped blaming herself for the violent acts enacted against her.

The dynamic that arises in these women's experience of seeking care for rape highlights that the woman Veteran is not the "typical" Veteran patient and faces "unique" circumstances that male Veterans do not encounter. Furthermore, in cases like Theresa's, we see that the stigma of being a substance user outweighed her suicide attempt and her suffering as a victim of rape, violence, and abuse.

Distortion of Women's Feminine Character Traits

While clinical practices worked to exaggerate gender difference placing women Veterans in marginalized positions in VA care, everyday social interactions with VA staff and male Veterans encapsulated them into stereotypical gender roles, distorting their behaviors and social identities and exaggerating socially undesirable images of women. For instance, Shirley, who was emotionally and psychologically abused by her husband of 20 years and beaten to near death by a boyfriend, alluded to images of women as "whiney and complaining" as she retold her substance use treatment experience:

> Everybody liked me. I'm a likeable person really. I'm naïve and get taken advantage of, but the guys, they liked me opposed to girls that had been there before me because I just went with the flow. I didn't *complain*, "Oh he tried to do this. He said this." They would say in a public forum that they liked and appreciated me because I was just like one of the guys.

Shirley's words provide insights into how women Veterans in VA health care settings are stereotyped as possessing socially unacceptable feminine behavioral characteristics—words that have also been used to describe feminine characteristics in military cultures (Whitworth 2008). Similar to other women in male-dominated spaces, she did not engage in practices that would draw attention to herself as a woman (Stead 2013).

Other women recounted different stories, illustrating what happens when women engaged in practices that drew attention to their gender. Theresa, who accessed the VA inpatient substance use program shortly after accessing VA emergency care for being gang raped, illustrated this point:

> I had one guy who kinda, not really assaulted me, but almost assaulted me. And I went to staff, and they did do something about it as far as call the police. But I still felt like a *tattle tale*. I felt like some of the staff looked at me differently after I did that, like, "Why would you do that? It wasn't that big a deal." Well not to you but to somebody who's been raped, it's a big deal!

LISTENING TO THE VOICES OF WOMEN VETERANS

Women Veterans with trauma histories and co-occurring substance abuse and mental health disorders area highly marginalized and stigmatized population of Veterans accessing VA services. As a collective social group, these women experience what Bourdieu (2001) has referred to as "symbolic violence" in which gender inequalities reproduced through everyday social practices and patriarchal structures of power disempower women; they share the social condition of oppression. While it is important to understand the social origins of women's ill health and uncover the ways in which gender and structures of power inform women's VA health care experiences, it is also critical to recognize what can and should be done to improve women Veterans' well-being and health care experiences.

An essential component of developing policies and programs that incorporates the unique needs of women Veterans requires listening to women and giving voice to their concerns. Indeed, the women's narratives underscore that they do not want to exist at the margins of the largest health care system in the country and they will fight to renegotiate their social positions in the VA health care system. As Melinda, a Euro-American woman in her fifties who struggled with the aftermath of being "pimped out" (in references to being sold for sex) by a fellow soldier and raped by two men, said:

> Once I decided I was gonna get clean and do whatever I needed to do, then I was determined I was gonna get it [treatment]. So being around all those men, sometimes it was like, the men were more important. But, when I had issues where I needed more information about, I made it clear that I needed the information. So you had to deal with me. And that's the attitude I had in there, "Look, I'm here too. And, yeah I'm surrounded by men but I'm a Veteran just like they are. And, yeah they need help, guess what, I do too. My thing was: I don't wanna go back to using so I'm gonna fight and get what I need.

Women Veterans want their voices heard and they believe that our work, which provided them an opportunity to share their insights on how to improve care for women with similar histories, can do that. As Jessica told us, "You're our only hope."

The Importance of All-Women VA Settings

An underlying theme that threaded their narratives together was the discrimination they experienced as women, as victims of rape, and as "drug addicts." While women indicated that male Veterans were perpetrators of sexual harassment and attempted assaults in VA settings, they also perceived staff as discriminating against them because of their gender. Several of the women talked about their vulnerability to sexual harassment and sexual assault in VA settings and expressed their desire for staff to understand the significance of unwanted sexual attention and harassment and of the potential enactment of violent acts against them. Jessica explained:

> You can go to the staff and the staff will be like "Well that's just kind of how it is around here." ... They act like there's nothing they can do ... We probably don't know who to take it to. If there was someone specifically designated for harassment of any kind for any patient, and we were educated about that and knew who to go to, we'd go to them. But, we're told to go to the staff members.

The everyday clinical practices and social interactions that contributed to the women's experiences of gender-based discrimination alert us to the importance of all-women VA settings. The VA has redesigned health care to accommodate the unique needs of women Veterans by designating primary care providers for women and assuring care delivery in sensitive and safe environments in VA Women's Health Clinics, clinical spaces where women receive gender-specific care in women-friendly settings (United States Department of VA 2010). Women Veterans' emotional and psychiatric needs are complex, necessitating treatment from multiple providers across diverse settings. Because of the complexities of these women's illnesses and treatment needs, they spent most, if not all, of their time outside women-friendly settings where they were highly visible, felt out of place, and were marked as "different" from the typical Veteran patient.

This was especially true in women's experiences of accessing the VA inpatient substance use program where they were the "only female" or one of two women among a group of men. In these contexts, women were often isolated and reexperienced sexual harassment, bearing the brunt of sexual innuendos and degrading comments, and some were revictimized by male Veteran peers and providers. In addition, as the "only female" or one of two women in all-male groups, these women rarely shared their stories of rape, sexual abuse, and/or intimate partner violence even if they needed to: "If a question came up that I didn't want to discuss, I wouldn't. I needed to, but I wouldn't." Melinda shed light on what can and does happen when women with histories of rape share their stories in male-dominated spaces:

> Men don't want to hear it, some of the issues that I was going through because it didn't pertain to them and they don't go through them, those kinds of issues [sexual assault and sexual abuse] but they was real to me . . . The men were like 'Ah we don't deal with that, we don't want [to discuss it]. But it was real for me and it was important to know how to deal with it.

Women Veterans expressed their desires to receive treatment in safe and secure environments surrounded by other women where they can "talk about women's issues." As Shirley explained

> When you're one or two women with twenty guys [in the in-patient substance abuse program], no way they can understand . . . the way men treat women and experiences in the military . . . Some [women] had been raped or been sexually harassed.

Within all-female settings, women indicated that they have felt a sense of belonging and connection with other women. Others have noted that women Veterans want to connect with women Veteran peers and share their military and postmilitary experiences in therapeutic support groups, but they do not always feel welcome or entitled to VA services because of beliefs that "The VA is a place where wounded men or retired men go" (Mattocks et al., 2012:7).

Furthermore, all of the women suffered from co-occurring substance use and mental health problems, including PTSD, depression, anxiety, and/or borderline personality disorder. However, their care, similar to male Veterans' care, was not integrated and their mental health problems were not addressed in the inpatient substance use program. Both in and outside the VA, interpersonal and gender-based trauma exposure is high among women in substance use treatment and women need trauma-specific approaches that simultaneously treat substance use, PTSD, and trauma (Cohen et al., 2013). Jessica's ideal model of care emphasized the importance of treating trauma and co-occurring substance use and mental health disorders in the same program:

> The PTSD and the MST they all tie in together and the SUD they tie in together too . . . If you're just gonna do the MST, that's like one symptom treating maybe the fever when

you've got the flu. All you're gonna treat is the fever and not the rest of it. Treat the whole package which would be PTSD, MST, and SUD all at once. And MST and PTSD classes and training and things like that are inter-related. You wouldn't have to create three or four different units. PTSD, substance use, and MST all wrapped up in one that would be so awesome!

RETHINKING CARE FOR WOMEN VETERANS ACCESSING VA SERVICES

The stories of the women Veterans in our study are not unique, but reflect the reality of many servicewomen and women Veterans who have experienced and endured violent acts against them. Similar to other women Veterans (see Suris and Lind 2008 for a review), these women endured repeat exposure to gender-based violence, which, for some, began as sexual abuse in childhood or early adolescence, continued as rape in the military and again as rape postmilitary. Others were raped and/or sexually harassed for the first time during their military service and again after leaving the military. In these narratives, we see how the roots of their trauma run much deeper and wider than the victimization(s) that occur during military service and that the origin of their distress and illnesses are embedded in and shaped by gender and structures of power.

While the women's narratives raise a number of concerns, first and foremost, they illuminate the complex nature of women's trauma exposures (Zinzow et al., 2007) and offer insights into the social processes (i.e., gender and power) that can compromise women Veteran's emotional, psychological, and physical health and shape their VA health care use (Sadler et al., 2004). As the women's narratives highlight, women's exposure to violent acts and repeat traumas can greatly affect women's relational experiences, influencing their sense of comfort and safety in the therapeutic environment (Rosenbaum and Varvin 2007). In cases like Jessica's, we see how everyday clinical practices intended to ensure sensitive and safe environments for women Veterans such as locking the door and asking women to adhere to dress codes had the opposite effect: It reified images of woman as sexual objects drawing attention away from their suffering and recovery efforts.

It is critical that clinical staff, irrespective of their gender, are sensitive to how gender-based violence can influence women Veterans' experiences in the clinical environment and how their own gender-based biases and stereotypes influence their interactions with female patients and the delivery of care (Salgado et al., 2002). For instance, we see in cases like Theresa's, how gender stereotypes (e.g., women are tattletales) and stigma around substance use (e.g., crackhead whore) were reproduced in the ways clinical staff related to female patients, greatly affecting women's experience in VA healthcare settings. The women in our study endured the stigma and shame of being labeled as an "addict," but also as a rape victim, and/or victim of intimate partner violence, which they believed influenced how providers and staff treated them.

As their narratives highlight, substance abuse was linked to chronic exposure to sexual harassment and/or sexual assault during military service, incidences of gang rape both during and after military service, and/or histories of abuse and intimate partner violence. Many articulated links between their trauma and substance abuse (e.g., "The drugs were to escape everything that happened to me") and their stories are similar to those of other women Veterans who used drugs to cope with the anxiety and emotional stress of victimization during military service (Mattocks et al., 2012). Thus, it is critical that health care professionals in the VA recognize the social origins of substance abuse to understand how and why social inequalities, specifically gender-based violence, impact the lives of marginalized persons and the choices they make (Singer 2006).

Investigators in the VA Women's Practice-Based Research Networks are working hard to implement an educational intervention to increase health care professionals' knowledge of and sensitivity to women's experiences in health care settings (Vogt, Barry et al., 2008). But, clinical staff and leadership in VA need to understand that everyday clinical practices that reproduce structures of power and gender inequalities are only part of the problem. The narrative data from both men and women in our study evidence how negative images of women in the military are mirrored in VA settings, creating discriminatory and potentially unsafe environments of care for women Veterans. Thus, more work needs to be done to develop interventions that can educate staff and male patients on how violent acts against women Veterans are embedded in culturally specific beliefs about gender roles and norms and structures of power present in military cultures and VA health care settings.

Additionally, by tracing the roots of women Veterans' trauma exposures, we can begin to see the limitations of current VA practices in the treatment of sexual trauma. Since 2000, providers have used the MST screener—a two-item tool assessing the occurrence of harassment and assault occurring "while the victim was in the military"—to detect exposure to sexual trauma. But, in cases like Jessica and Theresa, we see that despite procedures for treating women Veterans reporting MST, there were limited (if any) procedures for treating women Veterans with rape postmilitary service (e.g., rape kits were not used in emergency care in the VA), highlighting breakdowns in care for victims of postmilitary sexual assault. Over the years, investigators have highlighted the rather high rates of (re)victimization among women Veterans postmilitary service (Campbell and Raja 2005; Sadler et al., 2004) and have identified it as one of the root causes of homelessness in this population of Veterans (Hamilton et al., 2011).

But even in light of evidence that a significant amount of women Veterans with histories of sexual assault tend to use the VA for all of their health care needs and that so many of these women were sexually assaulted pre- and postmilitary service (Mengeling et al., 2011), MST remains the focal point of Veterans' sexual trauma exposures and treatment regimes. This begs the question: What does MST mean to VA leadership, VA providers and staff, and the Veterans accessing VA services? Is it perceived as a system of care designed to treat only "in military" experiences of sexual harassment and sexual assault or does it also address lifetime exposure to rape and sexual assault? How might current conceptualizations of sexual trauma in VA be problematic for the male and female Veterans accessing VA services, especially those with complex sexual trauma histories and those in need of emergency care for sexual trauma-related injuries, including physical, psychological, and emotional wounds?

The VA has traditionally served a male patient population; however, in the last decade the number of women using VA services has increased rapidly (Friedman et al., 2011). In 2009, estimates indicated that approximately 32 percent of the 1.5 million women Veterans were enrolled in the VA health care system and of those enrolled about 19 percent used VA health care—the percent of women Veterans using VA health care services in 2009 signifies an 83 percent increase since 2000 (National Center for Veterans Analysis and Statistics 2011). In general, women Veterans accessing VA services tend to report positive perceptions of VA care (Mengeling et al., 2011), and even women Veterans with MST histories have reported overall satisfaction with VA care (Kimerling et al., 2011). But, when examining the finer details of women's care, women Veterans with histories of MST using VA services have reported substantially and significantly lower satisfaction regarding certain aspects of VA care—specifically aspects tied to care coordination and patient-provider interactions (Kimerling et al., 2011). As we learned, women Veterans seeking sexual trauma-related care often use services, including specialty mental health care and SUD clinics, outside of women-friendly settings. In these settings, we see how gender inequalities emerged from institutional hierarchies and relations of power in the VA health care system, shaping their experiences of suffering and treatment seeking as well as contributing to disparities in care for women Veterans in the VA.

The discipline of anthropology and anthropologists have much to add to ongoing debates on how best to care for women Veterans receiving VA care. As we have highlighted throughout this article, anthropological frameworks of gender and violence can shed light on the ways in which military- and VA-specific constructions of gender roles and norms and power dynamics embedded in institutional hierarchies (e.g., military, VA health care system) shape violent acts against servicewomen and women Veterans. The critical lens we bring to our work prepares us to engage in conversations about why and for what purposes investigators need to consider the role of gender in the delivery and effectiveness of mental health care (Strauss et al., 2012). Our training also qualifies us to engage in debates on what gender-sensitive models of care mean and how best to address culturally specific constructions of gender and structures of power in the delivery of health care to women Veterans.

Applied and practicing anthropologist in VA can play an important role in helping to alert VA leadership and health care professionals to the ways that gender, power, and trauma shape women Veterans' help-seeking and treatment experiences in the VA, and in helping to design interventions sensitive to the needs of marginalized populations of service members and Veterans accessing VA care. In addition, our disciplinary training uniquely qualifies us to interpret and make sense of the nuances of Veterans experiences in ways that empower and give voice to Veterans, bringing their needs and preferences to the forefront.

In the next phase of our work, we will do exactly that: we will synthesize the narrative data from Veterans and present their preferences for treatment to other service members and Veterans during focus group discussions to elicit potential users' thoughts and feedback on intervention ideas. The final stage of our research will involve a multistakeholder product development meeting where service members' and Veterans' ideas regarding models of care will be presented to a team of clinical researchers, health services researchers, VA treatment providers and staff, military leaders, soldiers, and Veterans who will evaluate and prioritize the intervention ideas (Langford and McDonagh 2003). In the case of women Veterans with histories of gender-based violence, this means that their own perspectives will be incorporated into models of care and interventions will be sensitive to their unique histories as women, addressing the complex webs of power that women Veterans face.

NOTES

Acknowledgements. This material is based upon work supported by the Department of Veterans Affairs, Veterans Health Administration, Office of Research and Development. The views expressed in this article are those of the author and do not necessarily reflect the position or policy of the Department of Veterans Affairs or the United States government.

1. We have used pseudonyms throughout the article to protect Veterans' identities and maintain confidentiality. We have also included pieces of women's stories to disguise their identities, but have done so in a way that preserves the themes present in their narratives.

2. We are aware that violence against women is not always based on their gender and that men are also victims of gender-based violence. This holds true in the military: investigators are increasingly drawing attention to reported rates of MST among men (Hoyt et al., 2011).

3. Investigators have sought to flesh out military persons' sexual trauma exposure(s), employing more specific terms to indicate attempted and/or completed sexual assault, such as rape in military and sexual assault in military. In this article, when possible, we avoid clinical vocabularies and use women's words to best describe their sexual trauma experiences. Furthermore, it is important to note that men also experience MST; however, servicewomen are 20 times more likely to be exposed to sexual assault during military service than men (Suris and Lind 2008). In our study, we interviewed over 50 participants, most of whom were men, and we inquired about negative experiences during military service. Only women shared their stories of MST, thus we report on their experiences.

4. In 2013 the Department of Defense rescinded the ban on military women serving in ground-combat positions, and since leadership across the branches of the military have taken steps to open up military operation specialties that were once only available to men (see http://www.defense.gov/news/newsarticle.aspx?id=119100 for more information).

5. All of the participants completed two standardized interviews, the Mini International Neuropsychiatric Interview (MINI) and the SF36V. The MINI involved a series of structured questions assessing the participants' mental health status, including, but not limited to, major depression, generalized anxiety disorder, and PTSD. The SF36V is the shortened version of a more robust health survey designed to measure individual's perceptions about their health status and ability to function. It consists of 36 questions that fall within eight subscales, ranging from physical functioning to general health to mental health.

6. Although the interview focused on service members' and Veterans' violence exposures during military service, several of the women Veterans recounted histories of gender-based violence prior to entering the military (e.g., intrafamily sexual abuse) and after leaving the military (e.g., gang rape, intimate partner violence). Their stories illustrate that women with prior exposure to gender-based violence are at an increased risk for revictimization and poor health outcomes.

REFERENCES CITED

American Psychiatric Association (APA)
    2000 Diagnostic and Statistical Manual of Mental Disorders. 4th edition. Washington, DC: American Psychiatric Publication.

Barrett, Frank J.

    1996 The Organizational Construction of Hegemonic Masculinity: The Case of the US Navy. Gender, Work & Organization 3(3):129–142.

Booth, Brenda M., Michelle Mengeling, James Torner, and Anne G. Sadler

    2011 Rape, Sex Partnership, and Substance Use Consequences in Women Veterans. Journal of Traumatic Stress 24(3):287–294.

Bourdieu, Pierre

    2001 Masculine Domination. Stanford, CA: Stanford University Press.

Campbell, Rebecca, and Sheela Raja

    2005 The Sexual Assault and Secondary Victimization of Female Veterans: Help-Seeking Experiences with Miltiary and Civilian Social Systems. Psychology of Women Quarterly 29(1): 97–106.

Cheney, A. M., Booth, B. M., Davis, T., Mengeling, M., Torner, J. C., Sadler, A. G.

    2014 The Role of Borderline Personality Disorder and Depression in the Relationship between Sexual Assault and BMI among Women Veterans. Violence & Victims 29(5).

Cheney, Ann M., Brenda M. Booth, Michelle A. Mengeling, James Torner, and Anne G. Sadler

    N.d. "Let's Get Together and Solve This Problem": Servicewomen's Strategies to Staying Safe While Deployed. Department of Psychiatry, University of Arkansas for Medical Sciences.

Cohen, Lisa R., Craig Field, Aimee N.C. Campbell, and Denise A. Hien

    2013 Intimate Partner Violence Outcomes in Women with PTSD and Substance Use: A Secondary Analysis of NIDA Clinical Trials Network "Women and Trauma" Multi-Site Study. Addictive Behavior 38(7):2325–2332.

Connell, Robert W.

    1987 Gender and Power: Society, the Person, and Sexual Politics. Stanford, CA: Stanford University Press.

Csordas, Thomas. J.

    1990 Embodiment as a Paradigm for Anthropology. Ethos 18(1):5–47.

Dichter, Melissa E., Catherine Cerulli, and Robert M. Bossarte

    2011 Intimate Partner Violence Victimization among Women Veterans and Associated Heart Health Risks. Women's Health Issues 21(4):S190–S194.

Farmer, Paul

    2003 Pathologies of Power: Health, Human Rights, and the New War on the Poor. Berkeley, CA: University of California Press.

Firestone, Juanita M., and Richard J. Harris

    2003 Perceptions of Effectiveness of Responses to Sexual Harassment in the US Military, 1988 and 1995. Gender, Work & Organization 10(1):42–64.

Forman-Hoffman, Valerie L., Michelle A. Mengeling, Brenda M. Booth, James Torner, and Anne G. Sadler

    2012 Eating Disorders, Post-Traumatic Stress, and Sexual Trauma in Women Veterans. Military Medicine 177(10):1161–1168.

Friedman, Sarah A., Ciaran S. Phibbs, Susan K. Schmitt, Patricia M. Hayes, Laura Herrera, and Susan M. Frayne

    2011 New Women Veterans in the VHA: A Longitudinal Profile. Women's Health Issues 21(4):S103–S111.

Green, Gill, Carol Emslie, Dan O'Neil, Kate Hunt, and Steven Walker

    2010 Exploring the Ambiguities of Masculinity in Accounts of Emotional Distress in the Military among Young Ex-Servicemen. Social Science & Medicine 71(8):1480–1488.

Hamilton, Alison B., Ines Poza, and Donna L. Washington

    2011 "Homelessness and Trauma Go Hand-in-Hand": Pathways to Homelessness among Women Veterans. Women's Health Issues 21(4):S203–S209.

Hampf, Michaela M.

    2004 "Dykes" or "Whores": Sexuality and the Women's Army Corps in the United States during World War II. Women's Studies International Forum 27(1):13–30.

Hauser, Orlee

    2011 "We Rule the Base Because We're Few": "Lone Girls" in Israel's Military. Journal of Contemporary Ethnography 40(6):623–651.

Herbert, Melissa A.

    1998 Camouflage Isn't Only for Combat: Gender, Sexuality, and Women in the Military. New York: New York University Press.

Holmstedt, Kirsten

    2007 Band of Sisters: American Women at War in Iraq. Mechanicsburg, PA: Stackpole Books.

Hoyt, Tim, Jennifer Klosterman Rielage, and Lauren F. Williams

    2011 Military Sexual Trauma in Men: A Review of Reported Rates. Journal of Trauma & Dissociation 12(3):244–260.

Inhorn, Marcia C., Tine Tjørnhøj-Thomsen, Helene Goldberg, and Maruska la Cour Mosegaard

    2009 Reconceiving the Second Sex: Men, Masculinity, and Reproduction. Oxford: Berghahn Books.

Kanter, Rosabeth M.

    1977 Some Effects of Proportions on Group Life: Skewed Sex Ratios and Responses to Token Women. American Journal of Sociology 82(5):965–990.

Kelly, Megan M., Dawne S. Vogt, Emily M. Scheiderer, Paige Ouimette, Jennifer Daley, and Jessica Wolfe

    2008 Effects of Military Trauma Exposure on Women Veterans' Use and Perceptions of Veterans Health Administration Care. Journal of General Internal Medicine 23(6):741–747.

Kimerling, Rachel, Joanne Pavao, Courtney Valdez, Hanna Mark, Jenny K. Hyun, and Meghan Saweikis

    2011 Military Sexual Trauma and Patient Perceptions of Veteran Health Administration Health Care Quality. Women's Health Issues 21(4):S145–S151.

Kimerling, Rachel, Amy E. Street, Joanne Pavao, Mark W. Smith, Ruth C. Cronkite, Tyson H. Holmes, and Susan M. Frayne

    2010 Military-Related Sexual Trauma among Veterans Health Administration Patients Returning from Afghanistan and Iraq. American Journal of Public Health 100(8):1409–1412.

Kleinman, Arthur, Veena Das, and Margaret Lock, eds.

    1997 Social Suffering. Berkley, CA: University of California Press.

Langford, Joe, and Deana McDonagh

    2003 Focus Groups: Supporting Effective Product Development. London: Taylor & Francis.

Levin, Dana S.

    2010 "You're Always First a Girl": Emerging Adult Women, Gender, and Sexuality in the Israeli Army. Journal of Adolescent Research 26(1):3–29.

Lewis, Patricia, and Ruth Simpson

    2010 Revealing and Concealing Gender: Issues of Visibility in Organizations. Basingstoke, UK: Palgrave Macmillan.

Matthews, Michael D., Morten G. Ender, Janice H. Laurence, and David E. Rohall

    2009 Role of Group Affiliation and Gender on Attitudes toward Women in the Military. Military Psychology 21(2):241–251.

Mattocks, Kristin M., Sally G. Haskell, Erin E. Krebs, Amy C. Justice, Elizabeth M. Yano, and Cynthia Brandt

    2012 Women at War: Understanding How Women Veterans Cope with Combat and Military Sexual Trauma. Social Science & Medicine 74(4):537–545.

Mengeling, Michelle. A., Anne G. Sadler, James Torner, and Brenda M. Booth

    2011 Evolving Comprehensive VA Women's Health Care: Patient Characteristics, Needs, and Preferences. Women's Health Issues 21(4):S120-S129.

Mott, Juliette M., Deleene S. Menefee, and Wendy S. Leopoulos

    2012 Treating PTSD and Disordered Eating in the Wake of Military Sexual Trauma: A Case Study. Clinical Case Studies 11(2):104–118.

National Center for Veterans Analysis and Statistics

    2011 America's Women Veterans: Military Service History and VA Benefit Utilization Statistics. Washington, D.C.: Department of Veterans Affairs, National Center for Veterans Analysis.

Pavao, Joanne, Jessica A. Turchik, Jenny K. Hyun, Julie Karpenko, Meghan Saweikis, Susan McCutcheon, Vincent Kane, and Rachel Kimerling
  2013 Military Sexual Trauma among Homeless Veterans. Journal of General Internal Medicine 28(2):536–541.
Rosenbaum, Bent, and Sverre Varvin
  2007 The Influence of Extreme Traumatization on Body, Mind and Social Relations. International Journal of Psychoanalysis 88(6):1527–1542.
Sadler, Anne G., Brenda M. Booth, Michelle A. Mengeling, and Bradley N. Doebbeling
  2004 Life Span and Repeated Violence against Women during Military Service: Effects on Health Status and Outpatient Utilization. Journal of Women's Health 13(7):799–811.
Salgado, Dawn. M., Dawne S. Vogt, Lynda A. King, and Daniel W. King
  2002 Gender Awareness Inventory-VA: A Measure of Ideology, Sensitivity, and Knowledge Related to Women Veterans' Health Care. Sex Roles 46(7/8):247–261.
Scheper-Hughes, Nancy, and Margaret M. Lock
  1987 The Mindful Body: A Prolegomenon to Future Work in Medical Anthropology. Medical Anthropology Quarterly 1(1):6–41.
Singer, Merrill
  2006 The Face of Social Suffering: The Life of a Street Drug Addict. Long Grove, IL: Waveland Press, Inc.
Stead, Valerie
  2013 Learning to Deploy (in)Visibility: An Examination of Women Leaders' Lived Experiences. Management Learning 44(1):63–79.
Stecker, Tracy, John Fortney, Francis Hamilton, Cathy D. Sherbourne, and Icek Ajzen
  2010 Engagement in Mental Health Treatment among Veterans Returning from Iraq. Patient Preference and Adherence 4:45–49.
Strauss, Jennifer, Jennifer Runnals, Natara Garovoy, Monica Mann-Wrobel, Susan McCutcheon, Allison Robbins, and Alyssa Ventimiglia
  2012 Systematic Review of Women Veterans' Unique Mental Health Needs. Spotlight on Women's Health, Women's Mental Health Section, Mental Health Services. http://www.hsrd.research.va.gov/for_researchers/cyber_seminars/archives/sowh-101012.pdf, accessed April 20, 2014.
Street, Amy E., Dawne Vogt, and Lissa Dutra
  2009 A New Generation of Women Veterans: Stressors Faced by Women Deployed to Iraq and Afghanistan. Clinical Psychology Review 29(8):685–694.
Suris, Alina, and Lisa Lind
  2008 Military Sexual Trauma: A Review of Prevalence and Associated Health Consequences in Veterans. Trauma, Violence, & Abuse 9(4):250–269.
Turchik, Jessica A., and Susan M. Wilson
  2010 Sexual Assault in the U.S. Military: A Review of the Literature and Recommendations for the Future. Aggression and Violent Behavior 15(4):267–277.
United States Department of Veterans Affairs (VA)
  2010 Health Care Services for Women Veterans. VHA Handbook 1330.01.Washington, DC: Women Veterans Health Strategic Health Care Group. http://www1.va.gov/vhapublications/ViewPublication.asp?pub_ID=2246, accessed April 20, 2014.
Valdez, Courtney, Rachel Kimerling, Jenny K. Hyun, Hanna F. Mark, Meghan Saweikis, and Joanne Pavao
  2011 Veterans Health Administration Mental Health Treatment Settings of Patients who Report Military Sexual Trauma. Journal of Trauma & Dissociation 12(3):232–243.
Vogt, Dawne S., Amy A. Barry, and Lynda A. King
  2008 Toward Gender-Aware Health Care: Evaluation of an Intervention to Enhance Care for Female Patients in the VA Setting. Journal of Health Psychology 13(5):624–638.
Vogt, Dawne S., Rita E. Samper, Daniel W. King, Lynda A. King, and James A. Martin
  2008 Deployment Stressors and Posttraumatic Stress Symptomology: Comparing Active Duty and National Guard Personnel from Gulf War 1. Journal of Traumatic Stress 21(1):66–74.

Whitworth, Sandra

    2008 Militarized Masculinity and Post-Traumatic Stress Disorder. *In* Rethinking the Man Question: Sex, Gender and Violence in International Relations. Jane Parpart and Marysia Zalewski, eds. Pp. 109–126. New York: Zed Books.

Wies, Jennifer R., and Hillary J. Haldane

    2011 Ethnographic Notes from the Front Lines of Gender-Based Violence. *In* Anthropology at the Front Lines of Gender-Based Violence. Jennifer R. Wies and Hillary J. Haldane, eds. Pp. 1–17. Nashville, TN: Vanderbilt University Press.

Yoder, Janice, Jerome Adams, and Howard Prince

    1983 The Price of a Token. Journal of Political and Military Sociology 11(2):325–337.

Zinzow, Heidi M., Anouk L. Grubaugh, Jeannine Monnier, Samantha Souffoletta-Maierle, and B. Christopher Frueh

    2007 Trauma among Female Veterans: A Critical Review. Trauma, Violence, & Abuse 8(4):364–400.

AFTERWORD: PUBLIC SECTOR ANTHROPOLOGISTS AND NEW DIRECTIONS FOR A PUBLIC ANTHROPOLOGY

SARAH S. ONO

Department of Veterans Affairs, Center for Comprehensive Access & Delivery Research and Evaluation (CADRE), Iowa City VA Health Care System

SAMANTHA L. SOLIMEO

Department of Veterans Affairs, Center for Comprehensive Access & Delivery Research and Evaluation (CADRE), Iowa City VA Health Care System

In this final contribution in the edited volume on anthropologists working in the Veterans Health Administration within the Department of Veterans Affairs (VA), the authors reflect on how developments in recent years have brought us to this moment in time from the "insider" perspective of VA anthropologists. These collected papers provide ethnographic evidence for the innovative ways in which anthropologists employed in the public sector constitute a public anthropology that is theoretically informed, actionable, and cognizant of its role in the production of authoritative knowledge. The "afterword" makes connections between the chapters, with their varied topics, and addresses how this volume points to new destinations for engaged and ethical research in the growing field of public sector anthropology. [applied anthropology, public anthropology, health services research, Veterans, and health care]

The Annals of Anthropological Practice is an ideal venue for the discourse presented in this volume. The pieces herein demonstrate the varied ways contributors apply an anthropological approach to research under the umbrella of the Veterans Health Administration of the Department of Veterans Affairs (VA) Health Services Research and Development (HSR&D) service. The current volume is the most recent installment in a conversation we began several years ago, shortly after taking our current positions at the Iowa City VA. As nascent VA anthropologists, we set to puzzling out the embedded meanings in our new identity as "VA anthropologist" and how this was impacting our interactions with academic colleagues, other anthropologists in VA, and the larger disciplinary community. As addressed by authors in this volume (see Fix, and McCullough et al., this volume) there is conflict and contestation when it comes to the language and framing applied to our work in this federal setting. This negotiation around our identity as anthropologists in the public sector is something that is shared by our cohort, as well as a question that we see anthropologists new to VA (re-)engaging. Having set out to write a manuscript reflecting our conversation and those we began to have with other VA anthropologists, it was apparent how expansive the discussion became and how

ANNALS OF ANTHROPOLOGICAL PRACTICE 37.2, pp. 172–180. ISSN: 2153-957X. © 2014 by the American Anthropological Association. DOI:10.1111/napa.12025

important it was to incorporate others' perspectives. This volume does just that. This volume provides a collection of examples to illustrate the work anthropologists are doing in VA and reflects the tensions that accompany the decision to work as an anthropologist in the public sector.

In 2009, as Iowa City VA's HSR&D center began to build its qualitative research core, a group that currently has one of the largest concentrations of anthropologists nationally among VA HSR&D centers, we partnered with other VA anthropologists (notably Heather Schacht Reisinger and Gemmae Fix) to formalize and cultivate a professional network within VA. Our first step was to better identify who was out there in this national network full of coded job titles, none of which was "anthropologist." In November of 2009, the VA-Anthropology listserv was launched. In subsequent years it has grown from the original 9 participants to almost 60 members. Along with the listserv we initiated a regular national conference call to provide an informal forum for discussion of scholarly and professional issues specific to anthropologists in VA research. Perhaps this speaks to our shared nature as anthropologists and the need to have a more personal, tangible connection. Through these discussions, we began to build a national, virtual community, and in 2010, Reisinger and Ono organized the first all-VA anthropology panel at the annual meeting of the American Anthropological Association (AAA) that included contributing authors to this volume (Reisinger and Ono 2010). Since that time we have used this network to collectively organize social and scholarly events at professional anthropology and health services research meetings. These face-to-face interactions have been a way to foster our growing sense of connection and support, as well as to motivate ourselves and each other to generate submissions that create dialogue with the larger discipline and share the work we do in VA.

In 2011, we became contributing editors, along with our colleague Heather Schacht Reisinger, of the monthly column Anthropology in the Public Sector for the AAA publication Anthropology News (AN, http://www.anthropology-news.org/index.php/tag/anthropology-in-the-public-sector). Through this column, we have spotlighted anthropological research and professional development issues faced by VA anthropologists. Now in our third year, we are expanding beyond VA anthropologists to include our colleagues in other federal departments to contribute (see Fix this volume, which addresses anthropologist presence in other federal departments). Through the process of inviting colleagues to think with us about where the work we currently do is located in the larger landscape of the discipline, we have learned that much of our local dialogue about positioning ourselves as engaged members of anthropology's professional community as well as VA researchers is shared with our fellow VA and public sector anthropologists. We have also identified a shared developmental progression that anthropologists seem to move through when entering the VA that involves the familiar debate about what is at stake when it comes to being an anthropologist and taking a position in the public sector (see McCullough et al., this volume).

Building on these discussions, we organized a roundtable session entitled "What's at Stake? A Discussion of Transparency, Authenticity, Application, Theory, and Accessibility in Public Anthropology" at the 112th Annual AAA meetings (Ono and Solimeo 2013).

For the roundtable, we invited a diverse group of anthropology colleagues to discuss the larger goals of public anthropology and the slippage or disconnects that exist around this discursive idea of public anthropology and the work we all do. As one might anticipate, the muddiness of language was a predictable part of this discussion. The panelists and audience represented all of the categories we had hoped to engage—applied, academic, practicing, professional, engaged, un/employed, and public in both the United States and abroad; several sharing multiple monikers. Our goal of moving beyond the discussion of what to call ourselves, in order to think about what is to be gained through our efforts to think beyond classrooms and into our potential place in the expanse of public discourse was achieved, only scratches the surface of a topic that is likely to be ongoing. Emerging from this roundtable discussion was recognition of an increasing overlap among the categories we as anthropologists use to demark ourselves and the increasing presence of anthropologists working outside of academic institutions.

Characterizing VA Anthropology and Anthropologists in the VA

The papers collected in this volume build upon the discipline's ongoing dialogue about what constitutes public anthropology and highlight the unique contributions of public sector anthropologists in several critical ways. First, they illustrate some personal and professional benefits of conducting research under the VA umbrella. Second, the papers demonstrate the range of theoretical and topical issues engaged by VA anthropologists. Finally, in reporting on recent research, they make public sector anthropology more accessible to the wider anthropological audience and bring the insights provided by recent, anthropologically informed VA research into the broader disciplinary conversation. In order to orient this selection of manuscripts, it is helpful to know a bit about the broader context in which the work is being generated.

Before joining VA, many of our anthropologist colleagues were, like us, unaware of its complex research infrastructure. Being anthropologists, we often come to a new environment and start by trying to get a lay of the land, or a sense of "the big picture." Looking at VA, the picture is very big indeed, and complex. In addition to providing health care for more than 8.75 million Veterans, the Veterans Health Administration (VHA) operates a considerable research program, administered through four services housed under the Office of Research and Development. A majority of anthropologists employed by VHA are housed under one of these services, HSR&D, which at the time of this writing is composed of four organizational units—The Center for Implementation Practice and Research Support (CIPRS); the Quality Enhancement Research Initiative (QUERI); Resource Centers (Center for Information Dissemination and Education Resources, VA Information Resource Center, and the Health Economics Resource Center); and Centers of Innovation (COIN). At the time of publication there were 10 QUERI centers and 19 COINs. Within these research units, anthropologists are most typically employed as data analysts, methodologists, or independent investigators. Analysts and methodologists are generally responsible for data collection, processing, and research design. Investigators design research studies, write grants, analyze data and prepare findings for scholarly and internal dissemination, and perform various administrative activities.

As noted above, the number of anthropologists employed by VA has increased in recent years. Understanding of our value as researchers and interdisciplinary team members is also increasing and qualitative research is becoming more integrated throughout VA research. The growth of qualitative research in VA, and in particular the presence of anthropologists in health services research, has been acknowledged and addressed by high-level, national administrators at VACO, VA's Central Office in Washington D.C.; "Both HSR&D and QUERI benefit from the presence of anthropologists on various research teams" (Atkins 2013). This is a significant development and one that has not gone unnoticed. In his October 2013 Forum, HSR&D Director David Atkins evoked the observation of late Senator Daniel Patrick Moynihan who said, "The central conservative truth is that it is culture, not politics, that determines the success of a society." This is a sentiment that resonates with anthropologists.

We have been known to joke that the proverbial grass is not necessarily greener for applied anthropologists, but it is growing. With the exception of teaching, the substance of work performed by VA anthropologists does not differ significantly from colleagues in academic positions, but the value of anthropological work and issues of work life balance differ. As Fix (this volume) notes in her piece on career trajectories, anthropologists new to public sector work often identify a mismatch between their doctoral preparation and the skills necessary for applied work. Once applied anthropology skills have been mastered, many anthropologists come to appreciate the work–life balance and opportunities for intellectual diversity afforded by the VA system. While we do not have summers off, a majority are expected to hold regular hours (i.e., "tour of duty") and not necessarily expected to be responsive to e-mail and other work requests during off hours (with the notable expectation of grant deadlines). In the VA setting, our content areas of expertise become broader and more diverse over time as we collaborate with investigators and research centers locally and across the country, an aspect of research life that many anthropologists find satisfying.

The positives of work–life balance, working in an interdisciplinary environment, conducting research with direct practice applications, and developing a diverse research portfolio are not unaccompanied by negatives. Perhaps the most prevailing challenge faced by public sector anthropologists is the dominance and status afforded the randomized control trial (RCT) (see Sobo 2009). Despite increased integration of qualitative and anthropologically informed research, RCT is the gold standard for research design. This is unsurprising given the larger culture of clinical research and, certainly, we are not likely to see a time when qualitative or ethnographically informed research becomes the norm. At the same time, we are often not fully integrated in anthropological circles, either. Despite assurances in the literature and at professional meetings that we do not need to prove that we are "real" anthropologists (Sobo 2010), each of us routinely encounters other anthropologists who make offhand comments that reflect the disciplinary suspicion or bias against public sector work.

This suspicion is well described in the article by McCullough, Hahm, and Ono (this volume). Their piece is interesting for what it says about anthropologists in the VA and also for what it reflects that might not be explicit. The three authors are in themselves representative of something that we find in the population of anthropologists working in the VA. Among VA anthropologists, we find practitioners who hold doctorates as well as masters in anthropology. We also have a significant representation of anthropologists who have trained in specifically applied anthropology programs and terminal masters programs. For the small number of such programs nationally, there are a large number of graduates working in the public sector. A fact that is important as those of us who have contact with students think with them about options for those who pursue degrees in anthropology. Two of the three (McCullough and Ono) were part of the sample interviewed by Fix in this volume and each took a different path to arrive at the VA after completing theoretically rigorous graduate programs that tend to track graduate students toward the ultimate goal of a tenure track teaching position. Of the three, Hahm holds an MA in Applied Anthropology and has been in the VA the longest to date.

McCullough et al. and Fix's articles (this volume) communicate to readers what is at stake for anthropologists in the VA when they interact with the larger professional community as public sector employees, but such debates are not exclusive to those working in the VA. They are attitudes and fears that have been encountered by applied anthropologists in other sectors (e.g., private industry or NGOs) as well and are not new or unique. Perhaps the larger question is why do we so often encounter these feelings when we choose different types of work or applications for our knowledge as anthropologists? Or even better, how do we move past these anxieties and present a unified discipline that claims and embraces all of our contributions, even those that are consumed more widely than our own? One way that we in VA are finding to do this is through our work as illustrated by several of the authors in this volume.

Public Sector Anthropologists Challenge Traditional Representations of Anthropology

In the space between the recognized disciplinary journals and popular, publicly circulating work labeled "anthropology" there is a current of research that is more challenging to locate, but of increasing significance. It is the work of anthropologists who inhabit the borderlands that are home to much of applied anthropology. To some degree, our VA work may not be visible to other anthropologists because we typically publish in clinical journals, under the auspices of *qualitative* rather than explicitly *anthropological* or *ethnographic* research. This writing typically employs a less disciplinary-bounded discourse and a register and utilizes reporting structures more commonly seen in clinical research such as—Introduction, Methods, Results, Discussion. The rationale for this approach comes from the purpose of our work, often conducted to improve health care delivery, and from the context of our work, conducted in clinically oriented research environments. As Sobo noted in the foreword to this volume, publications not indexed in PubMed are typically not "counted" in the VA research environment. While VA anthropologists are most likely to aspire to PubMed indexing, it is likely that there is a similar, underused, resource for anthropologists working in the nonprofit arena or other areas of the public sector. Perhaps it is time for anthropologists to look harder and in new locations for models and application of ethnographic practice. Volumes like this one remind us to look for these less familiar contributions.

In Haun et al.'s (this volume) work evaluating the experience of Veterans using secure messaging to better understand how the VA might encourage greater use, we find an example of how qualitative elements in a mixed methods study are presented, often targeting a more clinical audience. For anthropologists less familiar with working as part of large, interdisciplinary teams, this is also an example of how the qualitative contribution is framed using medical anthropology. One thing that VA anthropologists encounter is the use of models that are largely borrowed from other disciplines; in this case the Health Behavior Model and the Technology Adoption Model are employed in the study design. While anthropology is not without models, our models tend to be of a more theoretical nature or on the scale of kinship, which makes them difficult to incorporate in a research environment that focuses on more measurable and actionable outcomes, in this case improving an element of communication in a patient-centered care model. Haun et al.'s paper (this volume) illustrates how ethnographic techniques are deployed to identify barriers to the use of secure messaging. Their work adds to the knowledge base regarding patient receptivity to and motivation for these emerging technologies. Similarly, Cotner et al. (this volume) demonstrate how an ethnographic approach is modified in the VA setting to evaluate the barriers and facilitators specific to a particular program or intervention. Their ethnographic study aimed to understand Veterans' experiences with maintaining employment (i.e., SCI assistance program). Using social capital theory, the authors "unpack" the notion of social support and show how critical certain forms of support are to Veterans working to maintain paid employment.

Lind et al. (this volume) also present their compelling research on the sociocultural concept of personal dignity in a format less familiar to anthropologists. The authors show the relationship between the organizational mandate to provide Veteran- or patient-centered care and the research conducted to identify shortcomings of that care or ways to improve it. This mixed methods study examined the definition and operationalization of patient dignity in samples of both Veterans suffering from spinal cord injury and VA staff. Not only do they report compelling information depicting the clustering and representation of threats to dignity for each, the comparison of the two samples, embedded in a framework derived from Kleinman's (1985) illness episode, allows them to illustrate the importance of these categorizations for the meaning of caregiving and receiving in the context of long-term injury.

Anthropologists and Anthropology are Socially Located

One assumption we have encountered as VA anthropologists is the suspicion by academic anthropologists that our thoughts and research are no longer organically driven by our individual and disciplinary yearning, but by the needs of the state. To some degree, this is another exercise of anthropology's disciplinary hierarchy, in which academic standpoint is made conveniently invisible. Academically appointed anthropologists are just as embedded in systems of power and knowledge production that shape their work as public sector anthropologists are presumed to be. In many ways, the papers in this volume demonstrate that anthropologists in VA have academic freedom, use theory, and think critically about knowledge production in the work they share here.

Finley (this volume) uses a macro structural approach to describe the relationships among prevalence, therapeutic regimes, and benefits administration in the context of posttraumatic stress disorder (PTSD). Her sophisticated discussion of the meaning effect is integrated within a treatment of how one bureaucratic logic (reducing Veteran's need for financial disability assistance) runs counter to another (reducing Veteran's suffering from PTSD). This framework of competing bureaucratic logic is echoed in the article on help-seeking among military chaplains, authored by Besterman-Dahan et al. (this volume). This study, based on qualitative research with currently active military chaplains, explores the consequences of increased utilization of chaplains for mental and social support for the chaplains themselves. While VA has ostensibly reduced the stigma of help-seeking from military chaplains for some Veterans, the high demand for their services has led to increased suffering among chaplains themselves. Notably, military chaplains in this study reported a degree of stigma associated with their own help-seeking, revealing the fault lines of organizational need for a robust caregiving workforce and the mental health and respite care required for that workforce to maintain their capacity.

As feminist anthropologists, it does not escape our attention that both Cheney et al. and Hamilton et al. (both in this volume) incorporate gender into their research and integrate theory that enriches their discussions of gender-based violence as it relates to Veteran homelessness and help-seeking for substance use treatment. Having both of these pieces included in the volume allows readers to see how the complex system of Veterans health care is being approached from multiple perspectives and how rigorous analysis is locating various points of intersection. Cheney et al. (this volume) use theory in a sophisticated analysis of barriers to help-seeking by women Veterans. She uses a lens that contextualizes these Veterans in a way that brings greater understanding to the structural position of women Veterans in the military and in VA health care settings. Hamilton et al. (this volume) consider pathways to homelessness among women Veterans within the web of contributing factors that are connected to power, gender, and trauma. These authors connect to Cheney et al. (this volume), developing the role of mental health and introducing employment status as experienced by women Veterans. Besterman-Dahan et al. (this volume) also address gender differences in their discussion of military chaplains and, while it is not the focus of their research, the exceedingly small number of women in these positions compounds the effects of deployment in this population. All of these authors succeed in giving voice to the profoundly gendered experiences of women Veterans.

These pieces taken together affirm that there are not simple answers when confronted with complex problems. The consideration of power, gender, and trauma in order to understand the complex connections between substance use, military sexual trauma, gender violence, structural inequality, and homelessness, marks these works as anthropology. In a research environment that places the highest value on RCTs, it can be a challenge to introduce research that is as complex and messy as what anthropologists bring to the table. This, however, does not lessen the importance of the work. Instead, the increasing number of anthropologists in the VA is educating research and operational partners about what can be gained *that is different* when anthropologists are included.

Perhaps the most significant characteristic of the work presented is the explicit address of how findings can be put into practice. Cheney et al. (this volume) engage help-seeking among women Veterans postdeployment for the purpose of developing treatment programs that take into account Veterans' preferences. The strength of this work is that it does not shy away from the complex challenges experienced by women Veterans. The authors present a critical analysis that includes structural factors and anthropological theory, while still moving toward a goal that involves developing a new treatment program in conversation with stakeholders in the VA and military leadership. Similarly, the work presented by Finley (this volume), Besterman-Dahan et al. (this volume), and Hamilton et al. (this volume) also illustrate this direct application of research into practical use. This step of moving toward action—action informed by critical analysis—is essential and central to the work being conducted by VA anthropologists. As anthropologists, we strongly believe that the insights gained through an ethnographically informed approach are valuable and hold the potential to have a real and significant impact on the populations we collaborate with to better understand lived experience. As anthropologists in the public sector, we understand that research needs to connect to practice. After reading the works in this volume, it is clear that there is a need for anthropologists in the public sector *and* that the work we do here has a real impact on health care.

New Directions for a Public Anthropology

The collective work that has served to formalize and make visible the VA anthropology community has instilled a degree of pride among practitioners and an awareness about the growth of VA anthropology, in numbers as well as in recognition from colleagues, both anthropologists and clinical collaborators alike. These efforts along with the persistent engagement of colleagues, notably Hamilton and Besterman-Dahan in their work on this volume, have developed into a steady expansion of our intra-VA collaborations and our ongoing engagement with the larger community of anthropologists and ethnographically minded researchers.

We are not alone in having grand aspirations for our contributions through the research we do that impacts Veterans, nor in the hope we bring to our professional goals as anthropologists and the desire to share our unique form of understanding and perspective with a broad public audience. This is why a volume of this kind is important, timely, and, as said at the outset of this Afterword, well suited to AAP and its readership. As a journal that has roots in the National Association for the Practice of Anthropology and strives to unite practical problem-solving and policy applications with anthropological knowledge and methods, this is an ideal venue for presenting the work of anthropologists in the VA. Anthropologists in the VA are demonstrating innovative ways in which anthropologists employed in the public sector constitute a public anthropology that is theoretically informed, actionable, and cognizant of its role in the production of authoritative knowledge. The authors in this volume point to new destinations for engaged and ethical research in the growing field of public sector anthropology, where we are also striving to unite practical problem-solving and policy applications with anthropological knowledge and methods.

NOTE

Acknowledgements. Drs. Ono and Solimeo receive support from the Department of Veterans Affairs, Center for Comprehensive Access & Delivery Research and Evaluation (CADRE), Iowa City VA Health Care System. The views expressed in this article are those of the authors and do not necessarily reflect the position or policy of the Department of Veterans Affairs or the U.S. government.

REFERENCES CITED

Atkins, David
    2013 Director's Letter. VA Health Services Research & Development Service: FORUM — Translating Research into Quality Health Care for Veterans. October 2. http://www.hsrd.research.va.gov/publications/internal/forum10_13.pdf, accessed March 11, 2014.

Kleinman, Arthur
    1985 Interpreting Illness Experience and Clinical Meanings: How I See Clinically Applied Anthropology. Medical Anthropology Quarterly 16(3):69–71.

Ono, Sarah S., and Samantha L. Solimeo
    2013 What's at Stake? A Discussion of Transparency, Authenticity, Application, Theory, and Accessibility in Public Anthropology, Roundtable organized for the 112th Annual Meeting of the American Anthropological Association, Chicago, IL, November 23, 2013.

Reisinger, Heather S., and Sarah S. Ono
    2010 Anthropologists in the Veterans Health Administration (VHA). Paper presented at the 109th Annual Meeting of the American Anthropological Association, New Orleans, LA, November 18, 2010.

Sobo, Elisa J.
    2009 Culture & Meaning in Health Services Research: A Practical Field Guide. Walnut Creek, CA: Left Coast Press, Inc.
    2010 Anthropologists in the VHA: So What? Paper presented at the 109th Annual Meeting of the American Anthropological Association, New Orleans, LA, November 18, 2010.

BIOSKETCHES

Karen Besterman-Dahan, Ph.D., R.D., is an applied medical anthropologist currently working at the Center of Innovation for Rehabilitation and Disabilities Research (CINDRR) at the James A. Haley VA Medical Center in Tampa, FL. She received her doctorate in applied biocultural medical anthropology from the University of South Florida (USF), and also received a master's in adult education from USF and a bachelor's in nutrition from Florida International University. She has over 15 years of health research experience, having collaborated on a variety of research focused on rehabilitation, trauma, cancer, and nutrition. She is currently the Director of the Qualitative Research Core at CINDRR and has a track record of funding. Her research interests include reintegration, operational stress, and traumatic brain injury.

Brenda M. Booth, Ph.D., is Professor of Psychiatry in the Division of Health Services Research at University of Arkansas for Medical Sciences, and for more than 25 years was a core investigator in Health Services Research & Development at the Central Arkansas Veterans Healthcare System as well as has been continuously funded by National Institute on Alcohol Abuse and Alcoholism and National Institute on Drug Abuse. She is a biostatistician and conducts mental health and substance abuse health services research. Over the past 15 years, she has conducted research on women Veterans' health and use of mental health care services and has published widely on issues of sexual and physical assault among women Veterans.

Margeaux A. Chavez is a dual degree graduate student at the University of South Florida working toward an M.A. in applied biocultural anthropology and an MPH in community and family health. Her current research focuses on food insecurity among urban poor and high school students' perspectives of standardized testing in education. She served as a consultant on this research and made significant contributions to qualitative data analysis.

Ann M. Cheney, Ph.D., is a core investigator in Health Services Research and Development at the Central Arkansas Veterans Healthcare System and an assistant professor in the Department of Psychiatry at the University of Arkansas for Medical Sciences. She is a medical anthropologist with training in women's studies. Her research has focused on how social and gender inequalities shape the experience of illness and behaviors in help-seeking. She has expertise in conducting multisite, ethnographic fieldwork and in-depth, qualitative data collection and analysis. She has designed and implemented ethnographic projects on disordered eating (e.g., anorexic behavior and bulimic behavior) among minority women in the United States, and women in rural communities in southern Italy. Her current research focuses on how trauma is linked to emotional and psychological distress and co-occurring substance abuse, and how these complex conditions and histories shape women's relational experiences in the clinical environment.

ANNALS OF ANTHROPOLOGICAL PRACTICE 37.2, pp. 181–188. ISSN: 2153-957X. © 2014 by the American Anthropological Association. DOI:10.1111/napa.12026

Bridget A. Cotner, has a Ph.D. in Educational Measurement and Research from the College of Education at the University of South Florida. She is the lead qualitative researcher for an ethnographic substudy on a multisite Veterans Affairs study exploring a vocational rehabilitation intervention for Veterans with spinal cord injury: SCI-VIP: Predictive Outcome Model over Time for Employment (PrOMOTE). Before that she was a faculty research associate with the Department of Applied Anthropology at the University of South Florida, during which time she conducted educational research and coauthored several book chapters and articles on educational issues. As part of the PrOMOTE study, Dr. Cotner is interested in issues related to community reintegration for Veterans with spinal cord injuries and using community-based participatory research methods, such as PhotoVoice, to involve Veterans as active participants in research.

Theresa Crocker, Ph.D., is a Health Services Research and Development (HSR&D) fellow at the James A. Haley VA, Center of Innovation on Disability and Rehabilitation Research in Tampa, Florida. She is a medical anthropologist with a background in nutrition and cancer prevention research. Her research interests include implementation science and evaluation research, and the utilization of mixed methodologies to provide a more comprehensive and holistic understanding of the issues and challenges facing Veterans in this rapidly evolving health care environment.

Geoffrey Curran received a Ph.D. in medical sociology from Rutgers University in 1996. After two years of postdoctoral fellowship funded by the National Institute on Drug Abuse at the University of Michigan and the Department of Veterans Affairs (Little Rock), he joined the faculty in the Department of Psychiatry, College of Medicine, University of Arkansas for Medical Sciences. He is currently a core investigator in Health Services Research and Development at the Central Arkansas Veterans Healthcare System and professor of psychiatry and associate director of the Division of Health Services Research with the Department of Psychiatry. For the last 16 years, he has been conducting mental health and substance abuse services research. He studies and publishes manuscripts primarily on (1) adaptation and implementation of evidence-based practices in mental health settings, and (2) the broader area of perceived need, treatment utilization, treatment retention, and outcomes in mental health/substance use disorders. Currently, he is PI or Co-PI on VA and National Institute of Health grants that are testing implementation strategies to assist both primary care and specialty care settings in adapting and adopting evidence-based mental health practices. In addition, he is also PI or Co-I on three qualitatively focused grants focusing on perceived need for treatment and treatment-seeking among persons with substance use disorders or mental health disorders. He is PI of the parent grant for the chapter by Cheney et al.

Audrey Dunn is a junior at Tufts University majoring in anthropology and international relations with a concentration in global health, nutrition, and the environment. She is interested in pursuing studies in public health or anthropology. She worked with the Clinton Foundation under the Regional Director of the Health Matters Initiative during the summer of 2013 where she worked on projects promoting healthy lifestyles. She is currently employed by the Tufts University Office of Sustainability.

Erin Finley, Ph.D., is medical anthropologist who has worked extensively in clinical and public health settings. Her research has explored the impact of stress and violence on physical and mental health in Guatemala, Northern Ireland, and among refugee, substance abusing, and Veteran populations in the United States. In 2012, she received the Margaret Mead Award from the American Anthropological Association and Society for Applied Anthropology in recognition of her 2011 book *Fields of Combat: Understanding PTSD among Veterans of Iraq and Afghanistan*. In addition to being Assistant Professor in the Departments of Medicine and Psychiatry at the University of Texas Health Science Center at San Antonio, Dr. Finley is also a health services research investigator with the South Texas Veterans Health Care System and a 2012–2013 Fellow with the NIMH/VA Implementation Research Institute. Her research interests include PTSD, the implementation of evidence-based treatments in inpatient and outpatient settings, and interventions promoting resilience at individual and family levels.

Gemmae M. Fix, Ph.D., is a research health scientist with the U.S. Department of Veteran Affairs Center for Healthcare Organization and Implementation Research (CHOIR) and a research instructor at Boston University's School of Public Health. She received her doctorate in anthropology from SUNY Buffalo and completed a VA postdoctoral fellowship in Health Services Research. Dr. Fix's research centers on patients' experiences of illness, with an emphasis on chronic, co-occurring conditions. She uses ethnographic methods to understand patient and provider behaviors and has a developing focus on implementation science. Dr. Fix is currently working on VA studies investigating patient-centered care initiatives and Veteran experiences of HIV care.

Marsha A. Fraser has been with the James A. Haley VA Medical Center since 2009 as a research project manager. She is a doctoral student in the Department of Public Affairs at the University of Central Florida. She is specializing in governance and policy research. She is interested in interdisciplinary alliances that improve health care and mental health, and reduce criminal recidivism. Ms. Fraser is adept at interviews involving sensitive topics, such as sexual assault; mental health; suicide; child abuse; and dignity. She has been involved in various VA and non-VA research projects concerning spinal cord injury, traumatic brain injury, post-traumatic stress disorder, depression, sexual assault, child maltreatment, and criminal recidivism.

Katharine E. Frith, B.A., is a research coordinator in Health Services Research and Development at the Central Arkansas Veterans Healthcare System and in the Division of Health Services Research, Department of Psychiatry at University of Arkansas for Medical Sciences. She has a bachelor's degree in anthropology and is currently completing work on a master's in public health with an emphasis in epidemiology. She has experience in qualitative methodologies in both research and evaluation/impact assessment applications. Her previous work experience includes the collection of qualitative data through field observation and interviews in east and central Africa and the development and publication of an epidemiological profile of substance use in Arkansas.

Bridget Hahm, M.A., M.P.H., graduated from the dual MA/MPH program in Applied Anthropology and Epidemiology at the University of South Florida in 2003.

Since 2002, she has worked at the James A. Haley Veterans Hospital as a research study project and data manager for a regional-level program evaluation team (2002–2007), the HSR&D/RR&D Center of Excellence: Maximizing Rehabilitation Outcomes (2008–2013) and the newly funded HSRD Center of Innovation on Disability and Rehabilitation Research VISN 8 (CINDRR). Certified as a clinical research coordinator since 2011, Ms. Hahm also supervises the CINDRR Tampa project management staff and participates in studies as a qualitative data manager and researcher. Her research experience has been in the areas of falls injury prevention, informatics research with the VA's electronic health records, and program implementation and evaluation.

Alison B. Hamilton, Ph.D., M.P.H., is lead of the Qualitative Methods Group and a research health scientist with the VA Health Services Research & Development Center for the Study of Healthcare Innovation, Implementation and Policy at the VA Greater Los Angeles Healthcare System. She is also an Associate Research Anthropologist in the Department of Psychiatry and Biobehavioral Sciences at the University of California Los Angeles (UCLA). She received her Ph.D. in medical and psychocultural anthropology and her master's degree in public health from UCLA. She had an NIH/NIDA Career Development Award (K01) from 2006 to 2011. Her current research focuses on women Veterans' health care decision-making and utilization, as well as mental health services, homelessness, and implementation science. Dr. Hamilton serves on the editorial board of *Implementation Science.*

Jeffrey Harrow, M.D., Ph.D., has worked in Spinal Cord Injury (SCI) for 18 years. He is board certified in Internal Medicine and SCI Medicine. He currently serves as Chief of Spinal Cord Injury at the San Antonio VA, having worked at the Tampa VA for 14 years and Palo Alto for three years. He has a Ph.D. in bioengineering, and completed a VA Research Career Development Award. His research interest is pressure ulcer prevention. He served as vice-chair of the University of South Florida IRB for eight years, and on the VA Research & Development Committee for three years. Dr. Harrow is a colonel in the U.S. Army Reserves, and served in combat operations in Saudi Arabia, Iraq, and Kosovo.

Jolie Haun, Ph.D., Ed.S., is a research health science specialist at the HSR&D Center of Innovation on Disability and Rehabilitation Research at the James A. Haley VA Medical Center in Tampa, Florida. Dr. Haun's program of research focuses on advancing the science of interpersonal health communication by meeting the communication needs of patients and providers through assessment and innovative strategies, including assessment and eHealth-based interventions. Dr. Haun's previous work within the VA included testing and implementation of a health literacy screening tool in the electronic health record, and mixed-methods research evaluating Veterans' experiences using Secure Messaging. Dr. Haun is currently engaged in several projects evaluating the use and implementation of electronic health technology resources to promote patient self-care management; and she is conducting a national database study evaluating outcomes associated with patient health literacy. Dr. Haun received her Ed.S. from Florida State University in the College of Education, her Ph.D. in Health Behavior with a Certification in Health Communication from the University of Florida in the College of Health & Human Performance, and completed her postdoctoral training as an NIH-National

Center for Complementary and Alternative Medicine fellow at the University of Arizona in the College of Medicine.

Jennie Keleher, M.S.W., has worked in the field of employment for persons with disabilities since 1998. Her initial training occurred while participating in a multisite, randomized, controlled trial of the Individual Placement and Support model (also known as Evidence-Based Supported Employment, or EBSE), where implementation guidance and oversight was provided by the Dartmouth-based developers of the model, Deborah Becker and Robert Drake. Subsequently, Ms. Keleher provided consultation and training to community-based programs in Florida to improve their fidelity to the evidence-based model, and she later served as Research Assistant on the Mental Health Treatment Study undertaken by the Social Security Administration, examining employment outcomes of disability payment recipients receiving EBSE services. As national clinical supervisor for PrOMOTE, Ms. Keleher works closely with the Vocational Rehabilitation Specialist staff at the study's seven sites as they provide direct services to Veterans in keeping with the model's fidelity standards.

Jason D. Lind, Ph.D., M.P.H., is an applied medical anthropologist with a background in public health currently working at the HSR&D Center of Innovation for Rehabilitation and Disabilities Research at the James A. Haley VA Medical Center in Tampa, FL. He has over 15 years of research experience in the health sciences, having collaborated on a variety of research focused on health disparities and infectious disease prevention among underrepresented populations in Latin America, as well as the United States. His is currently a qualitative health science researcher at the VA where he is active in the design, collection, analysis, and dissemination of research related to PTSD, eHealth, Traumatic Brain Injury, and Spinal Cord Injuries in Veteran populations.

Megan B. McCullough, Ph.D., is a research health scientist at the U.S. Department of Veterans Affairs Center for Healthcare Organization and Implementation Research (CHOIR) and a visiting scholar at Brandeis University. She received her Ph.D. in anthropology from New York University. Her early research focused on cultural competence, health inequalities, and Aboriginal women's health and well-being in North Queensland, Australia. Currently, her research focus is on clinical pharmacy, pharmacy-run specialty clinics, patient experiences of warfarin therapy and Medication Therapy Management, organizational change, and implementation science.

Danielle R. O'Connor, M.A., M.P.H., has been engaged in research for 18 years and is currently a qualitative researcher collecting and analyzing qualitative data from seven sites for a Veterans Affairs multisite study, "SCI-VIP: Predictive Outcome Model over Time for Employment." She has had field experience in Puerto Rico, working on an excavation; Jamaica, where she recorded and transcribed oral histories from elderly members of the community; and Costa Rica, where she conducted ethnographic research on the prevalence of diabetes in Quepos. More recently she has worked on programs in Florida for Latinos with diabetes and on a CDC-funded program for pregnant black women. She also founded a fair-wage clothing line that upcycles traditional Guatemalan Mayan clothing into children's clothes that are sold around the world and donates part of the profits to school children in Guatemala.

Sarah Ono, Ph.D., is the Director of the Qualitative Core at the Iowa City VA Health Care System. Dr. Ono is a cultural anthropologist with extensive ethnographic and interview experience, specializing in the complementarity of interview, observational, and focus group methods in health services research settings. Her current projects involve rural access to health care; HIV telehealth care delivery; VA use of new media; smoking cessation interventions; infection prevention; policy implementation; comanagement of patients using multiple health care systems; Patient Centered Medical Home implementation; and military sexual trauma. Prior to joining the VA, Dr. Ono's research focused on the Hollywood community, where she conducted fieldwork at film festivals and iconic Hollywood events.

Lisa Ottomanelli, Ph.D., is Psychologist at the James A. Haley VA Hospital in the HSR&D Center of Innovation on Disability and Rehabilitation Research (Veteran Integrated Service Network 8) and an associate professor of rehabilitation and mental health counseling at the University of South Florida in Tampa. Dr. Ottomanelli completed her doctoral degree in clinical psychology at Texas Tech University and her internship at University of Oklahoma Health Science Center. With over 15 years of clinical and research experience in the area of spinal cord injury (SCI), disability, and rehabilitation, Dr. Ottomanelli currently focuses on restoring community integration to severely injured Veterans. She is the principal investigator of a multicenter study funded by the Department of Veterans Affairs Office of Rehabilitation Development: "SCI-VIP: Predictive Outcome Model over Time for Employment" (PrOMOTE), which is exploring a vocational rehabilitation intervention to improve employment outcomes among Veterans with SCI.

Gail Powell-Cope, Ph.D., is section chief of Rehabilitation Outcomes Research, and Tampa Site co-director of the VA HSR&D Center of Innovation on Disability and Rehabilitation Research. She serves as Chief, Nursing Research at the James A. Haley Veteran's Hospital, and adjunct faculty at the University of South Florida Colleges of Nursing and Public Health. Dr. Powell-Cope has over 30 years of nursing experience and 24 years of experience in health services research, nursing research, survey and qualitative research methods, and quality improvement in patient safety.

Stephanie L. Shimada, Ph.D., is a research health scientist at the VA eHealth Quality Enhancement Research Initiative (QUERI) and at the Center for Healthcare Organization and Implementation Research (CHOIR), a Veterans Health Administration Research Center of Innovation. She is a research assistant professor in the Department of Health Policy and Management at the Boston University School of Public Health and adjunct assistant professor at the University of Massachusetts Medical School. Dr. Shimada's research focuses on the evaluation and implementation of patient-facing eHealth technologies, with additional interests in quality measurement, patient safety, and disparities in health care. She is currently engaged in several studies evaluating the implementation of secure messaging from both the patient and provider perspectives, and is conducting a national database study of Personal Health Record adoption in VA. Dr. Shimada received her Ph.D. in Health Policy from Harvard University and completed her postdoctoral training as a health services research fellow at the Center for Healthcare Quality and

Outcomes Research (CHQOER). Dr. Shimada is the recipient of a VA HSR&D Career Development Award.

Steven R. Simon, M.D., M.P.H., is chief of the Section of General Internal Medicine in the VA Boston Healthcare System and Associate Professor of Medicine at Brigham and Women's Hospital and Harvard Medical School. His research focuses on interventions to improve the quality and safety of health care, with special emphasis on the use of educational programs and health care information technology to improve the delivery and receipt of care for common primary care conditions. A practicing internist, Dr. Simon serves on the Massachusetts Medical Society's Committee on Medical Education. A California native, Dr. Simon attended Stanford University and graduated with honors from Yale University School of Medicine. After completing internal medicine residency training at University of California San Francisco and a chief medical residency at the University of Hawaii, Dr. Simon completed a fellowship in general internal medicine at Harvard Medical School, during which he received a master's degree in public health from the Harvard School of Public Health.

Elisa (EJ) Sobo, Ph.D., is Professor of Anthropology at San Diego State University (SDSU). Dr. Sobo, who has worked for the Veterans Healthcare Administration and Children's Hospital San Diego, has written numerous peer-reviewed journal articles concerning medical anthropology and health services research. In addition, she has authored, coauthored, and coedited 12 books, including *Culture and Meaning in Health Services Research: A Practical Field Guide* (2009). Dr. Sobo is on the editorial boards of *Anthropology & Medicine, Medical Anthropology,* and *Medical Anthropology Quarterly.* Previously, she served on the executive board for the Society for Medical Anthropology and as cochair for the American Anthropological Association's Committee on Public Policy.

Samantha L. Solimeo, Ph.D., M.P.H., is a medical anthropologist and investigator with the VISN 23 Patient Aligned Care Team Demonstration Lab and the Center for Comprehensive Access & Delivery Research and Evaluation (CADRE), Department of Veterans Affairs, Iowa City VA Health Care System. Her research interests include health care organization and delivery; chronic illness; aging; risk perceptions; long-term care; anthropological research methods; and gender. In addition to her ethnographic work on the perception of normal aging and risk, *With Shaking Hands: Aging with Parkinson's disease in America's Heartland* (2009), she has published in the *Gerontologist,* the *Journals of Gerontology: Social Sciences, Generations,* the *Journal of General Internal Medicine,* the *American Journal of Managed Care,* the *Journal of Men's Health,* and *Osteoporosis International.* Dr. Solimeo is a fellow of the Society for Applied Anthropology, president of the Association for Anthropology & Gerontology (2012–2014), coeditor of "Anthropology in the Public Sector" for Anthropology News, and co-convener of the informal VA masculinity research working group.

John K. Trainor, M.S., is a Ph.D./M.P.H. candidate in Applied Anthropology and Community and Family Health at the University of South Florida. He is a qualitative researcher for an ethnographic substudy of a multisite Veterans Affairs study exploring a vocational rehabilitation intervention for Veterans with spinal cord injury: SCI-VIP: Predictive Outcome Model over Time for Employment (PrOMOTE). He is also an adjunct instructor at Seattle University in the Department of Anthropology, Sociology and Social Work. Before that he was the evaluation coordinator at the Florida Prevention Research Center, during which time he conducted implementation and evaluation research focused on childhood obesity and coauthored several publications on physical activity, the built environment, and program sustainability. As part of the PrOMOTE qualitative substudy, Mr. Trainor is interested in how the built environment affects the interactions that spinal cord injured Veterans have with medical services, vocational rehabilitation services, and potential employers to understand the impact of built environment on employment outcomes.

Donna L. Washington, M.D., M.P.H., a general internal medicine physician and health services researcher at VA Greater Los Angeles Healthcare System (GLA), is the Women's Health Focused Research Area lead and leadership committee member for the VA GLA Health Services Research and Development Center for the Study of Healthcare Innovation, Implementation & Policy, and professor of medicine in the David Geffen School of Medicine at UCLA. Dr. Washington's research focuses on access to health care, quality of care, and health care disparities for women and racial/ethnic minorities. She is a nationally recognized expert in women Veterans' health care. Dr. Washington serves as a faculty mentor in the UCLA-VA multicampus fellowship program, as well as codirector of the GLA Women's Health Fellowship.

Jessica Zuchowski received her Ph.D. in anthropology from Princeton University and her M.P.H. from University of California. Currently, she is a health science specialist at the VA Greater Los Health Services Research & Development Center for the Study of Healthcare Innovation, Implementation and Policy (CSHIIP). A medical anthropologist by training, Dr. Zuchowski specializes in qualitative methods including research design, data collection, and analysis. Drawing on her doctoral background doing long-term ethnographic research in women's health and access to care in the United States and England, her interests include women's health, women's mental health, health care organization, implementation science, primary-specialty communication, and care coordination. Mentored by Dr. Alison Hamilton, Dr. Zuchowski currently contributes to five research and quality improvement projects including studies related to the VA's patient-centered medical home initiative, hepatitis C health services, cardiovascular risk reduction among women Veterans, and education and support for VA women's health primary care providers. She is a core member of the CSHIIP Qualitative Methods Group.